Alexander the Great versus Julius Caesar

Alexander the Great versus Julius Caesar

*Who was the Greatest Commander in
the Ancient World?*

Simon Elliott

Pen & Sword
MILITARY

First published in Great Britain in 2021 by
Pen & Sword Military
An imprint of
Pen & Sword Books Ltd
Yorkshire – Philadelphia

ISBN 978 1 52676 564 2

Printed and bound in the UK by CPI Group (UK) Ltd, Croydon, CR0 4YY.

Pen & Sword Books Limited incorporates the imprints of Atlas, Archaeology,
Aviation, Discovery, Family History, Fiction, History, Maritime, Military, Military
Classics, Politics, Select, Transport, True Crime, Air World, Frontline Publishing,
Leo Cooper, Remember When, Seaforth Publishing, The Praetorian Press,
Wharncliffe Local History, Wharncliffe Transport, Wharncliffe True Crime and
White Owl.

For a complete list of Pen & Sword titles please contact

PEN & SWORD BOOKS LIMITED
47 Church Street, Barnsley, South Yorkshire, S70 2AS, England
E-mail: enquiries@pen-and-sword.co.uk
Website: www.pen-and-sword.co.uk

Or
PEN AND SWORD BOOKS
1950 Lawrence Rd, Havertown, PA 19083, USA
E-mail: Uspen-and-sword@casematepublishers.com
Website: www.penandswordbooks.com

Contents

By the same author:

Sea Eagles of Empire
Empire State: How the Roman Military Built an Empire
Septimius Severus in Scotland
Roman Legionaries
Ragstone to Riches
Julius Caesar: Rome's Greatest Warlord
Old Testament Warriors
Pertinax: The Son of a Slave Who Became Roman Emperor
Romans at War
Roman Britain's Missing Legion: What Really Happened to IX Hispana?
Roman Conquests: Britain

To my amazing son Alexander and his wonderful new wife Crystal.
Congratulations on your wedding day!

Introduction

A lexander the Great and Gaius Julius Caesar are two of the greatest figures in world history. Comparing their careers, military and otherwise, has captured the academic and popular imagination for over two millennia. Even the great Plutarch, most prolific of the ancient world's biographers, began his parallel lives pairing of the two by apologizing for not being able to cover in full the enormity of their achievements, saying (*Lives*, Alexander, 1):

> The careers of these men embrace such a multitude of events that my preamble shall consist of nothing more than this one plea: if I do not record all their most celebrated achievements or describe any of them exhaustively, but merely summarise for the most part what they accomplished, I ask my readers not to regard this as a fault.

Such was the challenge I set myself when writing my own comparison of these two immense figures on the ancient world stage. Setting out to write the book, I had an inkling in the back of my mind who I would conclude was the greatest military commander in the ancient world. The clue might be in my now-adult son's name, Alexander. Despite my being an historian best known to date for my work on the Roman world, I have always had a lifelong fascination with Alexander the Great. The boyish conqueror of the known world whose exploits were more Game of Thrones than Game of Thrones, more Tolkien than Tolkien. Initially this bordered on hero worship, only partially tempered as I grew up to appreciate that not everyone viewed his exploits from the same philhellene perspective. I particularly remember the, for me, eye-opening sequence in Professor Michael Wood's superb 1990s television series *In the Footsteps of Alexander the Great* when he was travelling through modern Iran, where local traditions regarding Alexander were very different from those I grew up with. Similarly, when in one of the opening lectures as I began my Master's Degree in War Studies at King's College London in the mid-2000s, the discussion referencing what we today would call Alexander's war crimes rather than the usual eulogy to his cultural and geographic conquests. Nevertheless, despite such jarring challenges to the received wisdom I had grown up with, my faith in his capabilities as a military leader remained unshakeable.

Then, as my own publishing career gathered apace, I decided to write a military biography of another great figure of the ancient world, Julius Caesar. Here, what quickly became clear is that Caesar is a far more relevant cultural reference point in the modern world than Alexander. To that end, many feel they know his story intimately. Thus, as I began the research for my 2019 *Julius Caesar: Rome's Greatest Warlord*, I felt I also knew where that research thread would lead, and indeed what conclusions I would make. However, as this work continued, my eyes were slowly opened to what a truly astonishing story his was. Indeed it was this experience that set me thinking which of my hero Alexander and my new 'biographee' Caesar was the ancient world's greatest military commander.

In terms of housekeeping, in the first instance I am frequently asked why I chose Alexander and Caesar as the protagonists in this work rather than other great military leaders from the ancient world. Indeed I could have chosen from many (certainly from a western perspective given my own expertise), leading examples including Sargon the Great, Ashurbanipal, Cyrus the Great, Pyrrhus of Epirus, Hannibal Barca, Augustus (referenced many times in this work), Trajan and Belisarius. The truth is simple. It is my own opinion, nothing more and nothing less. I personally believe Alexander and Caesar were the greatest military commanders in the ancient world, and am perfectly happy for the reader to disagree.

Meanwhile, given the vast chronological and geographical scope of this work, sources of historical data are clearly of the greatest importance. Modern ones are too numerous to mention, but in terms of primary sources (and that is often a very loose definition given many were written hundreds of years after the event) the key five surviving works for Alexander include Arrian with his *Anabasis Alexandri*, Plutarch as detailed above, Diodorus Siculus with his *Library of History*, Quintus Curtius Rufus with his *The History of Alexander* and Justin with his *Epitome*. Most are based on contemporary histories of Alexander, for example by Ptolemy and Nearchus (see main text for detail). Meanwhile, for Caesar we can include his own *Conquest of Gaul* and *Civil War*, Cicero in his letters and various works, Sallust, Caesar's *legate* Aulus Hirtius who added a chapter to *The Gallic*

Wars and may have edited *On the African War* and *On the Spanish War* (both narrating Caesar's activities there), Velleius with his *Roman History*, Plutarch again, Suetonius with his *Twelve Caesars*, Appian with his *Roman History*, Cassius Dio with his *Roman History*, and Jordanes with his *Romana*. Livy also wrote about Caesar, but his works do not survive other than as excerpts.

Referencing again the chronology covered in this book, an understanding of key periods in Greek and Roman history is useful. For the former, those referenced are the Mycenaean period from 1650 BC through to the Late Bronze Age Collapse around 1250 BC, then the Geometric or Dark Age period through to the beginning of the ninth century BC, then the Archaic period, the latter then transitioning into the Classical period from the later sixth century BC, and finally the Hellenistic period following the death of Alexander in 323 BC. For the world of Rome, the periods referenced are the Republic from 509 BC, then the Principate phase of empire beginning with the Senate's first acknowledgement of Augustus as emperor in 27 BC, and finally the Dominate phase of empire from the accession of Diocletian in AD 284 through to the fall of the empire in the west in AD 476.

Regarding terminology, a few words find common usage throughout the book. For the reader less familiar with this period, these include:

- Hoplite, the standard heavy infantryman in the Classical Greek world, usually armed with the *doru* long thrusting spear and *aspis* large round body shield.
- Phalangite, the standard heavy infantryman in Macedonian armies, armed with the *sarissa* pike and *aspis* lighter shield.
- Phalanx, a deep formation of hoplites or phalangites (the latter usually in deeper formations), the standard line-of-battle formation in Classical Greek and Macedonian armies.
- *strategos*, a Greek or Macedonian general.
- Legionary, the standard line-of-battle heavy infantryman in mid and late Roman Republican (and later) armies, equipped with *pila* lead-weighted javelins, *gladius Hispaniensis sword* and *scutum* shield.
- *legate*, a Roman general.

In terms of the chapter flow, I begin with this short Introduction. Then, given the potential complexity in narrating and comparing the martial careers of two such high-profile figures in the ancient world, I have deliberately chosen a chapter structure that allows each to be considered in turn, before finally addressing the question set out in the title of this book once the facts have been set out for the reader. We therefore start with Alexander, and then consider Caesar. Each has four devoted chapters, these covering the background to their rise to greatness, then a biographical chapter (a difficult task for both given the huge amount of information to distil and impart), then a chapter on their military establishments, and finally a chapter specifically detailing examples of their highest profile campaigns and battles. Only then, in the Conclusion, do I set out to answer the question in the book title. Here I first examine their legacies then and now, then detail seven traits to enable the reader to judge their martial success, before finally addressing the matter at hand.

Lastly, I would like to thank all of those who have helped make this investigation into the military careers of Alexander and Caesar possible. Firstly, as always, Professor Andrew Lambert of the War Studies Department at KCL, Dr Andrew Gardner at UCL's Institute of Archaeology and Dr Steve Willis at the University of Kent. All continue to encourage my research into ancient Greece and Rome. Next, my publisher and friend Phil Sidnell at Pen & Sword Books. Also Professor Sir Barry Cunliffe of the School of Archaeology at Oxford University, and Professor Martin Millett at the Faculty of Classics, Cambridge University. Next, my patient and expert proofreader Richard Jeffrey-Cook, and my dad John Elliott and friend Francis Tusa, both companions in my various escapades to research this book. As with all of my literary work, all have contributed greatly and freely, enabling this work to reach fruition. Finally I would like to thank my family, especially my loving and tolerant wife Sara and children Alex (also a student of military history) and Lizzie.

Thank you all.
Dr Simon Elliott.
January 2021.

Chapter 1

Philip II and the Kingdom of Macedon

Macedon, later the traditional heart of the Hellenistic world was, until the mid-fourth century BC, the unloved northern neighbour of the celebrated Greek *poleis* city-states to its south and east. However, the 'barbarian' kingdom underwent a remarkable rise to dominance not only in the Greek-speaking world, but across the entirety of the then known world, under the rule of first Philip II and then his son Alexander the Great. This chapter sets out the background to Macedonia's extraordinary ascent to power, effectively in just two generations. In the first instance I consider the Hellenic world through to the accession of Philip II in 359 BC. I then detail the Argead dynasty, of which Philip and Alexander were the brightest-shining stars. Finally, I then consider the reign of Philip as he gradually rose to dominate the world in which he lived, setting the scene for the remarkable exploits of his son in the next Chapter.

The Hellenic World in the Mid-Fourth Century BC

The city-states of classical Greece, and the various regions under their control, were set out in a patchwork across the southern and central Balkan peninsula, in the various island chains of the Aegean Sea, and down the western Ionian coast of Anatolia. Note that, given the focus in this work is the kingdom of Macedon, the Greek colonies in Italy and the western Mediterranean are not considered here.

Poleis city-states were the dominant type of large-scale settlement in the ancient Greek world. They likely developed because of the physical geography of their Mediterranean region. The landscape there featured rocky, mountainous land and many islands. These physical barriers caused the population centres to be relatively isolated from each other, with the sea often the easiest way of moving from place to place. Each then strove to maintain their independence, and to unseat any potential tyrants around whom a region-wide monarchy might develop. Each *polis* featured an urban centre and surrounding countryside, the latter providing the produce to feed the wider population and much of the manpower for their armies and navies. The chief features of each city were outer walls for protection, an *agora* market, and a public space featuring temples and government buildings. The latter were often built atop a steep-sided hill called an *acropolis*. There were over 1,000 such city-states in ancient Greece, featuring many different systems of government. For example, Sparta was for much of the classical period ruled by two kings and a council of elders and featured a powerful army, while Athens valued education and art, is seen as the birthplace of democracy, and was for the most part a maritime power.

The key regions in the classical Greek world in the eastern Mediterranean, running clockwise from the south, were (Harwood, 1998, 2.07):

- Crete.
- The Peloponnese, featuring Sparta in the south, Arcadia in the centre, Elis to the west, Achaea to the north, and Corinth (one of the access-controlling 'fetters' of Greece) and Argos to the east.
- Moving across the narrow Isthmus of Corinth, Attica. Here could be found Athens, Laurion and Megara.
- To the north of the Peloponnese and Attica, central Greece. This featured, in the east, the Island of Euboea with its key cities of Oreos, Chalcis (another 'fetter') and Eretria, these home to many of the earliest Greek colonial adventures across the breadth of the Mediterranean, including to Magna Graecia in southern Italy and Sicily. Moving westwards, Boeotia and its key city of Thebes, then to its north and west Phocis where could be found the Temple of Apollo at Delphi with its famed oracle. Finally, to the west could be found Lokris and Aetolia. The northern region of central Greece is very mountainous and difficult to traverse for armies campaigning north to south, giving the resident Phocians and Aetolians much power there.
- To the northwest, Acarnania and Epirus, featuring broad coastal plains that, heading east, soon rose to become the north-south Pindos Mountain range. Off the coast here were the key Ionian Sea island city-states of Zakynthos, Kephallenia and Corcyra (respectively modern Zante, Kefalonia and Corfu), traditionally with four others called the Heptanese.
- Across the Pindos Mountains and above eastern central Greece, the broad plains of Thessaly, the key horse-breeding region in the

Balkan peninsula. Here was also located Mount Olympus, home of the Olympian Gods.

- To the north of Thessaly, the Kingdom of Macedon and its royal cities of Aegae (modern Vergina) and Pella. At its south-eastern tip sits the three-pronged Chalcidice peninsula, home to many Greek colonial cities, this region finally conquered by Philip II in 349 BC.
- Ranging above Macedonia, Illyria in the far north-west of the Balkans (where a key tribe, often in conflict with the Macedonians, were the Dardanians), then moving eastwards Paeonia, and finally heading into the region of modern Bulgaria Thrace. All were famed in the classical world for their fierce warriors, these detailed in Chapter 3. Above Thrace, along the Black Sea coast, could then be found the many Greek colonies established there from the seventh century BC onwards. Key examples included Tomis (modern Constanta in Romania), Istria and Boristhenis (modern Odessa).
- Crossing into Anatolia, the Greek colonial cities running down the Ionian coast and its hinterland. These included some of the leading cultural centres in the entire Greek-speaking world, examples including Pergamon, Ephesus, Priene, Miletus and Halicarnassus. By the time of Alexander the Great these *poleis* had long been vassal city-states of the Achaemenid Persian Empire.
- The various island chains of the Aegean Sea and beyond, including the large islands of Lesbos, Chios and Samos in the northern Aegean, the Sporades off Euboea, the islands in the Saronic Gulf south of Athens, the Cyclades in the south-central Aegean, and in the south-eastern Aegean the Dodecanese featuring the large island *polis* of Rhodes, one of the Greek world's leading naval powers.

A key point to note here, and a feature in both the campaigning of Alexander and later of Caesar, is how much the terrain of the Balkan peninsula and Anatolia impacted armies campaigning there, with much activity taking place along the coast and its hinterland, and down the major river systems. In particular, control of the 'fetters' proved vital, the two detailed above later joined by the city of Demetrias on the Pagasaean Gulf in south-eastern Thessaly. Additionally, the famous eastern-coastal pass at Thermopylae in central Greece was the scene of frequent conflict as the *poleis* in the Peloponnese and Attica strove to keep out northern invaders. Most famously, it was the scene of the heroic defence by the Spartan king Leonidas I against Xerxes I's vast Persian army in 480 BC.

Confusingly, the spread of the various dialects of ancient Greek spoken across the region did not correspond with the geographic distribution detailed above. This was because of the vibrant pattern of *poleis* colonial settlement throughout the eastern Mediterranean, and also because of the frequent conflicts in the region as the leading city-states strove for dominance.

In terms of the arrival of the ancient Greek language, the Balkan peninsula was always a place of transit for peoples and ideas entering Europe from the east and north. For example, Neolithic farming arrived around 6000 BC from Anatolia, while the Indo-European Proto-Greek language (the foundation of all Hellenic languages, Robinson, 1995, 118) arrived with peoples migrating from north of the Black Sea around 3200 BC. These were the ancestors of the Mycenaean civilization that dominated the Aegean from around 1650 BC to 1250 BC. Their culture, made famous by Homer in his *Iliad* and *Odyssey*, was based on a series of powerful proto city-state kingdoms, these spread throughout the Peloponnese, Attica and Boeotia. Leading settlements included Mycenae itself, Dendra, Pylos, Athens and Tiryns, with over twenty such kingdoms existing over the period of Mycenaean dominance in the region.

Mycenaean civilization came to a crashing end with the Late Bronze Age Collapse around 1250 BC, an event which saw many of its leading cities violently destroyed as they turned on one another in a time of catastrophic economic decline, now thought to be associated with climate change (Elliott, 2020a, 118). This ushered in the Geometric, or Dark Age, period of ancient Greek history that lasted through to the advent of the Archaic period which began in the eighth century BC. This Geometric phase was crucial in the development of ancient Greek given it featured the Dorian invasions from north-eastern Greece which began around 1150 BC, they bringing with them the Doric dialect which was the earliest dominant form of true ancient Greek. The various later dialects developed from this base, with writing in ancient Greek appearing in the eighth century BC for the first time through interaction with Phoenician traders in the Levant. By the time of Alexander, from this small base, ancient Greek had spread throughout the eastern Mediterranean and evolved into many different dialects. These included:

- The Western Group, featuring the oldest dialects, comprising -
  - North-western Greek, including (north to south) Epirus, Ambracia, Acarnania, and Phocis. This dialect was also spoken in the western Peloponnese, for example in Locris.

- ◆ Doric, by this time spoken only in the southern and eastern Peloponnese, including the key city states of Sparta, Argos and Corinth, and also on Crete.
- ◆ Achaean Doric, an antique form of the language spoken in the northern Peloponnese and the Ionian Sea islands.
- The Aeolic Group, comprising –
  - ◆ Aegean/Asiatic Aeolic, spoken on the northern Aegean Sea islands and along the northern Ionic coast of Anatolia.
  - ◆ Thessalian, spoken in Thessaly.
  - ◆ Boeotian, spoken in Boeotia in central Greece.
- The Ionic-Attic Group, comprising –
  - ◆ Attic, spoken in Attica and in the colonies of Athens in the northern Aegean, including the islands of Skyros and Lemnos.
  - ◆ Ionic, spoken around the Aegean. This sub-dialect was broken down into three specific groups:
    - Euboean, also spoken in the Chalcidice peninsula and in many of the colonies of Magna Graecia in Italy and Sicily.
    - Cycladic, spoken among the islands in the southern Aegean.
    - Asiatic Ionic, spoken in the *poleis* along the south-western Anatolian coast and its hinterland.
- The Arcadocypriot Group, the most primitive of the ancient Greek language groups, comprising –
  - ◆ Arcadian, spoken in the mountainous interior of the Peloponnese. This dialect retained strong links with the earlier proto-Greek spoken by the Mycenaeans and may have been a direct descendant.
  - ◆ Cypriot, very similar to Arcadian with additional influences from the various language groups in the Levant given the Cypriot maritime trading network in the eastern Mediterranean.
- Ancient Macedonian, this either a northern dialect of ancient Greek (with strong Euboean influences given the kingdom's proximity to the Chalcidice peninsula), or less likely a separate Hellenic language. This dialect gradually fell out of use in elite circles in Macedon in the fourth century BC through interaction with Athens, and by the time of Philip II and Alexander Attic Greek was the dominant dialect there. This proved a hugely important development as it formed the basis of *Koine* Greek, the *lingua franca* of the Hellenistic world following the conquests of Alexander.

The Argead Dynasty

In the wider family of classical Greek *poleis*, Macedon was long regarded as an uncouth northern outsider, with its mixed population of Macedonians, Greeks, Illyrians and Thracians (Haywood, 1998, 208). At best, the aloof Greek city-states to its south thought it a useful buffer to keep the uncouth 'barbarians' in the far north out of 'civilised' central Greece, Attica and the Peloponnese. As Green (1995, 5), details: 'Southern Greeks never lost an opportunity of sneering at Macedonian "barbarism", nor Macedonians at Greek effeteness.'

The early kingdom was split into two natural parts, a lowland/coastal region ruled by the Argead dynasty, and the highlands above reaching northwards to Paeonia. This upland zone featured tribal regions including Orestis, Lyncos and Elimaia, ruled by semi-independent dynasties that occasionally acknowledged the Argeads to their south as rulers. By the time of Philip II many of these highland kingdoms had been fully conquered by their more powerful lowland neighbour, a process he concluded. However, this did give the kingdom of Philip, Alexander and their Hellenistic successors a particular brittleness that continually required military success to maintain the authority of the monarch. Lane Fox best describes this later kingdom of Macedon as (1973, 28): '...a broad patchwork of kingdoms, stitched together by conquest, marriage, and the bribes and attractions of Philip's rising fortunes.'

In Macedon proper the Argeads had ruled unchallenged as kings since the seventh century BC when the dynasty had been founded, such monarchical rule one of the key points of difference with the Greek *poleis* to the south (Morkot, 1996, 72). The Argead name gives a clue to its origins, the word deriving via the Latin *Argīvus* from the Greek Ἀργεῖος, meaning 'from Argos'. This was the ancient Doric Greek-speaking city in the southern Peloponnese, first mentioned by Homer in *The Iliad*. Here, the Argead creation myth had a nobleman who claimed descent from Temenus, the great-great-grandson of the Olympian demi-God Hercules (himself the son of Zeus, head of the Olympian pantheon), who set out north from Argos to conquer a new kingdom which became Macedon. This link to Hercules and Zeus was heavily exploited by the Argeads, hence the local aristocracy rarely challenging the dynasty's hegemony. As Goldsworthy details, because of this illustrious heritage (2020, 15):

> ...only an Argead could be king of Macedon, a rule that was never
> broken until the final extinction of the line with the murder of

Alexander IV, son of Alexander the Great, in 310 BC. Something in the Argead bloodline was seen as so special and sacred, for the king had an important role as somehow more closely connected to the Gods.

This link to the Olympian pantheon, exploited to extremes by Alexander himself, was writ through every aspect of Macedonian kingship. For example, every Royal day began with the king personally sacrificing a beast by slitting its throat, wherever he was resident, even in the field. To that end, it was also the king's religious as well as royal duty to lead his army on campaign and in battle if at all possible, and to lead from the front by example at that. Given the kingdom was beset by potential enemies on all sides, with Epirots to the west, Illyrians and Paeonians to the north, Thracians to the east and the Greek *poleis* to the south, there was never a shortage of opportunity to do so.

This Argead dominance of elite rule in Macedon should have seen political stability quickly settle in northern Greece, but this proved not to be the case. This was because there was a simple flaw in the system of Argead hegemony, namely the size of the wider royal family. To that end, any male member of the Argead line could make a bid for power if they had enough support from the wider nobility and population. Although it was usual for an elder son, if of age and capable, to succeed his father to the throne, there was no legal requirement that this should take place. Indeed, given the Argead tradition of polygamy, there was never a lack of candidates for the throne given the profligacy of their offspring, hence for example the sense of jeopardy when Alexander himself succeeded his father Philip. The candidate simply had to put himself before his Macedonian subjects high and low, most often in the form of the nobility and army, to gain their acclamation. If he succeeded he became king, and if he failed he would die well before his time.

The earliest Macedonian rulers included the first Philip, though it is only by the late sixth century BC that we begin to get real insight into the kingdom and its monarchs. The first king of whom we know any real detail is Amyntas I who ruled from 540 to 498 BC. He was first ruler to have diplomatic relations with other states, including Athens. However, he is best known for allowing Macedonia to fall under the vassalage of Persia and its ruler Darius I in the context of the Greco-Persian Wars when, more often than not, the Achaemenid Persian king could rely on Macedon for free passage through to Thessaly (Green, 1998, 217). These early

Macedonian rulers revelled in their sense of difference when compared to their (as they saw them) physically weaker southern city-state neighbours. However, by the early fifth century BC the gradual osmosis of Greek culture from south to north had begun to change things substantially. To that end, Amyntas' son and successor Alexander I was able to participate in the Olympic Games, this based on his Temenid Argead lineage (Green, 1990, 5). He also benefited from the collapse of Persian interest in Europe following the latter's defeat at the Battle of Plataea in 479 BC by annexing the territories to the north of the Chalcidice peninsula between Amphaxitis and the Strymon river, formerly part of the short-lived Persian satrapy of Skudra (Thrace). This gave Macedon access for the first time to the silver-mines of Mount Dysoron, second only in terms of precious metal productivity to the gold and silver mines of Mount Pangaion to their south (Morkot, 1996, 73).

By the time of his grandson Perdiccas II, the Macedonian court had an even more overtly Greek flavour, he enjoying a short-lived treaty with Athens. With the accession of his son Archelaus I (whose mother was a slave, again showing the eccentric nature of Macedonian royal succession) this leaning towards Greek culture increased even more with the sweeping changes he made to state commerce, administration and the military. One major switch was to move the Macedonian capital from its traditional home at Aegae northwards to a new location at Pella, located next to a lake with river access to the Aegean, though the former location remained the ceremonial and religious centre of the kingdom. He also modernised Macedon's principal source of income alongside its rich timber resources (Green, 1998, 57), increasing productivity at the silver mines on the slopes of Mount Dysoron. Crucially, he now also had occasional access to the vast wealth available in terms of the gold and silver ore extracted from the mines of Mount Pangaion to the northeast of the Chalcidice peninsula, after expanding Macedonian interests in the region at the expense of the local Thracians and Greek colonies. The new influx of silver enabled him to start minting coins with a far higher precious metal content, such wealth proving a major attraction to the great and the good from the Greek *poleis* to the south, particularly Athenians fleeing Spartan revenge after the former's loss in the Peloponnesian War. Soon Archelaus' new court had acquired a thick veneer of Attic sophistication, with many resident Athenians supplanting earlier Greek inhabitants from elsewhere in the Greek-speaking world. These newcomers included the leading playwright Eurypides, with the historian Thucydides saying the king did more to modernise Macedon's state and military infrastructure than all of his predecessors combined (*The Peloponnesian War*, II, 100).

However, Archelaus' assassination in 399 BC plunged the kingdom into a period of chaos which saw four monarchs reigning in six years, all but one murdered. Little is known about this turbulent period until Amyntas III killed the previous incumbent and became king in 393 BC. Immediately he was forced to flee his kingdom when a massive Illyrian invasion from the north-west penetrated as far south as Thessaly. He soon returned with the help of Thessalian allies and secured his throne once more, remaining there until 370 BC. His reign was one of frequent conflict, which suited his nobles and subjects. As Green explains, despite the heavily Greek-leaning Macedonian court, the country (1995, 5) '… remained, in essence, sub-Homeric and anti-Greek, a rough and vigorous monarchy ruling, by main force, over ambitious barons whose chief interests were fighting and drinking'.

Amyntas III was later nearly overthrown by an invading army from the Chalcidian city of Olynthos, but he recruited the *strategos* Teleutias (brother of the Spartan king Agesilaus II) to lead the Macedonian army. In the subsequent campaign Olynthos was defeated in detail, being forced to surrender and to dissolve the Chalcidian League which the city had set up in 379 BC.

When Amyntas died in 370 BC he was succeeded by Alexander II, his eldest son by Eurydice I, the first of his two wives and possibly the daughter of an Illyrian tribal leader given her father's name was Sirras. Alexander's short two-year reign was again dominated by conflict given he immediately invaded Thessaly, targeting Alexander of Pherae who was the *tagus* (supreme military leader) in the region. The Macedonians quickly captured the key city of Larissa. However, far from being intimidated, the Thessalians determined to fight back, at the same time looking to unseat the unpopular Alexander of Pherae. To achieve their twin aims they turned to Thebes, the Boeotian city commanding the northern approaches to Attica and the Peloponnese. Led by the *strategos* Pelopidas, a Theban army was soon in the field, recapturing Larissa and forcing the Macedonians into a humiliating peace that saw Alexander II's youngest brother Philip (later Philip II) taken back to Thebes as a hostage along with thirty other sons of leading Macedonian noblemen. As detailed later in this chapter, this was an event that was to have major repercussions not just for Macedon and Greece, but the wider known world.

Paying the usual Argead price for military failure, Alexander II was assassinated in 367 BC. The rather gruesome event occurred during a religious festival when the king was participating in a ritual war dance called a *telesias*. There, a number of the participants stabbed him to death as part of a conspiracy led by his brother-in-law Ptolemy of Aloros. The latter then established himself as an overbearing *epitropos* regent for Perdiccas III, another younger brother of the former king. Ptolemy quickly had to deal with yet another intervention by Pelopidas who led an army of Thebans and mercenaries to challenge the regent after Alexander II's assassination. However, the wily Ptolemy bribed the mercenaries and Pelopidas quickly came to terms, taking a further fifty hostages back to Thebes including a son of the regent.

A further intervention proved more problematic though, with a pretender called Pausanias mounting a campaign from the Chalcidice peninsula. An exiled Argead from another branch of the royal family, he led a force of mercenaries and was soon gathering substantial support in the east of the kingdom where Ptolemy was viewed more as a usurper than the legitimate *epitropos*. Lacking the strength to defeat Pausanias, Ptolemy turned to an unlikely source of support. This was the great reforming Athenian *strategos* Iphicrates who had spent much of his life leading Athenian armies in the northern Balkans. At the time he was in command of a squadron of Athenian war galleys off the Chalcidice peninsula and saw an opportunity to further Athenian interests in Macedon. Accepting Ptolemy's request, he soon chased Pausanias out of the kingdom. This was an interesting campaign given it may have been the first time the Macedonians, including Philip who had returned to the royal court by this time, were introduced to Iphicrates' greatest military reform. The Athenian general was already well-known across the Greek world for the use of more *peltast* and *psiloi* light troops than usual when leading in battle, for example when defeating the Spartans at Lechaeum in 391 BC in the Corinthian War. Building on this success, he later began to arm his *peltasts* as pseudo-hoplites, though with a lighter panoply than the normal front-line hoplite warrior. This provided the dual function of giving the Athenians more line-of-battle troops to bolster the traditional citizen hoplites, but with the Iphicratean hoplites also able to deal more effectively with the lighter troops becoming more prevalent in Greek city-state armies. The most visible differences were the use by the new lighter hoplites of the smaller *pelte* shield (a round variant of the usual *peltast* crescent- shaped version with a leather facing), and to compensate for this lesser protection, a longer thrusting spear up to 3.6m long (see Chapter 3 for full details of these reforms). This weapon was effectively a proto-pike. To provide added mobility over the battlefield warriors armed in this manner were also equipped with *Iphicratid* long leather boots, again named after the *strategos*.

Despite Ptolemy's early successes in defending his regency, as soon as Perdiccas III came of age in 365 BC normal Argead succession politics immediately returned and the young king soon had Ptolemy executed. The remainder of Perdiccas III's reign was marked by financial and political stability until an Athenian invasion of southern Macedonia captured the cities of Methone and Pydna, and an Illyrian invasion once more penetrated deep into northern Macedonia. The latter proved the most damaging given that, according to the Greek historian Diodorus Siculus (*Library of History*, 16.2), Perdiccas III and 4,000 Macedonian troops were killed in 360 BC in a disastrous campaign of reconquest. Perdiccas was succeeded by his infant son Amyntas IV under the regency of Philip, by now returned from Thebes. However Philip, a young man with a true sense of destiny, soon usurped the throne in true Argead style to become Philip II in 359 BC.

Philip II: The Rise to Power

Amyntas III had three sons with his wife Eurydice I, Alexander, Perdiccas and Philip, the latter born in 382 BC. They also had a daughter called Eurynoe, while Amyntas also had three further sons called Archelaus, Arrhidaeus and Menelaus with another wife called Gygaea. Given the latter three weren't considered serious candidates for the Macedonian throne until much later it seems likely they were younger than Amyntas's children with Eurydice. The boys were ultimately eliminated by Philip when king because of their claim to the throne (see below).

While he was the youngest of the three sons of Amyntas and Eurydice, Philip was still raised with the expectancy that one day he might be king. Mortality rates in the ancient world were high among all classes of society, with the kingdom of Macedon particularly known for malaria given its extensive marshland. Therefore second and third sons were seen as key insurance policies to ensure a given Argead royal lineage had the best opportunity to thrive. Philip's upbringing was slightly unusual for a Macedonian royal court given his mother Eurydice had a greater influence there than was usual for an Argead queen. She is the first royal Macedonian woman to leave any trace of a public presence, this in the form of two inscriptions at Aegae in the temple there dedicated to Eucleia, the goddess of good reputation (Goldsworthy, 2020, 22). This may have been related to the Argead association with Hercules given the goddess was sometimes styled the daughter of the demigod. Further, Plutarch (*The Education of Children*, 20.12) says that although illiterate when she married Amyntas (supporting the idea she was originally Illyrian), she chose to learn to read and write alongside her children.

One of the perils of being the youngest son in a royal dynasty was being sent as a political hostage to a foreign power as part of a peace agreement. That was certainly the case for Philip. Even before he was sent by Alexander II to Thebes, he had already been the political hostage of a Dardanian Illyrian tribal leader called Bardylis, later as a 90 year old to defeat Perdiccas III in the battle which cost that king his life (and which is detailed above). However, it was Philip's time in Thebes that was to prove so important to the future of his country.

By 369 BC, the year Philip arrived there, Thebes had become the dominant military power in Greece. The Boeotian city lay to the north-west of Athens, situated on a low ridge dividing a surrounding plain with abundant springs, making the region one of the most fertile in Greece. Originally a Mycenaean settlement, it was the seat of the legendary king Oedipus and also the setting for many of the best known ancient Greek tragedies, for example Aeschylus' *Seven Against Thebes*. This original city was destroyed as part of the wider Late Bronze Age Collapse, but soon a new settlement was founded there. By the early fifth century BC this had risen to dominate the regional Boeotian League of local cities. Proximity to Athens quickly led to conflict, initially over control of the Plataea region, with Thebes first allying itself with Persia and later Sparta. However, at the end of the Peloponnesian War in 404 BC Thebes overplayed its hand, suggesting that Sparta should annihilate the Athenians. When the former declined such drastic action, a diplomatic schism developed with Thebes that eventually led to war in the early fourth century BC. Initially Sparta, still the most powerful land-based military power in Greece, was successful. The Boeotian league was disbanded in 386 BC, with the Theban citadel (called the *Cadmea*, named after Cadmus, the legendary founder of Thebes) captured in 382 BC. Thebes then found itself under Spartan vassalage, but in 379 BC the city revolted and refounded a new league along democratic lines.

War resumed, with Thebes this time ascendant following a series of military reforms that revolutionized hoplite warfare. The city was already famed across Greece for its elite *heiros lochos* Sacred Band of 300 paired warriors. However, from the later fifth century BC Thebes had begun experimenting with the deployment of its hoplite spearmen in deeper formations than usual. For example, at the Battle of Delium against the Athenians in 424 BC they deployed their phalanx twenty-five deep against their opponent's twelve-deep formation. Victory quickly ensued. Later, against the Spartans, they took this tactical innovation to extremes under their great *strategos* Epaminondas, forming their right flank fifty deep at the crucial Battle of Leuctra in 371 BC to smash the Spartan's twelve-deep left wing. Another Theban innovation here was to deploy their phalanx obliquely in echelon such that the over-deep right flank impacted the Spartan battle line first. Meanwhile, throughout its conflicts with Athens and later Sparta, Thebes and its Boeotian League allies also made increasing use of light troops and particularly cavalry to support their hoplites. A prime example of the latter was the deployment by Pelopidas of mounted troops to delay the formation of the Spartan phalanx at the Battle of Tegyra in 375 BC, where again the Thebans were victorious. The culmination of this ongoing success against Sparta was a Theban-led invasion of the Peloponnese in 370 BC under Epaminondas. Thus, by the time Philip arrived in Thebes, the military stranglehold Sparta had exercised across the Greek world for a century had been broken, with the Boeotian city now pre-eminent.

Philip was 13 when he arrived in Thebes. He was to stay there for three years. The future king spent most of his time there as a guest in the house of a well-connected and wealthy aristocrat called Pammenes, where he was very well-treated. It was completely normal among the Greek *poleis* for diplomatic hostages to be treated in this way, the hope being such benevolent treatment would foster mutual respect between individuals and states in the future. While there he received the same education as the other sons of the Theban societal elite, but crucially his relationship with Pammenes also gave him access to the very top level of the Theban military hierarchy given his host was a highly experienced military officer (and indeed a strong advocate of the Theban Sacred Band). Pammenes was also on very good terms with Pelopidas, the victor at Tegyra and protagonist behind Philip being a hostage given his earlier success against Alexander II. However, and much more importantly, Pammenes was also a close confidant of Epaminondas. It is from the latter many believe Philip learned much about the latest military thinking regarding strategy, tactics and technology, and also about diplomacy. The late first-century AD Greek orator and historian Dio Chrysostom reflected the classical world's view of how Philip benefited from his relationship with Epaminondas, saying (*Orations*, 49.5):

> Philip...witnessed the deeds of Epaminondas and listened to
> his words; and it was not mere accident that Epaminondas had
> acquired such power among the Greeks and had wrought so great
> a change in Greece as to overthrow the Spartans....this, I fancy,
> explains why Philip was far superior to those who previously had
> become kings of Macedonia.

The lessons suggested here that Philip learned from Epaminondas and his
fellow Thebans are many, and played a key role in the military reforms that
underpinned the meteoric rise of Macedon as a political and military force
under his later rule. This included the much wider use of combined arms
at a strategic and tactical level, and battlefield innovations including oblique
deployment and a new, deeper phalanx (Matthew, 2015, 43). With regard
to the latter, Macedonian *pezetairoi* phalangites in the armies of Philip and
Alexander were armed with the long *sarissa* pike held two-handed rather
than the standard long thrusting spear, this facilitated by the use of a
smaller round shield. Both the latter innovations were clearly influenced
by Philip's exposure to the lighter Iphicratean hoplite detailed above.
All of the above points are detailed in full in Chapter 3.

Back to the chronological narrative, Philip left Thebes and returned
to Macedonia when he was 17, just before Ptolemy's assassination. Soon,
with the regent dead, he was in the service of his elder brother Perdiccas
III. At some point Philip was then given charge of a Macedonian province,
almost certainly in the east where he held the frontier against the Thracian
tribes there. By this time Perdiccas had a young son of his own called
Amyntas, with Philip now once-removed from the official Argead line of
succession, though there is nothing to suggest he was anything but a loyal
supporter of the king. However, his sense of destiny soon came to the fore
when, out of the blue, Perdiccas was slain fighting the aged Bardylis and
his Illyrians.

This was a particularly shocking event for the Macedonians given
Perdiccas was their first king to die in battle. In addition, the 4,000 men
who died with him were most likely from the Royal Army which by that
time numbered 12,000 men, gathered to the king's standard to counter
Bardylis. Their crushing defeat left the kingdom wide open, the Illyrians
plundering deep into Macedonian territory and their many other enemies
suddenly sensing weakness. The Macedonians reacted with predictable
Argead decisiveness, in the first instance appointing Perdiccas' infant son
Amyntas as king, but with Philip as the *epitropos* regent. Goldsworthy

(2020, 33) says there is a possibility, and only that, that he may have been proclaimed king immediately, bypassing Amnytas entirely, but this seems unlikely to me. Even the Argeads, that most martial of dynasties, knew that an element of formality was important in the succession of their kings. Our only remotely near contemporary source is the later Latin historian Justin who wrote his *Epitome* summary of the kings of Macedonia in the reign of the first Roman emperor, Augustus. His narrative indicates Philip served as regent for two years (*Epitome*, 7.5.9-10), with Goldsworthy adding it would be unusual for him to make up such a specific fact (2020, 34).

However long Philip served as regent, soon external threats forced his hand. Once more the usurper Pausanias appeared on Macedon's eastern border, this time backed by a Thracian king. Then another challenger appeared called Argaeus, this time backed by Athens. In Pella, late in 359 BC, an *ecclesia* assembly of the great, good and soldiery was called and Philip swiftly declared the full *basileus* king. This was no time for the niceties of succession. An experienced leader of the Argead line was needed, and Philip was elected the man to lead the kingdom against its enemies, and back to political and financial stability. It is worth noting here that although only 22 at the time, Philip had already been the governor in an eastern province where he had seen active service leading troops against the Thracians there. He also had his experiences while a hostage in Thebes to call on, the Boeotian city still – though not for long – the leading military power in Greece. He was therefore as fully informed as possible on the latest concepts of military method in the Greek *poleis*.

Contemporary descriptions of Philip at this time are non-existent, though later accounts indicate he was a stocky man, around 1.7m tall. This was the average height for a well-to-do Macedonian or Greek man of the time. We have no indication of his complexion or hair colour, though one specific physical feature is always associated with the older king. This is the loss of his right eye during the siege of Methone in 354 BC, the last city on the Thermaic Gulf in the north-western corner of the Aegean then controlled by Athens. Here, while leading an assault from the front, the king was hit by an arrow in the face that injured the eye, it later being removed by surgery. The subsequent scarring gave him a fearsome countenance, communicated to modern audiences by lifelike facial reconstructions based on a remarkable modern archaeological discovery. This was the finding in 1977 at the ancient Macedonian burial grounds at Aegae near modern Vergina of three royal tombs hidden beneath a great burial tumulus. Strikingly, the bones buried in a golden *larnax* (a small closed coffin) in Tomb II featured the skeleton of a man of Philip's height with a serious injury to his right eye, and also an injury to the right leg. The latter is a particularly important piece of correlating evidence given the king also suffered a near fatal injury fighting the Thracians when a spear had been thrust through his thigh, penetrating through to his horse which was killed by the savagery of the blow. Based on an analysis of the remains, and the extremely fine grave goods also contained in the tomb (which included intricately decorated armour and weaponry), many have argued this is indeed the burial of Philip II. As Goldsworthy says in his recent consideration of the evidence (2020, 30): 'On balance, the occupant of Tomb II probably is Philip II, which means that the reconstruction of his face may give a hint of his real appearance.'

The finery of this martial panoply would certainly have been on display as Philip led his armies from the front to tackle the growing number of threats to his kingdom. No sooner were Pausanias and Argaeus dealt with, the latter's 3,000 Athenian hoplites almost wiped out, than the Paeonians in the north started infringing on Macedonian territory sensing easy plunder. Philip moved north to deal with this new threat, ejecting the Paeonians successfully, before finally turning his attention to Bardylis and his Illyrians still plundering Upper Macedonia. These were also defeated in short order, with any recalcitrant regions in this highland zone now formally brought under Macedonian hegemony.

Philip's swift military success firmly cemented him in power, his newly won reputation as a young, dynamic military leader soon spreading throughout Greece. A period of political and financial stability followed in Macedon, with any potential rivals to throne quickly eliminated. This included Archelaus, his eldest stepbrother through Amyntas III's second wife Gygaea. However, his former charge Amyntas IV was judged harmless, later thriving in the new king's court. He was ultimately to marry Philip's daughter Cynane, though was later murdered in the immediate aftermath of Alexander the Great's accession in the purges following the assassination of Philip.

Philip's real skills as a political leader and innovator now came to the fore. Building on the reforms of Archelaus I, and those planned in the short reign of Philip's eldest brother Alexander II, he first turned to his kingdom's principal source of wealth, gold and silver mining from Mount Dysoron, and occasionally Mount Pangaion. Archelaus I had already modernised the former in the late fifth century BC (Morkot, 1996, 73), but given the foreign policy tribulations in the reign of Alexander II, under the stewardship of Ptolemy, and later in the reign of Perdiccas III, the kingdom had become impoverished, with access to Mount Pangaion increasingly problematic. Time and again invaders had targeted the city of Amphipolis, an Athenian founding dating to 436 BC, which the latter had hoped would give them control of access to the silver and gold wealth to the north. The result was very few silver coins produced in Macedon in this period, let alone gold, the majority minted being bronze issues. By contrast, in the same period Bardylis was freely minting thousands of silver coins using his own mines in his native Illyria. However, with his borders now secure, Philip swiftly remedied this, setting his kingdom's finances on a secure footing once more. Firstly, he formally annexed the territory around Mount Pangaion, ensuring permanent access to the gold and silver mines there, which he further modernised. Soon these were producing an enormous 1,000 talents of precious metal a year (Green, 2007, 11). At the same time Philip also modernised Macedon's many iron-ore extraction operations, using the latest technological innovations through the recruitment of the finest mining and metallurgy experts from across Greece to help increase the output. Meanwhile, the ever-inquisitive Philip also sought advice on how to increase the agricultural produce of his kingdom. Unlike the regions in which the *poleis* to the south flourished, the climate of Macedon was more akin to that of continental Europe than the Mediterranean. It therefore enjoyed more rainfall, and was less prone to drought, with Philip soon ensuring that farms across his territory, great and small, were operating at full capacity. For the first time in generations Macedon began exporting arable produce and olive oil, adding to the wealth in the royal treasury.

It was this increased revenue that enabled Philip to initiate the series of reforms for which he is best known, namely those of the Macedonian army. This created the finest military machine in the known world at the time, and one which his son Alexander the Great later used to such great effect. The modernization programme is discussed in full in Chapter 3, but for context the key changes were to increase the size of the royal army, further increase the importance of the cavalry arm, innovate something entirely new in the form of the Macedonian pike-armed phalanx, and significantly improve Macedon's ability to engage in siege warfare. In the first instance, the army roughly doubled in size in the period from 359 BC to 352 BC, it now also benefiting from regular training introduced by Philip. Next, until the beginning of the fourth century BC Macedonian cavalry had been armed in a similar fashion to their Greek counterparts, though with a longer spear in addition to the usual javelins. However, early in the fourth century BC these mounted troops, particularly the *hetairoi* companion close bodyguards of the king, were re-armed as pure shock cavalry, now equipped with a long *xyston* lance often over 4m in length and fighting in a wedge-shaped formation designed to crack an enemy battle line. A key factor enabling this dramatic transition to such aggressive tactics was access to the finest horses and grazing land now provided by the wealth flowing into Philip's kingdom. This change proved so successful that, to increase their numbers, early in his reign Philip opened their ranks to anyone who could meet the wealth qualification, including non-aristocratic Macedonians and even Greeks. These new companions were then granted large estates in newly conquered territory, initially to the west, north and east, to ensure their absolute loyalty to the king. This was a bold move by Philip given, in Macedonian court tradition, the companions were allowed to address the king freely, including disagreeing with him, without fear of reprisal. Increasing their number only a short while after becoming king showed both Philip's self-confidence and his ambition.

However, it was Philip's principal military reform that was to revolutionize warfare in the Greek-dominated world for the next 200 years. This was to re-equip the foot component in his armies with the *sarissa* two-handed pike, the warriors now fighting in highly-trained deep phalanxes. This hugely transformative development followed Philip's exposure to the latest military developments in Thebes, and also the innovations of Iphicrates (detailed above). Some, including Matthew (2015, 42), have discussed whether the Macedonian pike-phalanx could have been introduced earlier, for example under Alexander II. However, it was Philip who history shows was the proven innovator here, and to my mind it was he who initiated the change. In so doing the king was displaying that most Roman of traits which was to cost later Hellenistic armies so dear, namely the ability to adapt the tactics and technology of others to one's own ends. As Lane Fox said graphically of Philip's new military establishment (1973, 73) '…great tactics are born less of originality than of a shrewd use of contemporary fashion, and Philip's army did not, like the Goddess Athena, spring fully armed from its parent's brain.'

Soon his phalanx was defeating all before it, with the king developing a specific combined arms tactic where the phalanx would first pin the enemy battle line. His lance-armed companions then charged in at the crucial moment when a weak spot in the enemy battle line was exposed to deliver the *coup de grâce*. Hammer and anvil indeed.

Additionally, and crucially as it turned out given most Greek cities had long had extensive wall circuits for their protection, Philip also acquired a modern siege train as good as any in the entire peninsula. To ensure he was able to make maximum use of it he then hired one of the finest military engineers of the day to oversee its many siege engines. This was Poleidus of Thessaly, it being likely that it was under Philip's auspices that the use of torsion in siege artillery was discovered, with sinew or horsehair springs innovated for the first time. This doubled the range of the recently invented arrow-catapult.

With military matters now in hand, Philip briefly turned to domestic matters, marrying the first of his seven wives in early 358 BC. This was Audata, great-granddaughter of Macedon's one-time nemesis Bardylis, king of the Dardanian Illyrians. She took the name of Philip's mother after the wedding, Eurydice. Soon the queen was pregnant, giving birth to a daughter called Cynane (later a noted warrior in her own right) in 357 BC. However, the king's happy matrimonials did not get in the way of renewed conflict between Macedon and Illyria, once more over disputed border territory, and later in 358 BC Philip marched again against Bardylis and his Illyrians in a pre-emptive strike. His successful campaign ended in 357 BC with a crushing Macedonian victory over the combined Illyrian tribal armies in an unnamed battle where 7,000 Illyrians died. Here, Philip used his new army for the first time, and to great effect. In particular, this was the first time we see the combined arms approach to battlefield tactics which he and later Alexander became famous for. First, he circled his cavalry around both flanks of the Illyrian spear-armed battle line, forcing them into a defensive square formation, thus negating their offensive capability. He then ordered his light troops forward to shower the Illyrian warriors with arrows, javelins and slingshot, while his phalanx pinned them in place. Finally, once a gap appeared in the square due to missile casualties and a subsequent collapse in morale, Philip's companion cavalry charged through, the king leading from the front as was the Argead way. This broke the enemy formation which then routed in disarray, with Illyrian warriors discarding their weapons as they fled. This total victory against the once-mighty Bardylis not only secured the territories of upper Macedonia once and for all, but also allowed Philip the opportunity to annex the Illyrian speaking regions even further north. Additionally, and equally importantly, his success against Bardylis removed the threat of an Illyrian invasion into Epirus in the west. This earned the favour of the Epirote king Neoptolemus I, not only securing Macedon's western borders but also freeing Philip to turn his attentions to the troublesome Greek *poleis* in the south, particularly Athens.

In that regard, to the south the Athenians were growing increasingly wary of Philip's martial success. For generations, whether in ascendency among the city-states or not, the ever-ambitious *poleis* had played a key role in keeping Macedonian ambitions in check, intervening in Argead dynastic troubles at every opportunity. However, having been defeated by Philip when supporting the usurper Argaeus at the cost of 3,000 hoplites, in 357 BC they now turned their attention again to Amphipolis, recently captured by Macedon after a siege in the context of the Social War between the Second Athenian League and the allied *poleis* of Chios, Rhodes, Cos and Byzantium. Here Philip now showed his growing skill as a statesman, leasing Athens access to the city which controlled Macedonia's gold and silver mines on the slopes of Mount Pangaion rather than risk another conflict. In return the Athenians ceded Pydna to Macedon, this the key one-time Macedonian port on the Thermaic Gulf, earlier lost in 363 BC. Sensing Athenian weakness, Philip then rescinded access to Amphipolis once he had placed a garrison in Pydna. Predictably Athens then declared war against him, though Philip easily countered this by forming an alliance with the latest incarnation of the Chalcidian League, established by the *poleis* of Olynthus. Together the new alliance conquered Potidaea, the Corinthian colony controlling the westernmost spur of the Chalcidice peninsula. Philip now felt so secure in his newly won position of regional superiority that he promptly ceded sole control of the city to his league allies, confident they would stay true to their word and protect this coastal region against Athenian predations. He then turned his attention south, to the broad coastal planes of Thessaly.

Here, the nobility had long set themselves apart as a mounted aristocracy, distinct from their hoplite citizen warriors. The *poleis* in Thessaly were therefore more susceptible to the rule of tyrants than the city-states further south. Such rulers always needed military success to maintain their rule, this often in the form of incursions into Macedon to the north. Philip now determined to stop this once and for all, though cannily not as martial conquest. Instead, he sequentially wed Nicesipolis of Pherae and then Philinna of Larissa, both from the leading aristocratic families in Thessaly. The new brides were his third and fourth respectively, the king having earlier married his second wife Phila who was the daughter of a leading upper Macedonian noble. It is noteworthy here that Philip had, in just a year and a half, married four wives. Clearly diplomacy through marriage was playing just as large a role in securing Philip's kingdom and its borders as was military campaigning.

However, it was Philip's next marriage that still resonates to this day, for in later 357 BC he married Olympias, daughter of the late Molossian king Neoptolemus I, niece of the then current ruler Arybbas, and future mother of Alexander the Great. This tribe traditionally associated itself in its origin myths with Achilles, greatest of the Greek heroes in the Trojan Wars, the match therefore linking this mighty warrior with the Argead dynasty's association with Hercules and Zeus. This was an auspicious match indeed, and so it proved. More practically, given the Molossians were the largest of the three tribes of Epirus alongside the Chaonians and Thresprotians, Neoptolemus I and now Arybbas were also the de-facto kings of Epirus, the marriage therefore further securing Macedon's western flank.

We have no detail of Philip's wedding to Olympias, or indeed of life at court where (unless Philip's mother Eurydice I was still alive) there appears to have been no hierarchy among the wives. Notably there were fewer slaves in Macedon than in the Greek *poleis* to the south (Goldsworthy, 2020, 74), though no doubt the royal palaces at both Pella and Aegae featured thousands of servants, all onerously employed to ensure the Argead resident there lived a life of luxury. Even more so than the royal courts of his immediate predecessors, Philip also ensured his court had a distinctly Greek feel to it, Macedon proving a natural home for the many city-state intellectual exiles falling foul of the ever-changing *poleis* ruling classes in the south.

However, one thing in Philip's court that would have jarred with his visitors from Greece was his continuing adherence to the Macedonian royal tradition whereby the young sons of the nobility, called *paides* (pages), served him at table, guarded his tent when on campaign and hunted with him. As Goldworthy says (2020, 88):

> ...Athenians and other southern Greeks found it baffling to see young noblemen serving at table or submitting to a flogging (which could only be carried out by the king) as if they were slaves. There was also concern that surrounding a king with so many young men and boys invited their sexual exploitation. Apart from affairs with women, Philip was said to have had numerous young men and boys as lovers, including a number of pages.

Despite this, Philip certainly continued to pay the closest attention to his wives and in 356 BC Olympias gave birth to a son, Alexander. It is because of his remarkable later exploits that we know more about his mother than any of Philip's other wives, or indeed any other woman at the Macedonian court earlier or later. Plutarch says that her real name was Polyxena, with Olympias actually a nickname, and that she was also variously called Myrtale and Stratonice, the former possibly adopted before her marriage as part of a mystery rite and the latter a much later sobriquet (*Lives*, Alexander, 3.4-5). Given Alexander's later career, classical historians attached many religious portents to his conception and birth after the event, including dreams by both Philip and Olympias, and the famous fire which allegedly destroyed the great temple of Artemis in Ephesus on the day he was born. However, at the time his birth would just have been yet another royal delivery, the new baby joining the ever growing number of Philip's infant offspring in the nursery at court. In addition to Audata's daughter Cynane, these also included Nicesipolis' daughter Thessalonike (named after 'victory in Thessaly', which given Philip had yet to win one means it was a later name) and Philinna's son Arrhidaeus. The latter, born in 357 BC and later given the royal title Philip III, was Alexander's elder brother and the only other legitimate male offspring. Notably, he was not taken seriously as a potential heir to Philip given he suffered from a learning difficulty of some kind, clearly an issue for the Macedonian nobility in an unkinder age.

Despite clearly fulfilling his royal matrimonial duties at court, like any Macedonian king Philip spent most of his time on campaign. It was vital to the continued success of his reign that he could show his fellow Argeads, and the wider Macedonian nobility, that he was not only virile in the bedroom but also on the battlefield. Thus his first move after the birth of Alexander was to invade Thrace on his eastern border, there swiftly conquering the city of Crenides between the rivers Strymon and Nestos. This Greek colony was close enough to Mount Pangaion to present a threat to the king's vital gold and silver mines there if controlled by an enemy, and he celebrated his success by renaming it Philippi, and then installing a large garrison there. Showing the growing size of Macedon's military establishment, at the same time the king also ordered his leading *strategos* Parmenion to invade Illyria where the latter also quickly achieved victory. This is the first time we hear of this leading man of Macedon who would later become Philip's most trusted military leader and advisor, and for much of his reign that of Alexander too.

Philip was never one to rest on his laurels and in 355 BC turned his attention to Thessaly where as detailed above he besieged the city of Methone which fell early in 354 BC, despite the Athenians sending two fleets to try to break the blockade. Here Philip displayed a trait that he and later Alexander used to great effect, namely the willingness to campaign out of season by continuing his siege over the winter when it was much harder to supply their own troops. His strategy evidently wrong-footed the Athenians, with Methone's fall setting up a lengthy period of Macedonian hegemony over much of Thessaly. However, it came at a price for Philip as it was here he lost his right eye leading an assault. The injury clearly healed quickly despite its severity, allegedly because of the skill of his physician Critoboulus, given later in 354 BC and into 353 BC the king once more switched his attentions to Thrace where he attacked the cities of Abdera and Maronea on the coast there.

Approaching the Argead Zenith in Greece

By this time the growing size of Philip's military establishment was outstripping his finances, despite the huge wealth mined in precious and other metals around Mount Pangaion and elsewhere, and he increasingly looked to foreign booty to make up the difference. This cast into sharp focus his relations with Illyria, Paeonia, Thrace, and also the Greek *poleis* to the south. With Philip's new, highly successful army, and the personal drive and ambition now evident in the king and his court, Macedon was no longer the victim. Instead it was the protagonist, casting its gaze farther and farther afield in its desire for military conquest. All of its neighbours failed to realise this until it was far too late, to their dramatic cost, most notably Athens.

Philip was soon casting around to find a cause that would legitimately allow him to intervene in central Greece, Attica and the Peloponnese. He found one in the Third Sacred War. This broke out in 356 BC when the Phocians, dominating mountainous central Greece, shocked the wider Greek world by seizing the Temple of Apollo in Delphi, using the vast treasure accumulated there to fund a series of mercenary armies. These they set against the Delphic Amphictyonic League, led by the leading Boeotian city of Thebes, this a pan-Hellenic 'council of neighbours' which had traditionally overseen Delphi and with whom they had a grievance over an earlier imposed large fine (Buckler, 1989, 16). This was just the sort of cause Philip had been looking for to legitimise his interests in the south, and in 353 BC he invaded Thessaly where he defeated a marauding army of 7,000 Phocian mercenaries. However, as soon as Philip's attentions were diverted elsewhere the Phocians went on the offensive again, defeating him when he returned in two encounters, one where they famously used concealed stone-throwing catapults against his army. The Macedonian king responded with massive force, knowing he could not afford a third failure. He re-invaded Thessaly with an army of 20,000 foot and 3,000 cavalry, this including many Thessalian horsemen and hoplites. The size of this army, which he fielded only five years after coming to power, is noteworthy, and he easily crushed the Phocians at the Battle of Crocus Field in late 353 BC or early 352 BC. Here over 6,000 Phocians fell, with 3,000 more captured. Many of these later drowned as they were being marched back to Macedon, the remainder enslaved to work in Philip's gold and silver mines. Such was the price of failure when standing up to the rising power of the Macedonian king.

Philip's success here earned him immense prestige among the Greek *poleis* given here he was representing a common cause with them against the Phocians, the latter now viewed as 'beyond the pale' after their seizure of the Temple of Apollo and its treasure. He was immediately recognised as the *tagus* in Thessaly, at the same time acquiring for Macedon the city of Pherae. More broadly, he also laid claim to the south-eastern Thessalian region of Magnesia, with its important harbour of Pagasae. Despite the goodwill Philip was enjoying with the Greeks in the south, this did set him against Athens given the port was in their sphere of influence and a vital maritime staging post for their exploits in the northern Thermaic Gulf. However, they were late in raising a naval force to intervene and instead opted to occupy the pass at Thermopylae. If Philip had intended to march further south, this was the route he would have taken. The way south blocked for now, he therefore decided to consolidate his position in Thessaly, leaving garrisons in key towns before marching north back to Macedon again.

He now turned to diplomacy to increase his influence among the Greek *poleis*, using his wealth to establish pro-Macedonian parties in the towns and cities of Euboea where they could threaten Attica if required. He then switched campaigning theatres again, from 352 BC to 346 BC campaigning against the Illyrians, Paeonians and Thracians, all the time looking for new territorial conquest, not least to provide estates for his growing number of companion shock cavalry. When campaigning in the east Philip also once more targeted the Greek colonial cities along the coastal regions of the northern Thermaic Gulf, and also the Thracian Sea as far as the River Maritsa in modern Bulgaria. Many of these considered themselves to be in the Athenian sphere of influence, further alienating

Philip with the leading city in Attica which increasingly viewed him their new chief rival for dominance across the Aegean.

By 349 BC the remaining major Greek colony in the region holding out against Philip was Olynthus on the Chalcidice peninsula. Although the city had originally sided with Philip when fighting against the Phocians in Thessaly, by this time Athens had invested much diplomatic and financial capital in convincing its rulers to ensure it would remain a pressure point in the Macedonian rear if Philip campaigned in the south in future.

The dynamic Philip could not let this remain unchallenged and in 349 BC he began an extensive siege that saw Olynthus fall within a year, the city and any nearby supporting settlements being raized to the ground. As an added bonus Philip also captured Arrhidaeus and Menelaus, his remaining two-step brothers through Amyntas III's second wife Gygaea. In true Argead fashion, he promptly had them killed. Athens lost further face here as the expedition it had planned to relieve Olynthus instead got diverted to Euboea to counter a revolt led by the various political factions set up with Macedonian gold to support Philip. The Athenians never forgot, and from this point until his death Philip was at war with Athens more often than not, even if only through proxies.

By 348 BC Philip could feel satisfied that in the decade since becoming king he had first secured Macedon's borders, and then significantly increased the amount of territory under its control at the expense of the Illyrians in the west, Paeonians to the north, the Greek cities in the Chalcidice peninsula and Thrace to the east. Further, Macedon was now the dominant power in Thessaly to the south, where it had also seized and garrisoned a number of key Greek cities. To celebrate, in the early autumn he hosted Macedon's own Olympic-style games at Dium on the foothills of Mount Olympus, specifically in honour of Zeus given the Argead link with the head of the Olympian Pantheon. Philip's offer of huge prizes and generous hospitality attracted leading athletes, artists, actors (one named in contemporary sources as Satyrus of Athens), and writers from across the Greek-speaking world.

Philip was clearly now riding high, though late in 347 BC he was again dragged back into the Sacred War which was still rumbling on between the Phocians and the Amphictyonic League. The former were behaving belligerently again in central Greece and southern Thessaly and, at the behest of Thebes and Boeotia, the Macedonian king began to gather his army to march south. Both Athens and its erstwhile enemy Sparta reacted with alarm, horrified at the prospect of Philip's ultra-modern army campaigning in Greece proper. The former voted to raise a force of citizen hoplites and sent a squadron of trireme war galleys to patrol the Thessalian coast, while the latter sent 1,000 of their elite full-time hoplites and supporting *periokoi* and *helots* (see Chapter 3 for distinction) north to block the pass at Thermopylae. However, events now overtook the Spartans. A change in leadership among the Phocians saw a faction in favour of ending the Sacred War take charge. These turned the Spartiates away and, according to Justin (*Epitome*, 8.4), sent gifts to Philip who responded positively by sending an Athenian captive from his Olynthus campaign with a message home to open peace negotiations (Diodorus Siculus, *Library of History*, 16.59, 2-3). The Athenians, still unclear if the Phocians themselves would block the pass at Thermopylae, decided to send ten ambassadors to Philip including a young Demosthenes, later one of the king's and Alexander's main protagonists. Eventually a peace agreement was reached, known as the Treaty of Philocrates (the latter the chief Athenian negotiator), with Philip receiving Athenian and other Greek delegations at the Macedonian capital of Pella in 346 BC. This clearly showed to all Greece who the major power in the Balkan peninsula now was (Morkot, 1996, 106). Crucially, Athens also now abandoned any claim to Amphipolis, though begrudgingly given the wealth of the mines in nearby Mount Pangaion. By this time Philip had also secured an alliance with Thebes in the context of the ending of the Sacred War the same year, this securing his army's passage through Boeotia into Attica and the Peloponnese whenever he desired. This sobering fact was not lost on Athens and Sparta who while now at peace with Philip, could clearly see the writing was on the wall for future conflict with Macedon if the king's ambitions weren't checked.

While in Pella Philip had time to visit his children by his various wives, including the young Alexander who was now 10. The court there was by now one of the most cosmopolitan across the Greek world, with the wealth of the gold and silver mines on Philip's eastern border attracting the finest academic, theatrical and artistic minds from *poleis* across the region (Lane Fox, 1973, 50). However, this mattered not to Alexander's mother Olympias who single-mindedly pursued her son's future success. It is clear from all the primary sources that Olympias had a profound impact on his upbringing, especially with his father permanently on campaign in the child's early years. As Goldsworthy says (2020, 137): 'For the young Alexander, his father was surely a distant figure, while his mother was far more familiar and important to him, even if her role was primarily to supervise his upbringing.'

Olympias is portrayed by classical historians as very strong-willed, to the point of ruthlessness, with a passionate nature which found an outlet in the Cult of Dionysius, the Greek God of the grape-harvest and wine, fertility, festivity and theatre. This cult had a strong association with the use of tame snakes in its religious ceremonies, in imitation of the Maenad female companions of Dionysius. These serpents occasionally made their way into contemporary narrative regarding the seemingly tumultuous relationship between Philip and Olympias, with Plutarch for example saying that Philip's ardour in the marriage bed was on one occasion cooled when he entered Olympias' sleeping chamber to find her with a snake stretched out at her side (*Lives*, Alexander, 4). Despite such setbacks, their marital relationship did result in the later birth of Cleopatra, Alexander's younger sister, in 355 BC or early 354 BC.

In the royal household Alexander was raised by his nurse Lanice, sister of leading royal companion Cleitus 'the Black'. Three of her sons would later go on to serve and die on campaign with Alexander. Meanwhile, his teachers included Lysimachus of Acarnania, well-known at court for his flattery of Philip and Alexander, and Olympias' relative Leonidas who was a strict disciplinarian.

By the time Philip visited his son in 346 BC there is no doubt he was the heir apparent, with his elder step-brother Arrhidaeus already displaying the symptoms which were to side-line him as a serious candidate for the Argead throne until much later in his life. Like many other key figures in world history, Alexander's early years are shrouded in hagiography, in his case perhaps more so than most. However, what is clear is that here was a young man who had definitely inherited his father's sense of destiny and ambition. This soon manifested to the point of precociousness, he excelling in the liberal Greek education that had long been the norm for male Argead children in the Macedonian court, including the young noble companions selected to become his educational peer group. Many of these as young men would accompany him on his later astonishing campaigns of conquest, including Ptolemy, Cassander and Hephaestion. Alexander's education specifically included a focus on the natural sciences, mathematics, music, rhetoric and literature. The latter was particularly important in that, with its focus on Homer and Athenian literature and drama, it emphasized Macedon's cultural association (whether a conceit or not) with the Greek *poleis* across the region.

True to his nature, Philip spared no expense in the education of his younger son, later famously recruiting Aristotle to become Alexander's tutor as he grew to early manhood. There was precedent here in that Aristotle's father had been a physician to Philip's father Amyntas III at Pella, and Philip had been friendly with Aristotle's former patron Hermeias, so perhaps the recruitment was not so unusual (Lane Fox, 1973, 53). Aristotle certainly benefited. Not only was he well paid, but also as part of his payment Philip agreed to rebuild his hometown of Stagira on the north-eastern coast of the Chalcidice peninsula after Macedon had earlier sacked it.

Meanwhile, for this later stage in Alexander's education, Philip chose the Temple of the Nymphs in Mieza as the classroom for the young man and his peers, one of the elite religious sites in the whole of northern Greece.

However, more importantly for an heir to the Argead throne, Alexander's education also featured a major focus on martial prowess. When later king he often quipped that Leonidas, tasked with his physical education, thought the breakfast should be a hard night's march and supper a light breakfast. Interestingly, Alexander showed fewer proclivities early in his education for the physical side of his tutelage, favouring the learning of Hellenic culture and music, but once he began his martial training he excelled with sword, bow and lance. He was soon an accomplished hunter, and at some stage in his early teens killed a boar single-handedly which allowed him to recline at table in an adult dining room when eating, an event no doubt stage-managed for his safety, even if unbeknownst to him. He was also famously a fine horseman, later taming the headstrong charger Bucephalus in front of his father and the king's companions. Here we have one of the most famous anecdotes about Alexander, with Plutarch saying that on seeing Alexander's bravery with the headstrong horse Philip said apocryphally (*Lives*, Alexander, 6.5): 'My boy, you must find a kingdom big enough for your ambitions. Macedon is too small for you.'

This fine stallion would be associated with Alexander throughout most of his adult life, even having the city of Alexandria-Bucephalous in the Indus valley later named after him in 326 BC.

The young heir's growing self-confidence is evident in a number of insightful vignettes detailed in classical literature. For example, Plutarch sets the scene for Alexander's later adult encounters with the Achaemenid Persian Empire, saying (*Lives*, Alexander, 5.1):

> On one occasion some ambassadors from the king of Persia arrived in Macedonia, and since Philip was absent, Alexander received them in his place. He talked freely with them and quietly won them over, not only by the friendliness of his manner, but also because

he did not trouble them with any childish or trivial inquiries, but questioned them about the distances they had travelled by road, the nature of their journey into the interior, the character of the king, his experience in war, and the military strength and prowess of the Persians. They came away convinced that Philip's celebrated astuteness was as nothing compared to the adventurous spirit of his son.

Through Plutarch's obvious 'after the event' flattery here we can see that Philip and the Argead court were grooming an heir fit to succeed a king who by this time was beginning to dominate the Greek-speaking world in the eastern Mediterranean.

Next, never one to rest on his laurels, in 346 BC Philip turned his attention back to Sparta which he correctly identified as the major land-based military threat to him (given his treaty with Thebes), not only in the Peloponnese but also given the *poleis* had recently sided with Athens, in Attica too. Here we have yet another anecdotal story about Philip, though one rather more ignominious. Before attempting any military intervention the king apparently tried to intimidate Sparta into accepting Macedonian hegemony, his message bluntly stating 'If I win this war, you will be slaves forever.' The Laconian reply was a suitably succinct 'If'. Sparta's concise reaction worked in the short term as Philip chose to leave the city alone for now.

Philip's focus on Sparta was short-lived. Soon his attention was pulled back towards more trouble along his eastern border with Thrace. He invaded in 342 BC, conquering the fortified settlement of Eumolpia which he renamed Philippopolis (modern Plovdiv in Bulgaria). Then, in the winter of 340–339 BC, Philip turned his attention to the north and the Scythian allies of the Thracians. These Indo-European nomads had settled on the Asian Steppe above the Black Sea and were renowned horsemen, noted for their skill with the bow. Their armies largely comprised skirmishing light horse and were notoriously difficult to bring to battle, and so it initially proved for Philip (see Chapter 3 for detail). However, ever the strategic innovator, he quickly deployed a small flying column of veteran cavalry to trap his Scythian opponents unexpectedly in their home territory. Here they were faced with confronting Philip's more experienced troops in a set piece battle, or fleeing and leaving their families to the king's mercy. They instead chose to submit, with Philip heading back to Macedon with a huge number of fine horses to add to the royal stables in Pella. However, it seems Philip's luck then failed him as he mistakenly chose to head home along a swifter route through the territory of the Thracian Triballi tribe. These, sensing the opportunity for loot, refused the Macedonians passage through the Haemus Mountains unless they received a share of the king's Scythian booty. Unsurprisingly Philip refused and tried to force his way through, in the process receiving the right-thigh injury detailed earlier in this chapter. Though again suffering a dreadful wound, he once more quickly recovered, with the Triballi then swiftly subdued.

In 340 BC conflict broke out again with Athens. Rather than target Attica directly Philip again headed east, this time to besiege the Athenian coastal colony of Perinthus on the Sea of Marmara in modern European Turkey. Philip's modernised army was highly proficient in siege warfare and he had no qualms about investing such a difficult fortified settlement, even though it stood on a peninsula connected to the mainland by a heavily defended 180m isthmus, and was surrounded by cliffs. Despite the city being repeatedly supplied during the siege by the Athenian fleet, the Macedonians eventually broke through the outer walls. However, much to the king's dismay, he then found a new and far more substantial wall had been built inside the original fortification, and after sporadic attempts to penetrate this decided it best to withdraw with his forces intact.

Philip was again back in the east a year later, with his target this time being Byzantium, another of Athens' key regional supporters. However, again he failed to capture his objective, though the event is better known for coinciding with Alexander's coming of age. The youth's education with his friends under Aristotle had ended on his sixteenth birthday, and this time when Philip went off to war he left his heir in charge in Pella as regent. Alexander quickly had the chance to test his skills in battle as, in Philip's absence, the Thracian Maedi tribe rebelled against Macedonian rule. Alexander, no doubt well-guided by the council of nobles appointed by the king to advise him, responded quickly. Leading a force to the northeast he drove the Thracians out of Macedonian territory and then colonised the region they had previously occupied with Greek settlers, founding a city there. This he famously named Alexandropolis, the first of his many foundings.

Chaeronea and After

While Philip had returned to Pella empty-handed from Perinthus and Byzantium, his wider campaigns in the east were broadly successful and he happily resumed rule in the royal capital, dispatching Alexander back to Thrace to get further experience of command and battle. However, to the south real trouble was brewing. In later 339 BC Philip's erstwhile allies Thebes reneged on their treaty with him. Though now fading as the leading military power in mainland Greece following the death of Epaminondas and his heirs apparent at the hands of the Spartans at the Battle of Mantinea in 362 BC, the *poleis* still occasionally flexed its muscles among its city-state neighbours. On this occasion it went too far though, deciding to supplant the Macedonian garrisons Philip had left behind to support the Thessalian-backed regime in the stronghold of Nicaea, one of the fortresses guarding access to the pass of Thermopylae. Though not a direct declaration of war, this was a warning to Philip that to pass further south to central Greece and onwards into Attica and the Peloponnese would now require the permission of Thebes. For Philip to do so would mean a huge loss of face among the city-states, all now wary of his growing power but also mindful of his recent setbacks in Perinthus and Byzantium.

The king cast around looking for cause to campaign in southern Greece to test Theban resolve. He found it in an obscure dispute in the *poleis* of Amphissa in Phocis where many of the regional powers, including Athens and Thebes, were being drawn into a dispute following the Sacred War over agricultural land being worked there which belonged to the recently re-consecrated Temple of Apollo at Delphi. This quarrel involved the Amphictytonic League once more, they being the accuser, and Phocian Amphissa, the accused. Philip sided with the former, Thebes the latter, with the Athenians officially remaining uncommitted though clearly favouring Amphissa and the Thebans.

There are differing accounts of how the king acted next. One school of thought has Philip ordering Alexander to muster an army to campaign in southern Greece, with the heir to the throne cannily disguising his preparations to appear as though Illyria was his actual target. This narrative says the plan backfired, with the Illyrians taking the Macedonians at face value and attacking first, only to be expelled by Alexander. This could of course be pure hagiography, written well after the event to show the future world-conqueror as a vigorous and cunning leader even in his youth. The other school simply has Philip completing his recuperation from his thigh wound while his army gathered under his auspices on the southern borders of Macedon.

Whatever the truth, when Philip's troops were ready he marched south in the late autumn of 339 BC, cleverly wrong-footing the Thebans by completely avoiding Nicaea and the pass at Thermopylae. Instead he chose to risk a crossing through the passes of mountainous central Greece, swiftly capturing Cytinium near the high Gravia Pass above Amphissa itself. With this route open, he then descended onto the border of northern Boeotia where he occupied the city of Elatea, situated between the middle of the narrows of the Cephissus River below Amphicleia. This was well placed to command any of the lowland access points through central Greece into Attica and onto the Peloponnese. Philip now consolidated, awaiting a large contingent of Thessalian allies which promptly arrived in good order. The wily king also ensured the local Phocians were well-treated, mindful that at any time he might have to retreat from whence he came at short notice.

With Philip now poised above Attica like a Sword of Damocles, panic gripped the city-states of southern Greece. In Athens pandemonium erupted among the ruling classes when news of the king's arrival to the north reached them, with Goldsworthy describing the scene, saying magistrates hurriedly left their dinner tables to set up an emergency meeting of the great and the good the following day at the Pynx place of assembly (2020, 169). It was here that Demosthenes, the Athenian statesman and orator now at the height of his powers and styling himself the spokesman for a Greece free from Macedonian interference, convinced those eligible to vote to seek an alliance against Philip with Thebes. Both Athens and the king then sent embassies to Thebes to win the Boeotian city's favour, with Athens winning the diplomatic contest. A Greek-Macedonian conflict was now inevitable, and this time it would not be fought out in Macedon's back yard in Thrace, the Chalcidice peninsula or Thessaly, but in southern Greece for the first time.

Philip once again deployed a stratagem to wrong-foot his enemies, making it known he planned to head back north to deal with a rebellion in Thrace. He then sent some of his army back towards the Gravia Pass to give the impression he was following this through. However, as soon as the mercenaries hired by the Athenians and Thebans to keep an eye on his camp at Elateia relaxed, he doubled his troops back south where, joined by the rest of his army, they swiftly occupied Amphissa. From this position he could threaten the lines of supply of the combined armies of the Athenians, Thebans and their allies who by now were gathering in northern Boeotia. They quickly withdrew out of Philip's immediate reach, setting up a new camp near the Boeotian city of Chaeronea. Both sides now paused for breath, with Philip sending envoys to Athens and Thebes to ask for peace. He probably thought his point had been made, making it clear to the *poleis* that if he wanted to campaign in southern Greece as he had earlier in the Peloponnese then he could at will. However, in Athens Demosthenes was in no mood to do a deal with the 'barbarian' Philip and again his fine oratory won the day in rejecting the Macedonian offer, this then stiffening the resolve of Thebes. Battle was now inevitable and by the beginning of August Philip again moved towards the allies. Soon the two armies were camped a few kilometres apart near Chaeronea.

Battle was finally joined on 2 August, with the Greek allies occupying a strong defensive position with their right flank covered by a marsh near a stream impassable for all but the lightest foot, and their left flank protected by rocky hills and the walls of Chaeronea itself. Their army totalled around 35,000 men, with the 12,000 far more experienced Thebans on the right including the 300 strong elite Sacred Band, then the Theban and Athenian allies positioned in the centre, and finally the 10,000 Athenian citizen levy deployed on the left. It is unclear if the army featured any cavalry on the day, with Head suggesting their best Boeotian cavalry were absent (2016, 147).

Philip's army deployed opposite, numbering 30,000 foot and 3,000 horse, mostly battle-hardened veterans of his recent campaigns. He divided his battle line into two, he commanding the right and the 18-year-old Alexander the left. The king clearly had a detailed battle plan from the outset, all based on his by now well-tried pike and shock cavalry 'hammer and anvil' tactics. In this context it seems likely he himself commanded the majority of his phalanx, with the experienced Thessalian allied cavalry covering their extreme right flank. This would leave Alexander with a small part of the phalanx to act as a fulcrum, perhaps with the guard infantry, and the companion elite *xyston* lance-armed cavalry. Alexander's extreme left flank then featured more allied cavalry, mainly fierce Thracians.

The frontage of both armies was screened with light troops using bows, slings and javelins, and given weight of numbers and experience their early skirmishing would likely have seen the Macedonians clear the enemy screen first. Philip then initiated his plan as the Greek allies gazed across the dusty battlefield, wondering what fate awaited them. Mathew explains what happened next (2015, 43):

> …Philip…advanced his right wing to engage first, creating a battle line extending obliquely to the left-rear, and then slowly withdrew his right behind the main frontage of the line to create a new oblique position extending to his right rear.

It cannot be emphasized how complicated a manoeuvre this was, the king's phalanx moving first forward to challenge the Athenian hoplites, then seemingly withdrawing. This was clearly done in good order and on purpose, with the phalangites slowly marching backwards, pikes forward, to create the reverse oblique. From the Athenians' point of view, given the clouds of swirling dust created by thousands of Macedonians marching first forward then back, they had no idea they were being lured by a cleverly-devised feint and took the bait. Urged on by an Athenian general called Stratocles, the part-time warriors gave up their secure position and surged forward to pursue what they thought was a fleeing enemy. They were soon proved wrong as Philip's phalangites promptly halted the 'withdrawal' as soon as the Athenians were proud of the Macedonian front line, the pikemen's front five ranks then stabbing viciously with their long pikes as soon as the Athenians were in range, the latter's front ranks pushed forward by those at the rear unaware at the sudden change of fortune. Here the Macedonians now had a huge advantage, with Goldsworthy saying (2020, 177): 'The Macedonian pikemen could reach their hoplite opponents, but unless they could break or push aside several sarissa heads in succession, it is hard to see how the allied hoplites (with their shorter spears) could harm their enemies.'

The allied hoplites in the Greek centre and the Thebans on their right viewed the Athenians' impetuous charge with horror, and as surviving stragglers began to stagger back to their start line the precariousness of their position now became evident given a massive gap had opened in the Greek line where the Athenians had once been. The Macedonian 'hammer and anvil' was about the snap shut with great force.

Either Philip, or Alexander himself, immediately saw the opportunity and the heir to the Macedonian throne now charged his companions into the exposed left flank of the allied hoplites in the centre, smashing them into the Thebans on their right who were already pinned to their front by a sharp advance by Alexander's foot. A massacre ensued, with Plutarch saying that Alexander was (*Lives*, Alexander, 9.29):

> the first man that charged the Theban's Sacred Band … This bravery made Philip so fond of him, that nothing pleased him more than to hear his subjects call himself their general and Alexander their king.

Diodorus Siculus, in his formal account of the battle, is more graphic, saying (*Library of History*, 16.86):

> Alexander, anxious to give his father proof of his valour ... was the first to break through the main body of the enemy, directly opposing him, slaying many; and bore down all before him ... and his men, pressing on closely, cut to pieces the lines of the enemy; and after the ground had been piled with the dead, put the wing resisting him in flight.

Engaged to their front by Alexander's foot, the Theban Sacred Band were butchered where they stood and died to a man as Alexander's lancers slammed into their left flank. Seeing this, the allied army then broke, leaving 2,000 dead Thebans and Athenians on the field, with around 4,000 taken prisoner to later be sold into slavery.

Only the fallen Sacred Band were accorded full funerary honours, with the Macedonians burying them in a mass grave known as the *polyandrion* (Plutarch, *Lives*, Pelopidas, 18.5). This was excavated in 1879-80 and found to contain 254 skeletons, most of which had visible unhealed wounds. These included several with puncture wounds to the skull, clearly caused by the *sauroter* butt-spikes of Macedonian *sarissa* as phalangites carried out a *coup de grâce* on the fallen hoplites (Dahm, 2020, 51). Meanwhile, Demosthenes and many other fugitives (mostly Athenians) fled over the nearby Kerata Pass to make their way swiftly south to Attica.

Philip's victory at the Battle of Chaeronea was total, with any Greek opposition shattered. The king and Alexander now marched unopposed through southern Boeotia into Attica and on to the Peloponnese. By this time the ever-ambitious Philip had his eyes on an even greater prize, namely Achaemenid Persia. He therefore needed to leave a stable Greece to his rear before looking eastwards. This meant first dealing with the main protagonists against him at Chaeronea, and then winning over the other city-states in southern Greece.

He first marched on Thebes which immediately surrendered, its leaders expecting the worst. However, instead of sacking his former home when a hostage, he simply expelled those Theban leaders who had opposed him, recalling any exiled pro-Macedonian Theban leaders and installing a Macedonian garrison. He also ordered the Boeotian cities of Thespiae and Plataea, destroyed by Thebes in previous conflicts, to be re-founded, and made the city pay for the return of its prisoners and to bury their dead. He treated Athens even more leniently. Although he abolished the Second Athenian League confederation of Aegean city-states, the leading city in Attica was allowed to keep its colony on Samos, and its own prisoners were freed without ransom. Perhaps here Philip hoped to make use of Athen's still-powerful navy in his future campaigns against the Persians.

Meanwhile, most of the other *poleis* in southern Greece were treated well, with Philip and Alexander welcomed in each city they visited except Sparta. Not having taken part in the earlier campaign against Philip, its military establishment was largely intact and clearly the Spartan leadership saw the demise of its recent nemesis Thebes and long-term enemy Athens as an opportunity to further its own ends. Still living on the reputation of their Greco-Persian War and Peloponnesian War exploits, the Spartans were emboldened to refuse Philip's invitation to engage in dialogue. The king therefore ravaged Lacedaemonia in the southern Peloponnese, though not Sparta itself which he again left well alone.

Philip next gathered the great and the good from across southern Greece at Corinth, where in 337 BC he established his Hellenic Alliance (called by modern scholars the League of Corinth) modelled on the old anti-Achaemenid Persian alliance dating back to the Greco-Persian Wars, with the members agreeing never to wage war against each other unless to suppress a revolt. The alliance included all of the leading city-states in central Greece, Attica and the Peloponnese except Sparta, which remained aloof from Philip's now otherwise unchallenged Macedonian hegemony in Greece. The king was soon declared the *hegemon* (supreme leader) of all Greece, and quickly turned his attention to the one subject he knew could unify all of the Greeks, namely his planned war with Persia. While some Greeks might still call him a 'barbarian', he knew the Achaemenids were the '...barbarians par excellence...' across the whole Greek-speaking world (Cartledge, 2004, 38).

Philip had long been interested in the vast Persian Empire, which by this time stretched from the western Anatolian coast in the west to the Indus valley in the east. Founded by Cyrus the Great around 550 BC, the empire was the heir to the lengthy tradition of monarchical and highly-bureaucratic regimes historically spread throughout the Levant and modern Middle East. However, what set this one apart from its Akkadian, Assyrian, Babylonian and Median predecessors was the speed with which it expanded on the path to empire (Elliott, 2020a, 49). Looking to continue this expansion westwards across the eastern Mediterranean, the empire considered the Greek *poleis* an irritating barrier. However, having twice been fought to a standstill in successive invasions of southern Greece under Darius I and Xerxes, subsequent Persian kings (who modestly styled themselves King of Kings) had resorted to diplomacy and bribery to achieve their aims in the west using the empire's vast wealth to wrong-foot the city states. Both the Persians and the Greeks knew the former's ambitions to conquer Attica and the Peloponnese was unfinished business though, and Philip felt a pre-emptive strike was the best form of defence, if only to free the Greek cities of Ionia from Persian rule. Martial success in the east would also secure his reputation as not only the champion of all Greece, but the greatest military leader of his generation.

Ever the careful planner, Philip knew his future enemy well. He was involved in Persian court intrigue from early in his reign, and by 353 BC at least three leading opponents of the Persian king Artaxerxes III were resident in his court. These were Artabazos II (the former satrap of Hellespontine Phryigia), the nobleman Amminapes who Alexander the Great later made the satrap of Parthia and Hyrcania, and another leading nobleman called Sisines. Through these, other frequent Persian visitors, and his extensive network of spies in Darius III's court, Philip had a good understanding of the Persian state and its military establishment. He also understood the myriad of issues faced daily by the Persian king. As detailed earlier, Alexander soon followed in the king's footsteps in this regard, getting to know his future Persian opponents from a young age.

In early 336 BC Philip appointed his right-hand man Parmenion as *strategos* to command an initial invasion force with orders to cross the Hellespont into Persian-controlled Anatolia. Comprising 10,000 veterans, and also featuring the experienced commanders Amyntas, Andomenes and Attalus, the force landed in Asia where it met minimal Persian resistance. Soon many of the Greek Ionian cities along the western Anatolian coast rebelled against Persian rule, throwing out the trappings of satrapal rule and welcoming the Macedonians and their Greek mercenaries. However, back in Macedon events suddenly took a dramatic turn for the worse.

This had begun earlier, as so often with the Argeads, with another royal marriage. Philip had already taken a sixth wife after marrying Olympias, the Thracian princess Meda of Odessa (who later committed suicide after the king's death). However, the primary sources say that when Philip later returned to Pella in 338 BC he fell in love with Cleopatra Eurydice, niece of Attalus, his general from one of the leading Macedonian aristocratic families (and shortly to accompany Parmenion to Anatolia). They married soon after, the event making the heir to the throne, Alexander, feel less secure, given if Philip and Cleopatra had a male child the boy might become the preferred candidate as next king given Attalus' pure Macedonian lineage and popularity at court. This insecurity was on full view when the wedding took place, the event ending disastrously for both Philip and Alexander. Plutarch provides specific detail of the occasion, saying (*Lives*, Alexander, 9.1):

> At the wedding of Cleopatra, whom Philip fell in love with and married, she being much too young for him, her uncle Attalus in his drink desired the Macedonians would implore the gods to give them a lawful successor to the kingdom by his niece. This so irritated Alexander, that throwing one of the cups at his head, 'You villain,' said he, 'What, am I then a bastard?' Then Philip, taking Attalus' part, rose up and would have run his son through; but by good fortune for them both, either his over-hasty rage, or the wine he had drunk, made his foot slip, so that he fell down on the floor. At which Alexander reproachfully insulted over him: 'See there,' said he, 'the man who makes preparations to pass out of Europe into Asia, overturned in passing from one seat to another.'

Context is important here, often overlooked in the contemporary sources that cover this event in the context of Alexander's later greatness. In Macedonian high society feasts, whether at weddings or otherwise, were always drunken events where kings could be praised but also mocked, particularly by those close to them. Angry and drunken exchanges were common, though usually forgiven and forgotten the following morning providing things did not get too out of hand. In that regard the king always had his companions (at least those remaining vaguely sober) and pages to look after his best interests. There is no doubt Philip was both proud and fond of Alexander, often expressing this publicly, but occasionally would remind the ambitious young man that he was not yet the king. Perhaps, in his cups, that was his intention here. However, given events at the wedding ended in humiliation for the king (indeed one recorded for all posterity), Alexander's position in the Argead court was now in jeopardy, even if only in the short term.

The heir now fled west with Olympias and his close friends. He left his mother in the safe hands of her brother Alexander I who was now the king of Epirus in Dodona, the Molossian capital. Alexander then escaped north-west to Illyria where he sought refuge, perhaps with the tribal leader Glaucias of the Taulantii. Here he and his entourage were treated as honoured guests. However, given the years Philip had spent grooming Alexander for the throne, and his genuine affection for his son, it seems unlikely that

Philip ever intended to severely punish his son, let alone remove him as heir. Accordingly, Alexander soon returned to Macedon after a six-month self-imposed exile.

Alexander was quickly back in favour with the king, but was soon in trouble again. The following year Pixodarus, the Persian satrap of Caria, offered his eldest daughter to Alexander's elder step-brother Arrhidaeus in marriage. Several of Alexander's close friends, together with the ever-wary Olympias, suggested this indicated Philip now intended to make the ill-favoured Arrhidaeus his heir. Predictably the young Alexander overreacted and sent an actor called Thessalus of Corinth to suggest to Pixodarus that he should offer his daughter's hand to himself instead. However, when Philip heard of this he reacted with anger, deciding to nip things in the bud immediately. He visited Alexander in his quarters in the royal palace at Pella, taking with him Parmenion's son Philotas in the hope someone of his son's generation might make him see sense. There Alexander was told that arranging royal marriages was the prerogative of the king only, and that a match for him with a mere local dynast's daughter was beneath the heir to the throne of Macedon. Such words may have come as a relief to Alexander, though the king still felt he needed to teach his heir a lesson. He therefore banished Alexander's close friends Ptolemy, Nearchus, Harpalus and Erigyius (the latter three notably Greek). He also ordered Thessalus to be brought before him in chains, though the actor shrewdly eluded capture to pursue his career elsewhere (Goldsworthy, 2020, 192). Pixodarus later married his daughter to another Persian satrap, wisely choosing to avoid any further engagement in Argead court politics.

One can sense an uneasy peace now descending in Pella, with Alexander on his best behaviour in the hope Philip would allow his friends to return. However, for the king disaster loomed. In October 336 BC, at the same time Parmenion was winning Ionian Greek hearts and minds, the great and the good from all over Greece gathered in Aegae to celebrate the wedding of Alexander I of Epirus and Alexander's full-sister (and Alexander I's own niece) Cleopatra. As part of the celebrations the 46-year-old Philip entered the town's theatre at the culmination of a procession of twelve statues of the key Olympian Gods, and one of himself. Philip was unarmed, wearing a simple tunic bleached pure white. He had no close-protection with him, the king's seven personal bodyguards ringing the arena at a distance. As he reached the centre of the arena, one of them suddenly ran towards him before anyone else could react. This was Pausanias of Orestis, a young man recently promoted to the post as recompense for very rough treatment (which may have included rape) at the hands of Philip's now father-in-law Attalus and his cronies. Pausanias, also a lover of Philip when a youth, felt Attalus had not been punished enough for his abuse. From that point, even as a close royal guard, he nursed a sense of grievance against the king. This was certainly encouraged by those in court who were set against Attalus, including Alexander and Olympias. Now, as Pausanias reached the king, he dropped his ceremonial javelin and drew a long dagger hidden beneath his cloak. He struck immediately, stabbing Philip viciously between the ribs before anyone could react. The *hegemon* of all Greece, set to lead the Greeks on their crusade against the Persians, died within seconds, his corpse bleeding into the sand of the arena.

After a shocked silence, pandemonium broke out. The assassin immediately tried to escape, racing towards associates waiting for him with horses near the arena entrance. However, closely pursued by three fellow guards, he tripped on a vine root and was quickly killed with javelins, his corpse subsequently crucified. Many have since speculated that Pausanias was part of a much wider conspiracy, potentially including Alexander and Olympias. However, at the time most commentators including Aristotle (*The Politics*, 1311b) concluded this was a tragic case of a former lover motivated by a sense of deep personal grievance against a close associate of the king.

Matters moved quickly from that point. The leading Macedonian noble Antipater, with Parmenion away, quickly presented Alexander to an assembly of the nobility and army as Philip's successor. Given the kingdom's many foreign policy commitments, all knew the last thing Macedon needed at that point was a contested Argead succession. The massed gathering swiftly acclaimed Philip's second legitimate son Alexander III of Macedon, who in short order thanked them by ensuring that any soldier whose salary had fallen into arrears while on campaign was paid in full. However, by this time the income from the gold and silver mines of Mount Pangaion and elsewhere was now only enough to pay a third of the cost of the enormous Macedonian army, while opportunity for local booty in Greece to make up the difference had dried up with the establishment of the Hellenic Alliance. Indeed, just to pay the arrears, Alexander had to borrow from the Macedonian aristocracy to make up the difference, he having already abolished direct taxation as a first act as king to boost early acceptance of his rule.

Alexander shared Philip's ambition to lead a crusade of all the Greeks against the Persian Empire, and he immediately turned his attention to his father's planned campaign. He soon had cause to personally engage there as, when word reached the Persians that Philip had been murdered, they quickly moved to crush the newly free cities on the Ionian coast of Anatolia. Further, the Achaemenids then defeated a Macedonian force under Parmenion near Magnesia, the Persians led by the mercenary *strategos* Memnon of Rhodes. Taking this in, Alexander realised that to have a remote chance of success in Asia he needed to gather the largest possible army he could from across Greece, and then lead his *anabasis* eastwards in person. He was also aware that the vast wealth available there as plunder would solve, once and for all, the problems he was having in paying the army. First though, as with any king of Macedon, he had to secure his borders at home.

Chapter 2

Alexander the Great: A Biography

In the annals of ancient history the light of Alexander the Great shines brighter than any other, inspiring generations of dynasts and despots. Thus we have Julius Caesar, his rival as a commander in this book, reduced to tears on seeing a statue of the Macedonian king and feeling diminished (Elliott, 2019, 82). Alexander was the embodiment of the Homeric warrior hero. A regent at 16, cavalry commander at 18, king at 20 and conqueror of the biggest Empire the world had ever known at 26. The explorer of mythical India at 30 where he reached the ends of his known earth, but wanted more. The man for whom achievable was never enough, and who later thought himself a God.

In this chapter I provide a concise biography of Alexander from his accession as Macedonian king in 336 BC through to his dramatic death in Babylon in 323 BC only a month shy of his thirty-third birthday. In the first instance, to provide context and set the scene for the astonishing story that follows, I detail his key opponent Darius III and his Achaemenid Persian Empire. I then chronologically consider each phase of Alexander's *anabasis* eastwards, this including an analysis of his Indian opponents as his conquests concluded in the Punjab. Finally, I detail his traumatic journey back to Babylonia where he finally met his fate.

The Achaemenid Empire of Darius III

The Empire ruled by Darius III, while not as powerful as that of his predecessors, was still mighty indeed. The early Achaemenid kings had built on the fearsome reputation of their former Median masters whose rule Cyrus the Great had usurped. The Biblical prophet Isaiah paints a grim picture of Median martial prowess when describing their turning on their former Babylonian allies with whom they had earlier defeated the Neo-Assyrian Empire, saying (Holy Bible, Isaiah, 13, 18):

Behold, I am stirring up the Medes against them, who have no regard for silver and do not delight in gold. Their bows will slaughter the young men: they will have no mercy on the fruit of the womb: their eyes will not pity children. And Babylon, the glory of kingdoms, the splendour and pride of the Chaldeans, will be like Sodom and Gomorrah when God overthrew them. It will never be inhabited or dwelt in for all generations: no Arab will pitch his tent there, no shepherds will make their flocks lie down there. But wild beasts will lie down there, and its houses will be full of howling creatures.

Cyrus' successors inherited this terrifying reputation, with the Persians time and again shattering the armies of their enemies and razing their cities to the ground as they expanded Persian territorial control from the eastern Mediterranean to the Indus. However, the defeat of Darius I's invasion of Greece at Marathon in 490 BC, and later that of Xerxes at Salamis in 480 BC and Plataea in 479 BC, removed the spell of Persian invincibility and from that point onwards Persian armies would more often than not meet their match when fighting the Greek *poleis* and their hoplite phalanxes.

Darius III is one of the great unfortunate figures of world history, forever remembered as the unworthy opponent of Alexander the Great and the last king of the Achaemenid Persian Empire. Born around 380 BC to a subsidiary branch of the royal family, he was originally called Artashata (and later Codomannus by the Greek city-states). His pathway to power was unusual, even for an eastern despot. His grandfather was one of the younger sons of Darius II, while his mother was a daughter of Artaxerxes II. Therefore, while he certainly had royal lineage, this was well-removed from the normal line of succession for an Achaemenid Persian monarch. Darius' early career reflected this, he serving as the satrap of the Persian province of Armenia, then leading campaigns against the distant Cadusii tribe in the mountainous district of Media Atropatene on the south-western shores of the Caspian Sea, before ultimately being given charge of the royal postal service which made use of the extensive network of Royal trunk roads to link all corners of the empire. This last posting was key to his later rise to power as it gave him a leading place in the royal court where he was improbably elevated to the throne after the royal grand vizier Bogoas poisoned the then king Artaxerxes III, with whom he had fallen out of favour, and then also killed his son and successor Arses (also known as Artaxerxes IV).

The main issue inherited by Darius III on his unlikely accession, aside from the instability of his rise to power, was the gradual eroding of the authority of the Achaemenid Persian kings over the satrap governors of the Empire's many far-flung provinces. While still styled 'slaves to the king' by the Greeks, by the mid-fourth century BC many ruled semi-independently of royal authority, especially in the most distant provinces. Some had even begun to institute a system of hereditary succession within their own territories. Further, from the fourth century BC some satraps had also started to keep a certain amount of the tribute collected from native peoples, usually paid directly to the king, for local defence, this further increasing their autonomy. Nevertheless, as Cartledge says (2004, 43):

> Even a weak king…such as Darius III looks to have been provided with enormous institutional and symbolic buttressing. He was, to quote the formula from an inscription of Darius II, 'the Great King, King of Kings (Shahanshah), King of peoples with many kinds of men, King of this great earth far and wide.' His person was sacred, and though not himself a god, he ruled by the grace of the great Zoroastrian God of Light Ahura Mazda.

The famous multilingual cliff-relief inscription found on a rock face at Mount Behistun in the Kermanshah province of western Iran, dating to the earlier reign of Darius I and later crucial to the decipherment of cuneiform, illustrates the crucial importance of this religious link for each Achaemenid monarch. Specifically, it says: 'Ahura Mazda is a great God, who created this earth, who created the sky, who created man, who created happiness for man, who made Darius king, one king among many, one lord among many.'

The Persian king's court was highly elaborate, inheriting many of the traditions of earlier empires in the region. This included a hierarchy of officials with a variety of titles which may, or may not, have reflected their actual responsibilities. Examples included a spear bearer, bow bearer, staff bearers, cup bearer (a role fulfilled for the king Artaxerxes I by the Old Testament scribe and priest Ezra), a grand vizier (for example Bagoas as detailed above) and large numbers of court eunuchs who managed everything from the day-to-day activities of the royal court through to the delicate task of controlling the king's harem. One of the most famous of Darius III's eunuchs was another Bagoas, this youth a royal consort who went on to become a famous paramour of Alexander the Great.

However, the most important individuals in the orbit of the King of Kings were, in descending order:

- His seven special counsellors, all leading noblemen and usually close family members.
- The Royal Judges.
- The Chief Priests of Ahura Mazda.
- His advisory group of Honoured Equals, King's Friends and Royal relations.

All helped him run his immense empire, broadly in the interests of his Persian subjects, who were clearly favoured over and above the huge number of other cultures and peoples within the empire's far reaching borders.

The Persian king was also commander-in-chief of the empire's vast military resources. Persian armies tended to operate on two levels. First, at the upper end the royal army was commanded in person by the king who would position himself in the dead centre of his multitude, though unlike an Argead monarch only fight if absolutely necessary. Second, at the lower end there were regional armies commanded by individual satraps. The resources available to each usually depended on the region in which a campaign was taking place, but generally they comprised various combinations of central army troops, mercenaries and regional troops, the latter depending on whether the army derived in the west or east of the empire. Royal armies tended to have a far larger contingent of central army troops, particularly guard units.

In terms of the central army troops, at their core were originally the Immortals, select warriors armed with short spears and bows. As with most Persian warriors who could afford them, sidearms included short swords, hand axes and war picks. The front rank in Immortal units were equipped with large pavise-style wicker body-shields that gave its name to this style of Persian warfare, *sparabara* ('shield bearer' in Old Persian). In this type of warfare, these front rankers used their pavises to form a physical barrier behind which the other Immortals (often in deep formations) used their bows to reduce their opponents to a state of disorder, after which the front ranks then discarded their pavises to engage hand-to-hand, followed by those behind. This pavise barrier-tactic proved particularly effective defending against aggressive cavalry, though much less so against the hoplite phalanxes of the Greek *poleis* in the Greco-Persian Wars. In the armies of Darius I and Xerxes, the Immortals numbered

10,000 troops who the Greek city-states wrongly thought were always kept at this number through the use of central reserves, hence the guard unit's name. It was also from within the ranks of the Immortals that the 1,000 picked elite warriors who formed the king's personal bodyguard were chosen. It is the appearance of these troops which has been preserved for posterity by the over life-size carvings which decorated the external façade of the Achaemenid royal palace at Persepolis, the ceremonial capital of the empire.

However, by the time of Darius III contact with other troop types, most notably hoplites, had led to a significant change in the panoply of Persian royal guard troops. Long gone were the pavise-equipped front rankers, and by this later period they tended to be provided with the finest equipment available at the time. This included helmets and armour in the style of Greek hoplites. There is also some debate about whether some were also equipped with Greek-style *aspis* shields, though the likelihood is that most were still equipped with the traditional smaller Persian crescent or round shield. The core weapons remained the same as with earlier Immortals, a short spear and bow. It is the former that gave these guards their 'apple bearers' contemporary name, this based on the elaborate spherical counterweight on the butt of their spears. The guard troops of Darius III numbered far less than those of his predecessors, perhaps the original 10,000 reduced to the core 1,000 close guards of earlier times.

The other key central army troop type in later Achaemenid Persian armies were the west Iranian cavalry which formed the main strike force (Cartledge, 2004, 45). These ranged from the elite mounted kinsmen of the king (including another guard unit of 1,000) through to Iranian levies, though all were broadly armed in the same way with short spears and a missile weapon, usually javelin though sometimes a bow if from further east. The better off, notably the nobility, wore fine armour including bronze and lamellar scale-mail coats adapted from those of the Scythians, and bronze cuirasses imitating those of the Greeks. Some mounts also featured horse armour, again copied from the Scythians and other horsemen of the central Asian Steppe, while most wore helmets (some again similar to those of the Greeks) and carried traditional round Persian shields. Notably, cavalry of this type had begun to charge to contact against their opponents by the time of Darius III rather than skirmish from a distance, particularly in the west of the empire. Guard units operating in this way had also begun to adopt the lance, perhaps copied from the *xystons* used by Macedonian companions.

Finally in terms of central army troops, one weapon type much commented on at the time and subsequently was the scythed chariot. This was the ultimate classical world wonder-weapon, though in reality proved next to useless against disciplined opponents. Drawn by four armoured horses and usually featuring a single armoured driver, scythed chariots had razor-sharp metal blades attached to their wheel axle-ends, yoke and shaft, the latter projecting forward of the horses. Alexander first encountered them at the Battle of Gaugamela when Darius III opened the battle with a charge of 200 such machines. They were later used in Hellenistic armies by the Seleucid Empire and the Pontic kingdom, and were also deployed by the Galatians. In Achaemenid Persian service they were supplied from royal estates called 'chariot land'. Under earlier Achaemenid Persian kings these estates had supplied the more traditional heavy chariots that had served as mobile missile platforms, and when required, shock weapons. Adding scythes and other bladed weapons was the ultimate development of this technology.

Meanwhile, by the fourth century BC Persian kings had increasingly begun to rely on Greek hoplite mercenaries (some later armed in the Iphicratean fashion) to form the core of their royal and satrapal battle lines. Despite the evident decline of the empire by the time of Darius III, the king could still call upon the vast cash reserves of the royal treasury to fund such recruitment. To provide context here, when Alexander the Great captured Darius' various treasuries in his *anabasis* eastwards the total amount accounted for was 180,000 talents of silver, weighing 4,600 tonnes and amounting to almost $4 billion in today's money (Elliott, 2020a, 273).

However, later Achaemenid Persian armies paid a psychological price for this reliance on the infantry tactics and technology of the Greek *poleis*. Specifically, that given the right circumstances and no matter what the disparity in numbers, they could be beaten by the Greeks. This lesson was emphasized by the remarkable story of the *strategos* Xenophon who was recruited to lead 10,000 Greek mercenaries fighting for the usurper Cyrus the Younger against his elder brother Artaxerxes II in his ill-fated challenge for the throne. As retold by Xenophon himself, although Cyrus lost the decisive encounter in 401 BC at Cunaxa given he died on the battlefield (*The Persian Expedition*, 1.8.29), his Greek hoplites defeated all they encountered there, and were later able to extricate themselves from the heart of the Persian Empire northwards to the safety of the Greek colonies on the southern shores of the Black Sea.

Moving on, the bulk of later Achaemenid Persian armies, whether royal or satrapal, were made up of local levies of varying quality, more often than not erring towards the lower end of capability. In the earlier armies of Darius I and Xerxes those drafted from near the Imperial centre included more *sparabara*-style foot, with the infantry in later armies instead equipped with short spears, bows and crescent shields. By the time of Darius III the latter had evolved into troops generically known as the *kardakes*, a semi-professional heavy infantry muster. Initially armed in the same manner as the crescent shield troops detailed above, Head (2016, 11) and others now argue that by the mid-third century BC many *kardakes* had been re-equipped to fight in a similar manner to the warriors fielded by their Greek *poleis* opponents. These included both those trained to fight in the line of battle as hoplites, and also lighter-armed warriors similar to Greek *peltasts* and *psiloi* (see Chapter 3). However, it seems likely that troops equipped in the normal crescent-shield manner also continued in use fighting alongside these Hellenised troops, especially in the east. Meanwhile, another traditional line-of-battle troop type called the *takabara* are also referenced in the primary sources fighting in later Achaemenid Persian armies, these again appearing more commonly in eastern armies

Later Achaemenid Persian armies also included local levies recruited from all of the peoples of the enormous empire. Here there was an even clearer differential between west and east in terms of those available. Those recruited to serve in the former included remnant Egyptian troops, Medizing Greeks, Thracians, Armenians, various Caucasian tribes, Scythian and Dahae horsemen, and various hillmen from the tribes of the Levantine interior. Bow-armed camel riders were also recruited from Arabia.

In the east such local levies featured a larger mounted contingent. These included Bactrians, Saka, Dahae, Paphlagonians and Arachosians. Additionally, eastern armies also often included a contingent from the Indian kingdoms of the Indus valley, including war elephants. Alexander first encountered these when fifteen were likely deployed, though not used, at the Battle of Gaugamela in 331 BC (see later in this chapter for detail on the Indian armies Alexander faced later in his *anabasis*).

Finally here, there has been much debate about the size of Achaemenid Persian armies, particularly those faced by Alexander. Unsurprisingly, the primary sources emphasise the size of the multitude deployed by Darius, for example at Gaugamela, which I use here as my example.

Table 1: Achaemenid Persian Kings

Cyrus The Great	559 BC - 530 BC
Cambyses II	530 BC - 522 BC
Smerdis	March - September 522 BC
Darius I	522 BC - 486 BC
Xerxes I	486 BC - 465 BC
Artaxerxes I	465 BC - 424 BC
Xerxes II	424 BC
Sogdianus	424 BC - 423 BC
Darius II	Early 423 BC - 404 BC
Artaxerxes II	404 BC - 358 BC
Artaxerxes III	358 BC - 338 BC
Artaxerxes IV	338 BC - 336 BC
Darius III	336 BC - 330 BC

At the battle Plutarch says the King of Kings fielded 1,000,000 troops (*Lives*, Alexander, 31.1), with Diodorus Siculus having the same total, he breaking this down as 800,000 foot and 200,000 cavalry (*Library of History*, 17.53). Meanwhile, Arrian (the source which mentions the fifteen Indian elephants) goes slightly further, having 1,000,000 foot and 40,000 cavalry (*Anabasis Alexandri*, 3.8). The only ancient world source to give a more reasonable figure for the size of the Persian army at Gaugamela is the first century AD Roman historian Quintus Curtius Rufus who argued Darius fielded 45,000 cavalry and 200,000 infantry (*The History of Alexander*, 4.12.13).

Continuing with Gaugamela as the example (and noting it was one of the larger, if not the largest, engagements in the later Achaemenid Persian period), most modern sources disagree about whether to take the primary sources at face value or not regarding the size of the Persian army. For example Cartledge (2004, 152) argues in favour of 250,000, while earlier Lane Fox (1973, 236) settled for 300,000. Most recently, Goldsworthy (2020, 325) focuses on the Persian cavalry, indicating there is a reasonable chance that the 45,000 mentioned by Quintus Curtius Rufus were present. With regard to the Persian infantry, no matter what their numbers, Head believes only around 8,000 were of reasonable quality (this including 2,000 mercenary hoplites, 2016, 150) at Gaugamela.

Crossing to Asia

At the time Alexander became king, all contemporary commentators describe his striking appearance. Plutarch says (*Lives*, Alexander, 4.10):

> Alexander possessed a number of individual features which many of his successors and friends later tried to reproduce, for example the poise of the neck which was tilted slightly to the left, or a certain melting look in the eyes...

Though shorter in height than the average Macedonian man of the time, Alexander stood out among the older warriors at court by choosing to remain clean-shaven rather than grow the traditional beard. He is described as having a fair complexion with a 'ruddy tinge' (Plutarch, *Lives*, Alexander, 4.11), with tawny-brown hair often likened to a lion's mane. Notably, his eyes were of different colours because of a condition called heterochromia iridum, with one brown and the other blue grey, giving him an unsettling stare that he used to great effect when needed. This disorder can be caused by trauma, either at birth or later in life, or very rarely by genetics. If trauma at birth, it is the only indication we have that his may have been a difficult delivery.

Alexander was already an accomplished warrior when he acceded to the throne, having commanded the elite companion cavalry for his father at Chaeronea in 338 BC where he had led the charge that cracked the allied Greek line. Now king, he knew that before he turned his attention eastwards he had to secure his rear, especially given the wretched circumstances of Philip's death. Alexander therefore quickly marched south to ensure the loyalty of Thessaly. Then, at a hastily convened assembly of the League of Corinth, he replaced his father as the *hegamon* in charge of the planned Greek campaign against the Persians. The new king then returned north to campaign against the Illyrians and Thracians to secure his borders there, before again heading south when rumours of his death prompted Thebes, urged on by Athens, to revolt against Macedonian rule. Alexander arrived after a forced march, sacked the city and then razed it to the ground after it refused to surrender. In total 6,000 Thebans lost their lives, with the rest of the population sold into slavery.

Alexander's actions as a military leader in dealing with this Theban revolt show a number of traits that came to define him as a military leader. First, the speed with which he acted at a strategic level, catching all by surprise when returning to Boeotia. Next the brutality he employed when required, here destroying the city his father had lived in as a youth. Finally, a towering level of self-confidence, later manifest in his overt sense of destiny as he pursued his *anabasis* eastwards.

The destruction of Thebes cowed any further insurrection in Greece. However, from that point an ever-deeper sense of distrust existed between the Macedonians and Greeks, verging on enmity in the case of Athens and Sparta (Green, 2007, 10). Alexander then left garrisons in Corinth, Chalcis and the *Cadmea* citadel of Thebes (which he had left still standing) before finally turning his attention to his father's planned Persian expedition.

In the first instance Alexander further increased the size of his military establishment, despite the strain already being placed on his treasury by the planned campaign. His own invasion army would now comprise 1,800 companion shock cavalry, 1,800 Thessalian cavalry, 600 Greek cavalry and 900 light cavalry. The latter included a mix of javelin-armed Greeks, bow-and-javelin-armed Paeonians and Thracians, and Macedonian *prodromoi*. The latter, fully detailed in Chapter 3, were lance-armed and principally employed to protect flanks from other light troops, perform a scouting function and to pursue a defeated enemy. Meanwhile, his infantry force comprised 12,000 Macedonians, 7,000 allied Greek warriors, 5,000 Greek mercenaries, 7,000 Thracian and Illyrian irregulars and 1,000 skirmishers. Of the Macedonians, 3,000 were *hypaspist* 'shield bearer' guard troops and 9,000 *pezetairoi* line phalangites organised in six provincial 1,500-strong *taxeis* (again, see Chapter 3). Meanwhile, most of the Greek troops were hoplites, either equipped in the Iphicratean fashion or with the more traditional panoply. As a final comment here on Alexander's invasion army for his Persian campaign, it is worth noting how unusual it was for its time given its very deliberate combined arms nature, with a far higher complement of both cavalry (Head, 2016, 43 notes that Philip had been building these numbers up for some time) and light/rough terrain troops than usual. It also included Philip's sophisticated siege train. Finally, as a statement that this invasion was far more than a simple punitive expedition, Alexander was also accompanied by large numbers of surveyors, architects, engineers, scientists, historians (including Callisthenes, Aristotle's great nephew) and court officials. Clearly Alexander intended to make his mark wherever he conquered Persian territory and elsewhere. This was 'Spear Won' land he had no intention of giving up.

Gazing across the Hellespont towards Asia ready to set out on his *anabasis*, Alexander now displayed the attention to detail in logistics, intelligence gathering and communications that were to be other key hallmarks of his military career. Philip had already initiated this level of planning with his earlier expedition under Parmenion. To determine the lessons the latter had learned in his initial campaigns, Alexander called him home, leaving his troops in place at Abydos on the Asian side of the Hellespont. Once debriefed Alexander then promptly appointed him second-in-command of his *anabasis*, securing the loyalty of the Macedonian high command.

In the spring of 334 BC all was ready and Alexander launched his full invasion force into Asia where they quickly joined the remainder of Parmenion's earlier army. Setting sail from the port city of Sestos on the Thracian Chersonese peninsula to cross the short distance to Abydos on the Helespontine Asian coast, he was accompanied by a cast of characters, some the same age and some older, who would go on to shape the future of the Hellenistic world. These included Ptolemy, Seleucus, Lysimachus, Eumenes, Antigonus *Monophthalmus* (the 'one-eyed'), Perdiccas, Craterus, Leonnatus and Peithon.

A lively debate continues as to the scale of Alexander's ambitions at the point he embarked on his *anabasis*. Green argues that Philip's initial plan was to only secure Asia Minor through to Cilicia, today the southern Anatolian coast (2007, 12). Control to here would have completed Philip's mastery of the Aegean and provided him with an additional 1,760 talents a year for the royal treasury, useful given the cost of maintaining his army. However, Alexander clearly wanted more, his goal I believe to conquer the whole of the Persian Empire. The primary sources are clear regarding his Panhellenic and Homeric intent in that regard. For example Diodorus Siculus has him standing in the prow of his ship in full armour as it approached the Achaean Harbour at Rhoeteum on the southern coast of the Hellespont (*Library of History*, 17.17.2.). This was home to the tomb of Ajax, a highly symbolic location. Here, making his landfall, the king threw a spear ashore and declared his acceptance of Asia from the Gods. Arrian goes further, having the young king taking the helm of his ship for the crossing, sacrificing a bull to Poseidon and the Nereids mid-channel, then disembarking in full armour and setting up altars to Zeus, Athena and Hercules (*Anabasis Alexandri*, 1.10.7). He then has Alexander travel the short distance to Troy. There the king first visited the local temple of Athena. Here

Arrian says he dedicated his armour to the goddess, taking in its place an antique set dated to the Trojan Wars. He next sacrificed to the Trojan king, Priam, in the temple of Zeus. Finally he laid a wreath on the tomb of Achilles, his closest companion Hephaestion doing likewise on the tomb of Patroclus. Green argues all of these vignettes are evidence that Alexander's intentions were far grander than those of his father (2007, 12).

Alexander moved quickly once in Asia. He sought battle with the local Persian army immediately when he learned it was gathering, especially given his force was only equipped with supplies for thirty days (Lane Fox, 1973, 116). The key engagement occurred at the Granicus River in May 334 BC. Here Alexander was confronted by the combined forces of a number of regional Persian satraps. This comprised 20,000 cavalry and 20,000 Greek mercenaries, the latter mostly hoplite heavy infantry, together with supporting Persian foot (Arrian, *Anabasis Alexandri*, 1.10.7, with the battle fully detailed in Chapter 4). Alexander led the Macedonian right flank. He crossed the river and gradually forced back the Persian horse to his front at considerable danger to himself. His phalanx then crossed and eventually engaged the enemy cavalry in the centre. This quickly broke, leaving the Greek mercenaries still unengaged at the rear. Arian has Alexander dealing with the mercenaries harshly (Arrian, *Anabasis Alexandri*, 1.16.2). In his account the young king attacked them to the front with his phalanx and in the flanks with his cavalry. The Greeks were massacred, excepting 2,000 sent back to Macedonia in chains to a short life as slaves in the mines.

This victory removed any immediate threat to Alexander and exposed much of western Anatolia to his army. Most cities opened their gates to the new conqueror. Tyrants were expelled and democracies installed. This underlined Alexander's Panhellenic goals. The only exception was Miletus which was encouraged to hold out by the close proximity of the Persian fleet. Alexander quickly captured the city using specialist troops to assault the walls. Again victorious, he next set about occupying the nearby coastal cities to deny the Persian fleet a regional base of operations. Only Halicarnassus in Caria resisted and was stormed. Alexander then moved quickly on. This was a young man in a hurry.

The king advanced to Perga in modern Antalya in the spring of 333 BC, sticking to the coast where he could rely on his fleet for supply. The region pacified, he then headed inland to Gordium where he famously cut the eponymous knot. This was a feat local tradition said could only be performed by the man who would rule Asia. Alexander then advanced to Ancyra (modern Ankara) before turning south again, passing through Cappadocia and the Cilician Gates. This was the vital pass through the Taurus Mountains that provided access from the Anatolian plateau to the coastal lowlands of Cilicia and Syria (Hornblower and Spawforth, 1996, 331).

Following the failure of his satraps at the River Granicus, and the subsequent fall of the Ionian Greek cities, a chastened Darius now determined to stop this Macedonian upstart once and for all. Gathering his royal army, bolstered by levies from his western and central empire (though not the east), he manoeuvred to interdict Alexander's lines of supply to their north, cutting the Macedonians off from their route home. This forced Alexander to turn back and force a battle with Darius at Issus in a narrow plain between the sea and mountains, given a retreat inland with the Persians so close was not an option (Goldsworthy, 2020, 283). An epic battle ensued, this fully detailed in Chapter 4. The result was again total Macedonian victory, with Darius' vast army (only just shy in terms of numbers of that used at Gaugamela by the Persians) defeated in detail, suffering up to 100,000 casualties. The Macedonians lost only 450 dead and perhaps 4,500 wounded.

In the battle Darius fled as soon as Alexander had turned his lancers towards the Persian centre to threaten the king. This had a crucial outcome as when the Persian army subsequently broke, its baggage camp immediately fell into Macedonian hands. This included the Persian royal family, with Darius' mother, principal wife and children captured, all treated with the utmost respect. Additionally, the imperial court was also seized including Darius' closest advisors. It was here that famously the women in Darius's family mistook Hephaestion for Alexander, and where the king bathed in Darius' own bath after returning from his pursuit of the broken Persian army.

To contemporary audiences such a victory for Alexander and his Greek allies was astounding, especially given the asymmetry of numbers involved in the battle where the Macedonians had been so heavily outnumbered. The young king lost no time in spreading word of his triumph across the Greek-speaking world, with Parmenion then capturing the satrapal capital of Damascus with a flying column of cavalry before the Persian treasury there could be evacuated. Here the Macedonians also captured Barsine, the wife of the Persian mercenary *strategos* Memnon who had earlier died at the siege of Mytilene. Parmenion sent her back to Alexander, and she soon became one of his long-term mistresses, allegedly bearing him an illegitimate son called Hercules. Also caught in Damascus were Theban, Athenian and Spartan envoys who had been there to seek audience with the King of Kings, they clearly expecting a Persian victory over the Macedonians. All were brought before Alexander who first freed the Thebans, saying that as they had no city to return to they were right to seek help wherever possible. He then decided to keep the Athenians in his entourage, though treated them with honour, this not surprising given the delegation was led by the son of Iphicrates. However, the Spartans he arrested. Here the king had learned that the *poleis* was not just indifferent to his crusade against Persia, but had begun to act with hostility towards Macedon. This included Agis III, one of its two kings, sailing to meet a Persian fleet off the island of Siphnos (modern Sifnos) in the Cyclades in the hope of obtaining vessels to raid Macedonian territory. However, while there word reached the gathering of Darius' shattering defeat at Issus, and the plan came to naught.

Alexander next marched south again, through Syria and Phoenicia. Here the king aimed to isolate the Persian fleet from its bases there. The cities of Arados and Marathos submitted quickly, after which the Persian king made a peace offering, this brusquely rejected by Alexander. Biblos and Sidon then fell as Alexander continued south. However, the important port of Tyre held out. This was subject to a famous siege, fully detailed in Chapter 4, where Alexander's specialist engineering troops played a leading role. While this investment was underway Darius made another peace offer, this including a ransom of 10,000 talents for his family, and the ceding of all Persian land west of the river Euphrates to the Macedonians. However, Alexander rejected the offer once more, despite Parmenion's advice to accept. Tyre was then stormed in July 332 BC, with 8,000 Tyrians losing their lives in the assault and 2,000 more crucified on the sea front. A further 30,000 were enslaved (Lane Fox, 1973, 191). Alexander's actions here in the aftermath of the siege show that, once more, he was never afraid of using brutality when he deemed it necessary. The Macedonian king left Parmenion to mop up resistance in Syria, continuing south down the Levantine coast where he was held up at Gaza for two months before finally capturing the city. Brutality followed yet again, all the men in the city being killed and the women and children enslaved.

By November Alexander had reached Egypt. The population there welcomed him as a saviour from Persian rule, with the satrap Mazaces quickly surrendering. The king then travelled to Memphis where he sacrificed to Apis, the Greek name for the sacred Egyptian bull Hapi. He was next awarded the double crown of the pharaohs and spent the winter setting up his own administration across the country. Early the following year he founded the city of Alexandria and then marched along the coast to Paraetonium. From there he headed inland on his famed visit to the desert oracle of Zeus Ammon at Siwa. This God was the Greek appropriation of the well-known Egyptian deity Amun-Ra. Here Alexander consulted on the success of his expedition. He revealed the answers to no one. However, from this moment he always associated himself with the god, gradually beginning to claim descent from Zeus.

Alexander returned to Tyre early in 331 BC having conquered the whole eastern Mediterranean. He appointed a Macedonian satrap for Syria and then advanced eastwards into Mesopotamia. Arrian details he did not follow the usual route but one avoiding the intense heat of the desert, allowing his army to re-provision (*Anabasis Alexandri*, 3.7.4). This northern route also drew him directly towards Darius, his ultimate target. The Persian king learned of the move and marched 480km up the Tigris to oppose him. The decisive engagement took place at Gaugamela, between Arbela and the old Assyrian capital of Nineveh, on a dusty plain northeast of the middle Tigris. The Persian king chose this battlefield as it would allow his enormous force, detailed earlier in the chapter, the chance of surrounding the Macedonians with a double envelopment (Devine, 1989, 104). However, the result was another astonishing victory for Alexander, with Darius escaping with his Bactrian cavalry and Greek mercenaries (the engagement fully detailed in Chapter 4). The Persian king fled northeast to Media with Alexander in hot pursuit until he finally lost contact. The Macedonians then occupied Babylonia and its principal city, Babylon. Here Alexander re-installed the regional satrap Mazaeus, a sign of things to come, alongside a Macedonian troop commander. Lane Fox described his welcome here as overwhelming (1973, 247). Alexander next captured the Persian capital Susa, this releasing a huge amount of treasure totalling 50,000 gold talents. No more would the army go unpaid, with the king again showing his generosity by distributing much of the wealth among the army and sending more home to Macedonia. He also installed Darius' family in Babylon to live in luxury.

Next Alexander moved against the Ouxian mountain tribe to the east, before pressing on over the Zagros Mountains into the Persian heartland itself in modern Iran. Here he forced the pass at the famous Persian Gates held by the local satrap Ariobarzanes, and then advanced rapidly to capture Persepolis, the spiritual heart of the Persian Empire. Here Alexander ceremonially burned down the palace of Xerxes to symbolise the end of the Panhellenic war of revenge.

While in Persepolis many in the Macedonian high command tried to convince Alexander that his father's envisaged mission was now accomplished and they should return home to a deserved hero's welcome. However, the king would have none of it. Even if he had not initially planned to capture the entire Achaemenid Empire at the outset of his *anabasis*, that was now exactly his plan. He sensed destiny calling and determined to hunt Darius down and force a final decisive meeting engagement to settle matters once and for all. Thus he marched north into Media in the spring of 330 BC, while there sending many of his Thessalian and Greek allies home, increasingly replacing them and others with local Persian recruits. This is the first manifestation of the vision many commentators then and now suggest he began to contemplate at this time, of an empire of equals uniting all of its component cultures and peoples. The re-appointment of Mazaeus in Babylon shows how his views on the future of the newly won empire were changing. This was to cause a growing schism with his closest advisors and the army, first manifest at this point when he decided to leave Parmenion in Media to control communications. Although a sensible move – it replicated his earlier similar positioning of Antigonus *Monophthalmus* in Phrygia – the Macedonians interpreted it as favouring the king's new-found Persian friends.

Alexander set out again at high speed in the summer of 330 BC, heading northeast. He travelled via Rhagae near modern Tehran through the Caspian Gates into the Caucasus Mountains. Here he learned that Bessus, satrap of Bactria, had deposed Darius. The Macedonians closed on the former Persian king. After a skirmish at modern Shāhrūd in north-eastern Iran the usurper had Darius stabbed. The King of Kings, earlier the richest man in the known world, was left to die in the mud next to a pool where he was found by a Macedonian soldier. Alexander, shocked, sent the body back to Persepolis for burial with all due honours in the royal tombs there.

The Macedonian king was now unchallenged, with a Rhodian inscription from this time calling him the 'Lord of Asia'. This remarkable statement highlights the astonishing success of his *anabasis* to date, he conquering the mighty Achaemenid Persian Empire of Cyrus the Great, Darius I and Xerxes I in just four short years. However, no doubt to the dismay of many of the Macedonians in his entourage and the army, his ambitions for further conquest were undimmed, with the ends of the known world beckoning.

Onwards to India

Alexander defined the phrase 'not resting on one's laurels'. Consolidating briefly to ensure his lines of supply were secure, he then set off eastwards once again. Crossing the Elburz Mountains in northern Iran he arrived at the Hyrcanian Ocean, today's Caspian Sea. He then seized Zadracarta in Hyrcania where he received the submission of the remaining Achaemenid Persian satraps and nobles. Again, as with Mazaeus in Babylon, he re-confirmed the most capable in their offices, knowing that as he headed ever further east on his *anabasis* stability in his rear was key. The king then briefly turned westwards to modern Amol, reducing a mountain people there called the Mardi in the Elburz Mountains. Here he also accepted the surrender of the last Greek mercenaries who had been in Persian employ.

Alexander continued east, advancing rapidly again and crossing into modern Afghanistan where he founded Alexandria in Ariana near modern Herat. However, next disaster struck at Phrada in Drangiana. Here the king discovered a plot to assassinate him. Worse, Parmenion's son Philotas who by now commanded the companion cavalry was implicated. He was tried and condemned by the army, and then executed. Alexander knew that Parmenion would seek revenge for his son's death and sent a secret message to Cleander, Parmenion's second-in-command back in Media. This ordered him to assassinate his superior, which Cleander duly did (Plutarch, *Lives*, Alexander, 49.121). All of Parmenion's close colleagues were also quietly dispatched. This episode once again shows the ruthless brutality of Alexander when confronted with a threat to his ambitions.

These actions caused widespread horror among the Macedonians given Parmenion's high standing. However, they also strengthened Alexander's position with the older officers who had served under Philip as their cards had now been marked. From now on anyone who crossed the king knew that no matter how senior they were, a miserable end was the likely outcome. Another result was the reorganization of the companion cavalry into two sections. Each now contained four new *hipparchia* squadrons (see Chapter 3 for detail), with one group commanded by the ultra-loyal Hephaestion and the other by Cleitus 'the Black', one of the army's most seasoned warriors.

From Phrada Alexander next marched ever further east, through the winter of 330 BC into 329 BC. Advancing up the valley of the Helmand River through Arachosia he passed the site of modern Kabul. The king then entered the territory of the Paropamisadae where he founded

Alexandria by the Caucasus. Bessus, murderer of Darius, was now in Bactria trying to raise a revolt in the eastern satrapies. Taking the title Great King he styled himself Artaxerxes V. Alexander acted with his usual efficiency, crossing the Hindu Kush via the 3,850m high Khawak Pass, and then heading north with his full field army. Despite bitter cold and food shortages the army soon arrived at Drapsaca in Afghanistan north of Kabul. Bessus, outflanked, fled again. He crossed the River Oxus heading back west, with Alexander in hot pursuit after appointing loyal satraps in Bactria and Aria to secure his rear. By the time Alexander again neared the fugitive, the Sogdian warlord Spitamenes had deposed Bessus. Captured and flogged, Bessus was handed to the Macedonians and then sent back to Bactria. There he was mutilated in the Persian manner, losing his nose and ears, and was then publicly executed at Ecbatana in western Persia (Arrian, *Anabasis Alexandri*, 4.7.3). Things also ended badly for Spitamenes, who was later killed by his wife who sent his head to Alexander.

Alexander now turned north again, reaching Maracanda (modern Samarkand) by way of Cyropolis. In short order he reached the River Jaxartes, the modern Syr Darya River, which was the most northerly border of the former Persian Empire. Here he fought the Battle of the Jaxartes against the local Scythian nomads. The site of this campaign straddles the borders of modern Tajikistan, Uzbekistan, Kyrgyzstan and Kazakhstan, lying south-west of Tashkent (the modern capital of Uzbekistan). In the battle Alexander used catapults to clear the Scythians from the north bank of the river. They were unused to such long-range firepower, one warrior being impaled through body and shield (Arrian, *Anabasis Alexandri*, 4.4.4). Alexander then forced the crossing, pursuing the Scythians northwards into central Asia. Dispersing them, he then returned south to the Jaxartes. Here he founded Alexandria Eschate (meaning 'the farthest') on south bank on the site of the modern city of Khodjend in Tajikistan.

Meanwhile, the emboldened Spitamenes had raised Sogdiana in revolt to Alexander's rear, also recruiting the Massegetai tribe to his cause. Alexander spent the next year through to the autumn of 328 BC crushing the uprising. He next attacked the remaining nomadic warlords resisting his rule in the hills of Paraetacene in Sogdiana near modern Tajikistan. One was the Bactrian Oxyartes who had established a fortress on a high crag dubbed the Sogdian Rock. The Macedonians captured it with a stratagem using volunteer mountaineers. Among the prisoners was Roxanna, Oxyartes' daughter. Alexander, ever the pragmatist, married her. He knew this was the quickest way to pacify a region so far from the centre of his growing empire, and ever likely to be a cause of trouble.

Back at Maracanda another incident occurred which radically widened the schism between Alexander and his Macedonians, particularly those of Philip's generation. This was the murder of Cleitus 'the Black' in a drunken quarrel. Arrian (*Anabasis Alexandri*, 4.8.9) says in his detailed account of the incident that the actual cause of the feud was unknown, though Plutarch (*Lives*, Alexander, 50.126) lays some of the blame with Cleitus for taking advantage of the king's anger and intoxication. In a more recent analysis Lane Fox (1973, 309) argued that Cleitus took offence at the older officers being insulted by the king's supporters. He has Cleitus accusing Alexander of taking personal credit for the feats of all of the Macedonians, including previously his father. The result was fatal. Alexander impaled him with a pike.

The king was full of remorse after the event. His public mourning led to the army passing a decree convicting Cleitus of treason posthumously. However, the damage had been done, with the split between Alexander and his troops widening.

This further manifest when Alexander started wearing Persian royal dress. This was a very visible expression of the eastern absolutist form of rule he was beginning to adopt. Shortly afterwards he tried to impose a Persian court ceremonial routine which involved *proscynesis*, a form of prostration. Normal for Persians when entering the king's presence, it implied an act of worship. The Macedonians and Greeks refused point-blank, even his most loyal supporters. In the short term at least, the multi-cultural experiment was put on hold.

Another plot against the king was soon uncovered which involved the royal pages. Callisthenes, Alexander's historian and Aristotle's great nephew, was also implicated. Tried and convicted, he either died of disease in captivity or was tortured on the rack and hanged, with the pages stoned to death (Plutarch, *Lives*, Alexander, 55.136). Relations between the king and his men worsened yet again.

Alexander now targeted India to the south. Before he did we have another of those curious incidents which the primary sources record with such relish. This was his order for the army to destroy the carts in the Macedonian baggage train laden with the soldier's loot. The aim here was clearly to allow a speedier advance into new enemy territory, unencumbered by plunder. Given the strain now being felt between the king and his men, one might expect this to cause a further schism. However, Plutarch says that the great majority cheered the fires being lit, with Alexander burning his own plunder first, and with only a few resenting it (*Lives*, Alexander, 57.138). Despite recent tribulations, the bond between the king and his men was clearly still strong when it needed to be.

Alexander left Bactria in the summer of 327 BC with the whole field army, less the garrisons left to secure his rear. He re-crossed the Hindu Kush through Bamiyan and the Ghorband valley and then divided his forces into two columns. Hephaestion and Perdiccas took charge of half of the army and the baggage train, heading through the Khyber Pass. The king himself led the remainder south. As they cleared the foothills of the Himalayas they now saw spread out before them the broad forested expanse of the Punjab. Fabulous India beckoned, one more stop on Alexander's road to destiny and greatness.

Porus and the Indian Kingdoms

Alexander's experience fighting the Indian kingdoms was very different to that when campaigning in Achaemenid Persian territory. There he had one clear opponent in Darius who, despite the latter's vast numerical superiority, provided a target for Alexander's campaigning strategy. Further, the set piece battles against the Persians tended to be on terrain that was agreeable to his army, with its reliance on the phalanx and shock cavalry.

India was a very different story. Here, instead of one dominant power there were a patchwork of kingdoms spread out across often inhospitable terrain, most of whom at one time or another were capable of tenuously uniting their neighbours to fight against an invader. So it proved against Alexander, who initially sought to subdue those kingdoms which opposed him, often dealing with them brutally to send a message to others that the price of confronting the Macedonians was high indeed. However, soon he came up against a ruler and kingdom that had the critical mass to rally real Indian resistance against him. This was Porus and his eponymous kingdom of Paurava, one of the largest Indian states. This was located between the rivers Jhelum and Chenab, the former a tributary of the latter which is itself a tributary of the mighty Indus.

Given Alexander's final set-piece victory in battle was against Porus at the Hydaspes River, the primary sources all speak very highly of this Indian king, clearly aiming to portray Alexander as heroically as possible. Arrian for example says Porus was well over 2 metres tall (*Anabasis Alexandri*, 29.2), while Plutarch talks of his '…size and huge physique…'

(*Lives*, Alexander, 60.42). All comment on his prowess and courage when fighting Alexander and the Macedonians from the back of his war elephant. This certainly impressed the Macedonian king who, in the aftermath of victory, treated him more as an ally than enemy after his vanquished foe told him he expected to be treated like a fellow king. In fact Alexander, ever the romantic, expanded Porus' territory to such an extent that by the time of the Macedonian king's death the Indian kingdom included all of the Sind (Hornblower and Spawforth, 1996, 1230). This vast territory stretched all the way from the Punjab through to the Indus Delta and Arabian Sea. Sadly, after Alexander's demise Porus failed to hold onto his expanded territories and the collapse of his kingdom opened the way for the rise of Chandragupta, founder of the Mauryan Empire.

Indian warfare was highly stylised in nature, with a chivalrous code of rules aimed at preserving the integrity of a defeated kingdom, even if only as a vassal. We have great insight into its various component parts thanks to the *Arthaśāstra* treatise on military strategy, statecraft and economic theory, this dating to after the time of Alexander (the first sections were written around 150 BC) but still relevant to the Indian armies of his day.

Classical Indian armies featured four main constituent parts, these being elephants, chariots, cavalry and foot. The former were the elite shock troops, relying on their psychological impact and huge size to fracture an opposing battle line. As a weapon of war they are discussed in full in Chapter 3 which follows their military evolution from the time of Alexander to the later Roman Republican period. However, at the time of his engagement with the army of Porus at Hydaspes they were deployed in traditional Indian fashion, his 200 beasts set out in a long line in front of his central infantry battle line. Elephants had been in use in Indian armies from at least the sixth century BC, with those aged around 60 thought best suited for warfare given their maturity and therefore suitability for training. This is notably late in the life span of an elephant as they rarely live beyond 80 years of age.

Indian war elephants were covered in highly decorated *hattatthara* cloth caparisons, often with a *paristara* padded covering atop. The latter, secured with ropes and straps, provided secure seating for the beast's fighting crew. This included the mahout driver sitting between the elephant's ears who, in addition to his *thotti* (bull hook), *valiya kol* (long pole) or *cheru kol* (short pole) used for controlling the animal, also carried javelins. In addition up to three further crew were also carried. The latter, sitting astride the elephant's back, were armed with bows and javelins, with one crew member often shown in art also carrying a parasol or other form of standard. Indian war elephants could also be accompanied by supporting missile-armed light infantry, though there is no mention of this in the accounts of Alexander's victory at Hydaspes. A final point to note here is that the noise and smell of elephants could prove particularly unsettling to cavalry horses if they were unused to them, as Alexander found in his campaigns in the Punjab (Goldsworthy, 2020, 427).

Chariots were also a feature of Indian armies at the time of Alexander, though less so later. Most were of the shock variety, sometimes used to bolster battle lines when elephants weren't available in any quantity, though most often used to support cavalry as at Hydaspes. Indian chariots were heavy two-wheeled vehicles pulled by four horses, with large crews armed with bows and javelins. Though this gave them plenty of momentum and impetus when well underway, it meant that otherwise they were slow and clumsy, especially in the soft soils of the Punjab. In such circumstances they were easy to pick off, as by Alexander's Macedonians, again at Hydaspes. Note should be made here that some argue Indian chariots were of the smaller, more manoeuvrable two-horse variety (and indeed the *Arthaśāstra* mentions seven different sizes of vehicle), but I have opted here to stick with the traditional interpretation given their performance against the Macedonians (see Chapter 4).

Indian cavalry were the least effective arm in the military establishments of the various Indian states according to contemporary sources. Most often unarmoured, at best they carried a shield of various shapes, and for offensive weaponry used javelins, though the *Mahābhārata* Sanskrit epic dating to the pre- and post-Christian era mentions mounted warriors throwing *prasa* barbed spears. For a sidearm cavalry also carried a short sword if wealthy enough. Their battlefield role appears to have been the seizure of key terrain features for foot troops, flank protection and the pursuit of defeated enemies. Interestingly, they were only infrequently employed in a scouting role, probably reflecting the inhospitable hilly or forested terrain in much of the Punjab.

Meanwhile, the vast majority of classical Indian armies comprised infantry which Head says were so subsidiary to the other arms that the *Arthaśāstra* provides little detail about them (2016, 126). Goldsworthy describes the majority facing Alexander at Hydaspes as archers carrying a long bamboo self-bow able to shoot a heavy 1.4m arrow made of reed or cane (2020, 433). These weapons were particularly effective at short range, though at Hydaspes the rain and slippery ground greatly reduced their effectiveness. The bowmen were usually totally unarmoured, lacking even a helmet, carrying their arrows in a long quiver set down the centre of their backs. Some of the better foot troops also carried a short sword as a sidearm, while elite warriors are often depicted in sculpture fielding a 1.4m-long, straight two-handed slashing sword. Some foot troops are also described by the primary sources carrying a short spear and long, raw ox-hide shield rather than a bow. These may have formed a front rank for the better trained bowmen formations, or may have been deployed in separate units interspersed with units of bowmen, though the primary sources are unclear on this.

Plutarch says that the best Indian warriors, of whichever arm, were mercenaries who served their masters loyally wherever they were hired, adding it was these troops who gave Alexander the most problems as he progressed slowly and sanguinely through the Punjab (*Lives*, Alexander, 59.141). The Macedonian king's solution here was again brutal, he first buying them off himself, and then annihilating them when they were on the march. They were thus denied to Porus for use in the Indian king's army at Hydaspes.

A further observation on the Indian military establishment at the time of Alexander relates to another manifestation of their stylised form of warfare, namely the use of formal camps when on campaign. These were in many ways similar to later Roman marching camps, built every night when in enemy territory. In that regard, at the beginning of a campaign the given Indian army would gather in a *skandhāvāra* base encampment, these called a *jaya-skandhāvāra* if the king was present. Such camps featured extensive defensive ditches, banks and palisades, with an inner bastion for the army's command staff. Then when on the march, a similar though smaller fort was built each night, these continuing to be manned as the campaign progressed to ensure that the army had a line of retreat given the often hostile nature of the terrain.

A final comment here relates to the size of Indian armies. Unlike Darius with his all-encompassing empire, which enabled him to field his vast armies, those of the Indian states were far smaller. Thus we have the key primary sources all emphasising the smaller scale of Porus' army at Hydaspes. For example, Arrian says he fielded 200 elephants, 300 chariots, 4,000 cavalry and 30,000 foot (*Anabasis Alexandri*, 5.15.4), while Diodorus Siculus details 130 elephants, 1,000 chariots and 50,000 foot (*Library of History*, 17.87.2) and Plutarch 2,000 mounted troops and 20,000 foot (*Lives*, Alexander, 62.2). Goldsworthy says that, taking these numbers into account, it is likely Alexander's army at Hydaspes was actually larger than that of Porus (2020, 427, with Diodorus' 1,000 chariots seeming particularly unlikely).

End of the Anabasis and the Road Home

Alexander's assault on India began with an advance through Swāt and Gandhara, he deploying his force in multiple columns with the spearheads again led by Hephaestion and Perdiccas. Following the strategy detailed above he gradually fought his way south and east through the Punjab, fighting multiple small-scale engagements, mostly short sieges of regional fortified towns and citadels. The Macedonian king continued to lead from the front when needed, and in the winter of 327 BC he was wounded fighting the Aspasioi in the Kunar valley by a dart striking his shoulder and penetrating his linen armour, though he soon recovered.

Eventually Alexander forced a route to the Indus, then storming the supposedly impregnable pinnacle of Aornos (modern Pir-Sar). This was within a day's march of the Indus itself, which he crossed in the spring of 326 BC near Attock, the army then entering Taxila. Here the ruler, Taxiles (also called Ambhi), gave the king elephants and Indian troops in return for his support against his rival Porus. This was the context for Alexander's last great victory, fought on the left bank of the Hydaspes, fully detailed in Chapter 4. In triumph Alexander was magnanimous with Porus as detailed above, also founding two cities near the site to celebrate the victory. These were Alexandria Nicaea and Bucephala, the latter named after his horse Bucephalus which died there.

After founding the latter, Alexander sacrificed to the Sun, showing his determination to continue ever eastwards on his *anabasis* (Lane Fox, 1973, 363). Fighting his way further into the Punjab, he soon reached the River Hyphasis (the modern Beas River) in late August 326 BC. However, here his exhausted and homesick army finally mutinied in the tropical rain, refusing to go any further. Alexander made a determined effort to change their minds, using fine oratory and calling specifically on the honour and reputation of his senior leaders, but finally had to accept the inevitable. He then erected twelve altars to the Olympian gods, and built a fort he named Alexandria Hyphasis on the western bank of the river near modern Amritsar. This last was an interesting initiative, he perhaps hoping he could one day return east and resume his *anabasis*. However, for now he realised that dream was over.

The Macedonian king now headed back to the Hydaspes where he built a fleet of 1,000 ships on which he embarked half the army, the other half marching alongside in three columns. The whole headed south-west towards the confluence with the Acesines River, from where he knew they could continue along the Indus and the coast. This was through particularly hostile territory. On the way any riparian communities Alexander came across were faced with the usual choice when confronted by the arriviste Macedonians, subjugation or conflict. Most chose the former given Alexander's reputation in the region for violent reprisal, but one chose the latter, which almost cost Alexander his life. These were the Mallians based near the confluence of the Hydaspes and Acesines who, with no king of their own, formed a loose confederacy with their Oxydracan neighbours. When the Mallians refused to submit, Alexander formed a sizeable campaigning force with half of the companion cavalry, his *hypaspist* foot guards, two regiments of the phalanx, his Agrianian light foot and locally-recruited mounted and foot bowmen. He ordered the rest of his riverine fleet and any troops remaining in the three columns to continue on their way.

With typical aggression Alexander then headed inland at speed, dividing his force into smaller flying columns to best negotiate the forbidding terrain. He soon caught a Mallian force against the walls of the nearest city which his troops massacred, he then killed another 2,000 when assaulting the settlement. Seeking a short campaign so his force could re-join the fleet and the columns on foot, Alexander pressed on, burning numerous local villages as he pursued the native Mallians towards the nearby 'city of the Brachmanes' (Arrian, *Anabasis Alexandri*, 6.6.6). This was quickly stormed, with Alexander leading from the front, the many Mallians seeking shelter there butchered or enslaved. Pressing on, the Macedonians next caught a Mallian army against the banks of the Hydroates River. Here Alexander pinned them in place with his cavalry which was then almost overrun before his foot arrived, forcing the Indians to flee. He pursued them to the nearby town of Malli which he quickly invested, storming it the following day. It was here, leading the assault in person, that he was hit by at least two of the long Indian arrows. The second proved a serious wound, causing a thoracic trauma that was for a short time life-threatening, the shaft's large iron barb penetrating the king's left lung and leading to a significant period of convalescence. However, he survived and although weakened, finally led his army down to the Indus Delta, building Alexandria on the Indus on the way.

Once on the coast Alexander constructed a new stone-built harbour and dockyard, and then divided his army once more for the journey home. One column, under Craterus, was sent through the Mulla Pass, Quetta and Kandahar into the Helmand valley, and then onwards to Drangiana with the aim of re-joining other elements of the main army on the Amanis River in Carmania in south-eastern Iran. This force included the baggage train, three battalions of the phalanx, the king's newly acquired elephants and the sick and wounded. Meanwhile, another force, under the Cretan admiral Nearchus, set sail in September 325 BC in 150 ships for the Persian Gulf. Alexander himself led the rest of the foot along the coast through Gedrosia (modern Baluchistan in south-western Pakistan). Some argue Alexander actually planned for Nearchus' fleet to supply this column, but it may have sailed too late due to the prevailing winds. In any event, the land force was soon forced inland away from the coast by the mountainous terrain, and the march west through the Gedrosian Desert became a disaster given the serious shortage of food and water. Additionally, many of the camp followers in the column died in a sudden monsoon that flooded their encampment in a wadi. Finally, after much suffering, the survivors re-joined Nearchus and the fleet on the Amanis. Such were the privations of Alexander's journey through the Gedrosian Desert that Plutarch says when Alexander finally returned to Babylonia it was with only a quarter of the force that had originally left for India, with a large number of the casualties occurring in this final phase of the campaign as he travelled home (*Lives*, Alexander, 60.149).

Alexander was back in Susa in western Iran by the spring of 324 BC. There he made his boldest gesture to date regarding his desire to see the fusing of Macedonian and Persian culture. This was the mass wedding of himself and eighty of his senior officers who were all married to Persian wives in the context of a feast to celebrate his conquest of the Persian Empire. At the same time 10,000 of his line soldiers with native wives were given substantial dowries. Yet despite this generosity, his policy of racial fusion continued to go badly with the Macedonians. Most had no sympathy for his concept of a cosmopolitan empire. In particular, his determination to add even more Persians into the army on an equal basis was bitterly resented. He pressed on with the plan anyway. Examples included 30,000 native youths who received Macedonian military training, and the introduction of Bactrians, Sogdians and Arachosians into the *hipparchies* of the elite Companion cavalry. Persian nobles were also accepted into the royal cavalry bodyguard. Only Peucestas, the new governor of Persia, gave the policy his full support. However, most Macedonians viewed it as a direct threat to their own privileged position.

Things came to a head later that year in the ancient Bablyonian city of Opis on the Tigris. Here Alexander announced his plan to send home, under the veteran phalanx leader Craterus, 10,000 phalangite veterans who were unfit for service, either through injury or age. This was a sensible plan but caused uproar among the Macedonians who mutinied again. The reaction should be seen in the context of the schism that, as we have seen, had continued to grow ever since the king had sent home the Thessalians and other Greeks in Media, followed by the execution of Philotas, assassination of Parmenion, demise of Callisthenes, murder of Cleitus 'the Black' and the 'mutiny' at River Hyphasis. Most recently, with the overt introduction of Persians into all ranks of the field army, the Macedonians were clearly feeling unloved by Alexander. The announcement of the veterans' return was the final straw. Nagle (1996, 151) says it was a far more serious mutiny than that on the Hyphasis, with only the royal bodyguard remaining loyal. Alexander reacted with fury, Arrian having him quicker to anger as he grew older (*Anabasis Alexandri*, 7.8.3). The king arrested the thirteen ringleaders there and then, pointing them out personally. He then withdrew from all contact with the army and began substituting even more Persians for Macedonians, also giving Macedonian military titles to Persian units. The army was aghast and the mutiny collapsed. An emotional scene of reconciliation followed outside the royal quarters, after which a vast banquet with 9,000 guests was held to celebrate the ending of the 'misunderstanding'. The 10,000 veterans were then sent back to Macedonia with gifts, and the crisis abated.

Alexander next tackled the problem of the thousands of mercenaries wandering throughout the Empire. Many of those from the Greek-speaking world who had accompanied the Macedonians at the beginning on the *anabasis* were political exiles from their own cities. He therefore sent the 'Exiles Decree' to be read at the Olympic Games in September 324 BC. This required the Greek cities of the League of Corinth to receive back all exiles and their families. He also indicated at this point his desire to replace Antipater as regent back in Pella with the returning Craterus, viewing the latter as a more loyal supporter than Philip's old friend.

However, disaster struck again for Alexander before the year was out when his favourite Hephaestion died in Ecbatana. The king was grief-stricken and indulged in extravagant mourning. A royal funeral was held in Babylon with a pyre that cost 10,000 talents. The king then gave a general order for all Greeks to honour the deceased Hephaestion, this linked with a demand that he himself be given divine honours. With this he was finally asking his troops to call him a living God.

Alexander next carried out a brutal punitive expedition against the Cossaeans of Luristan in the Zagros Mountains. The following spring he then received embassies from the Libyans, Bruttians, Etruscans and Lucanians, showing his fame was spreading to the western Mediterranean. Representatives from the Greek *poleis* also came, acknowledging his divine status for the first time. The king then started planning an expedition to Arabia, his next target of conquest where he intended to build new settlements on the Persian Gulf. He also established an Alexandria at the mouth of the Tigris, with plans to improve sea communications with India. Fully recuperated from his injuries and the brutal transit through the Gedrosian desert, at least ostensibly, and with his plans for further conquest well set in train, the future looked bright for the king. However, all was to come to naught as within a month Alexander the Great, conqueror of his known world, was dead.

The Death of Alexander

Alexander the Great died in the sweltering heat of a Babylonian summer in 323 BC. The king was taken suddenly ill after a prolonged banquet that featured the usual bout of Macedonian heavy drinking. Arrian has him imbibing late into the night, this an increasingly frequent occurrence (*Anabasis Alexandri*, 7.24.4). The cause of death is uncertain to us today, with the symptoms as described indicating a ruptured ulcer or perhaps malaria, made worse through prodigious alcohol consumption early in the illness. To contemporary audiences poison was also a candidate for his untimely demise, some accusing the Antipater's son Cassander of bringing it to Babylon, with his younger brother Iollas (the king's cup-bearer) administering it. Alexander's enemies in Athens certainly believed foul play was involved, later voting Iollas honours. Whatever the cause, his alleged last words had huge ramifications for centuries to come. First, when asked to whom he left his vast empire, he allegedly said to the strongest. Ambiguous indeed, this made his final utterance highly prophetic, with Diodorus Siculus (*Library of History*, 18.1) having him at the last say 'I foresee that a great combat of my friends will be my funeral games.' In the ancient world such games were the athletic events held in honour of a recently-deceased dignitary, the more senior the grander. Thus those of Alexander appropriately set the world he had created, an empire stretching from the Balkans to India, alight for two decades.

The king's unexpected death caused a huge outpouring of grief across most, if not all, of his recently won empire. In the immediate aftermath his future plans of conquest, for example in Arabia, were quietly shelved, as were the building projects he had spent much time on since returning to Babylon. Most importantly though, the king left no obvious heir. His first wife Roxanna was six months pregnant with the future Alexander IV, while another candidate was Alexander's elder though ill-fated half-brother Arrhidaeus. A more distant prospect was Hercules, the king's supposed bastard son with Barsine, and a small boy at the time. However, all each potential heir offered was the prospect of favour for those who championed them, and soon the band of brothers which had helped Alexander conquer the known world fractured. The Wars of the Successors soon followed, with the subsequent fall of Alexander's empire as a homogenous entity. This was a bitter end indeed for a man whose ambitions, when he was alive, knew no boundaries. However, subsequently his legacy has manifest in far more ways than he could have imagined, and these are discussed in the Conclusion in the context of my final comparison between Alexander and Caesar as military commanders.

Chapter 3

The Macedonian Army

T he Macedonian army of Philip II and Alexander was pre-eminent in the age in which they lived, in a way only later replicated in the classical world by the legions of the later Roman Republic (including those of Caesar) and the Principate Empire. Time and again it proved supremely effective on campaign and in battle against the widest variety of opponents, ranging from the vast armies of the Achaemenid Persians, the horse archers of the Asian Steppe and the elephants and chariots of armies in India.

Yet just as with the Roman legions, the story of how this supremely efficient military machine came into being was both lengthy and complex. In this chapter I therefore follow a chronological path, first looking at the origins and function of that most classical Greek form of combat, hoplite warfare. I then move on to examine each arm of the Macedonian army of Philip II and Alexander, starting with line-of-battle infantry and light foot troops, then cavalry, next siege warfare and finally naval combat. Where appropriate, in each specific section I additionally consider their development in the subsequent Hellenistic period for completeness.

Hoplite Warfare in Ancient Greece

The term phalanx is used ubiquitously today to describe any dense body of organised spear or pike-armed infantry. However, it is most commonly associated with the hoplites and phalangites that came to dominate conflict in the classical Greek and Hellenistic world. Hornblower and Spawforth (1996, 1153) say Homer was the first to use the term, this in plural form to detail 'ranks' of soldiers. This was to differentiate their formal organised form of combat from the individual duels he so often describes in the *Iliad* and *Odyssey*. Certainly in the Minoan and later Mycenaean cultures through to the Late Bronze Age Collapse around 1,250 BC highly-organised dense bodies of spearmen were a core element in a given army's battle line. These were usually armed with long thrusting spears (called an *eka-a* by the Minoans) and tower body shields, the latter later supplemented by enormous figure-of-eight shields (Elliott, 2020a, 114). However, this style of organised warfare disappeared amid the economic catastrophe of the collapse, to be replaced by the individualistic style of warfare most associated with Homer that had increasingly come to the fore in the later Mycenaean period.

Organised line-of-battle warfare in the Greek world only reappears with the onset of the Archaic period in the ninth century BC, when Hornblower and Spawforth say the term phalanx re-emerges again (1996, 1153). This time it is in the singular form we know today, being used to describe a totally new kind of warfare based on the newly emergent proto-hoplite. The first true Greek phalanx formations appear in artwork and literature after 700 BC, they playing a key role in the armies of the emerging Greek *poleis* whose origins are detailed in Chapter 1. This very specific formation had its origins in two developments, one economic and one political:

- First, the re-opening of trade routes after the Greek Geometric/ Dark Age. This led to the renewed establishment of colonies, for example in Italy, Anatolia and the Aegean Islands, increasing prosperity and thus the number of men within a city state able to afford the full panoply of hoplite armour and weaponry. At this early stage such equipment was principally (if affordable by the individual) bronze body armour and helmet, the *aspis* large round body shield and the *doru* long thrusting spear. Early proto-hoplites could also be armed with javelins, perhaps reflecting the transition from the Geometric-style of individualistic combat to the far more organised form of warfare associated with the phalanx.
- Second, the actual emergence of the *polis* self-sufficient autonomous state. This bound citizens more closely together within their communities than previously. Given the first duty of the *polis* was to defend itself in time of war, this development was the catalyst to organise the now more numerous fully-armed hoplites into what became the classic Greek hoplite phalanx.

In such a formation the front rank troops usually fought with their long spears held in an overarm thrusting position (see discussion below), covered by interlocking *aspis* large round body shields. Those at the rear added their weight to the formation, replacing those falling in battle at the front.

In terms of hoplite equipment, the most essential item was the *aspis* shield. This highly successful design had its origins in the bronze-faced and centrally-gripped shields originating in the Urnfield culture that dominated central Europe from 1,300 BC to 700 BC. Here, the vectors of cultural transmission were the Dorian invasions of mainland Greece in the Geometric period. It therefore seems likely that the mature *aspis* shield design predated its use by hoplites in the traditional phalanx, with the first to carry them being the proto-hoplites in the later Archaic period.

The hoplite *aspis* was a shallow bowl between 80cm and 100cm wide. A wooden design covered completely with bronze with an offset rim, it featured a double grip made from a metal or leather strap across the centre through which the left forearm was inserted, and a leather grip on the outer rim held in the left hand. Though seemingly a simply design the hoplite *aspis* is actually a complex piece of military technology, being expensive to make and requiring a variety of craftsmen skilled in different trades to complete (Manning, 2017, 46). Further, while surviving examples are broadly the same design, they are made in a variety of different ways and materials depending on what was available in a given locality.

The characteristic domed shape of the *aspis* was vital to the successful functioning of the hoplite phalanx. Such shields were often brightly decorated, either to identify a given nationality/unit (the *lambda* upturned V worn on the shields of Spartan *hippeis* and Spartiate-class hoplites are the best known example) or to display martial valour and wealth. Shields could also be fitted with leather or cloth skirts to protect the lower legs from arrows, these again often decorated. Hoplite *aspis* were so successful that they continued to be used until the disappearance of the traditional hoplite in the later third century BC, the only major change being its replacement by the smaller, leather-faced round *pelte* used by Greek line-of-battle troops equipped in the Iphicratean fashion. This latter could feature the double-grip of the hoplite *aspis*, or a simpler single central grip. If the warrior armed in this fashion held his spear two-handed, this central grip was replaced with a leather strap to enable the left forearm to pass through it, thus freeing this hand to help grip the spear.

For armour, those proto-hoplites and early hoplites who could afford it wore a bronze cuirass known simply as a *thorax*, usually comprising a breastplate and back plate which gave significant protection to the warrior from neck to hips. Early designs were comparatively primitive, the best known being the so-called 'bell cuirass' which dated to the later Archaic period. This was so called because of the distinctive bell-shape marking across the pectorals. By the classical period these early designs had significantly evolved, with the most popular being the muscled cuirass made from hammered bronze plates, designed to replicate the muscles of the upper-body. Boiled leather was also sometimes used to create the muscled cuirass design. However, by the time of Philip II and Alexander only cavalry, officers and elite foot units wore such expensive armour, with Head (2016, 201) highlighting the foot guards of Agathocles of Syracuse being so equipped.

By this time most hoplites who could afford armour had long-worn a stiff linen or leather *thorax* made from layers of material glued together to form a stiff shirt up to 5cm in thickness. Bronze or iron plates and scales could also be added to protect vital areas, for example the pectoral region or down the left and right sides where the chest and back plates were strapped together. Protective corselets made in this way often featured *pteryges* (meaning 'feathered' in Ancient Greek) layered linen or leather strips hanging from the base of the cuirass down to the thighs, these designed not only to provide additional protection for the lower abdomen and groin but also allow ease of movement. As with the *aspis*, corselets and *pteryges* were often brightly decorated, the former frequently with the head of a medusa to ward off the 'evil eye'. A fine example is that worn by Alexander in the Alexander Mosaic from the House of the Faun in Pompeii, the original now on display in the Museo Archeologico Nazionale di Napoli. Meanwhile, a final cuirass type had begun to appear from the beginning of the fourth century BC, this a lighter, quilted design of padded wool or cotton, the type being most associated with the Iphicratean hoplites and other lighter armed troops.

Hoplite warriors also wore additional forms of armour, especially early on. These included hand, arm, thigh and foot guards, all made from bronze. However, by the classical period the most common type of additional armour was the bronze or iron greave sprung on the calf to protect the knee and lower leg. Later many hoplites replaced these with high leather boots, for example the *Iphicratid* footwear detailed earlier in the context of the reforms of Iphicrates.

The other key item of hoplite protection was the bronze (or less frequently iron) helmet, this evolving over time into a variety of popular designs. The earliest complex post-Mycenaean type found in Greece was excavated in a late Geometric-period grave from Argos in the Peloponnese, and was dubbed the Kegelhelm type. It comprised five pieces that together formed a cone shape covering the head and cheeks. Though the design had disappeared by the beginning of the seventh century BC, it had evolved into two further types called Insular and Illyrian. These, and their later developments, survived in use with hoplites through to the fifth century BC, mainly in the Peloponnese and the islands of the eastern Mediterranean.

However, by far the most successful Greek helmet design was the Corinthian type whose lineage led directly to the many fine forms of head protection common by the time of Philip II and Alexander. The earliest Corinthian design comprised a bronze domed bowl cast in two halves that provided full protection from crown to neck, with eyeholes either side of a nose guard and opening for the mouth. As with the Kegelhelm type, these early designs also dated to the late Geometric period, though from slightly later. This initial Corinthian design finally fell out of use in the eastern Mediterranean in the later fifth century BC, though it continued in use in Magna Graecia in Italy for much longer. There, it developed into a very specific type of head protection called the Italo-Corinthian helmet. This featured the eyeholes moving much further back towards the scalp to become decorative features, with the design remaining in use until the first century BC.

The main failing of all early Greek helmet designs was the lack of ear apertures to enable hearing. Because of this the Corinthian design eventually evolved into the Chaldicean helmet after 500 BC, when the first of these new types start appearing on vase paintings. This featured a much-revised bowl with earholes and elongated cheek guards that were sometimes hinged and sometimes not. The former later evolved into a further design called the Attic helmet that lacked a nose guard, this appearing from the fourth century BC and seeing extensive use in Magna Graecia.

The final evolution of the classic Greek hoplite helmet emerged at the beginning of the fourth century BC and is today called the Thracian (or Phrygian) type. This combined design features of the leather cap associated with Thracian warriors of all types with the Chaldicean helmet it resembled. The most notable difference was the use of even more pronounced cheek guards that often met at the chin to resemble a beard, and the appearance of a central ridge to provide additional protection across the crown of the head.

Additionally, two further types of helmet were worn by hoplites. Both were very popular by the time of Phillip II and Alexander, they evolving completely separately from the design lineages detailed above. The first was the Boeotian helmet, a protective development of the classic *petasos* wide-brimmed Greek sun-hat, with the sides folded down. This was an open design allowing good peripheral vision and unimpaired hearing, with a domed skull surrounded by a wide, flaring, down-sloping brim which at the rear came down to protect the back of the neck. Downward pointing folds either side provided minimal cheek protection. The Boeotian helmet was much-used by Theban hoplites, and was also very popular as a cavalry helmet in Macedonian armies given the excellent vision and hearing it provided.

Meanwhile, the *pilos* helmet was a very simple conical design, based on the *pîlos* brimless Greek felt skull-cap. A bronze version began to appear at the beginning of the fifth century BC and by the time of Philip II and Alexander it was one of the most common forms of hoplite and phalangite head protection given its cheapness.

Greek hoplite helmets were often decorated with striking and distinctive crests. These served the dual purpose of adding to the height of the warrior, helping to intimidate opponents, and also to distinguish him or his unit. Their depictions in contemporary artwork on pottery and in sculpture, and descriptions in literature, testify to their ubiquitous use. Such crests were most often made from horsehair tied in bundles which were slotted into holes cut into a crest box atop the helmet, they then being dyed as required.

As a closing comment here on hoplite defensive body armour, it should be noted that in the citizen-levy armies of many of the *poleis*, most hoplites (perhaps excepting front-rankers and officers) would be unarmoured except for their *aspis* and helmet.

The primary weapon of the hoplite was the *doru* long thrusting spear. This could be anything from 2.5 to 4.5m long, the shaft (usually made from ash) tapering towards a small leaf-shaped blade of bronze or iron. At the rear was mounted the bronze *sauroter* spear-butt, this often spiked for use if the primary blade was broken or to set the spear in the ground. This usually weighed around twice as much as the blade, moving the point of balance about two-thirds down the shaft where a grip was then fitted. Such weight distribution extended the reach of the spear and reduced its overhang at the back to prevent the warrior behind the front-ranker being stabbed as the weapon was drawn back.

As detailed below in the descriptions of the hoplite experience of battle, the *doru* was most often held in the right hand above the shoulder to enable it to be thrust over the rim of the large *aspis*, though could also be used to thrust underarm or set in the ground to receive a charge. The most powerful and deadly thrust was that used overarm with the thumb pointed backwards, the spear being stabbed forward in an almost overarm throwing action. Meanwhile, some hoplites armed in the Iphicratean fashion may also have held their longer spears two-handed, these effectively proto-pikes given their likely later evolution into the Macedonian *sarissa*. Usually only one spear was carried by the hoplite, though spares were common in the baggage train.

A sidearm, usually a sword made from bronze or iron, complemented the hoplite's *doru*. These included the vicious looking *kopis* or *machaira* that featured a forward-curving 60cm blade that was used for slashing, the *xiphos* short stabbing sword, and the dagger-like Spartan *enchiridion* whose popularity spread to other regions in mainland Greece, particularly Boeotia. Earlier, simple leaf-shaped sword blades were also popular. Manning (2017, 46) explains that the size of the actual weapon fielded by the hoplite could depend on the region of its manufacturer, with those made in Macedonia (even before the time of Philip II) being potentially twice the length of those manufactured in the Peloponnese and Attica.

Each *polis* used the hoplite phalanx in differing ways. Sparta, the most militaristic, treated its entire male citizen population as lifelong conscripts forbidden from any other work except soldiering. At the most elite level were the *hippeis* knights and Spartiate citizens, followed by the *periokoi* who were recruited from the city's hinterland. Even Athens at its most democratic required all males between the age of 17 and 59 to serve in times of war. Other *poleis* also had elite units within their wider hoplite formations, for example Thebes with the Sacred Band.

The depth of the hoplite phalanx was a matter of city state preference and tactical expediency. Thucydides (*The Peloponnesian War*, V.68) says the Spartan phalanx at the First of Battle of Mantinea in 418 BC, when they and their allies defeated Argos, Athens and their allies, was eight deep. This was also the standard depth for Athenian phalanxes, though other states such as Thebes often deployed their phalanxes much deeper as detailed in Chapter 1, for example at the Battle of Leuctra in 371 BC, this later clearly making an impression on the young Philip II when a hostage there. Leuctra also illustrates the increasing use of tactical innovation in phalanx warfare, with the Thebans deploying obliquely and withholding their centre and left flank while using their extra-deep right flank to such great effect. This tactic of attacking with a strong wing, most often the right as set out above, while refusing another, was one which was readily adopted by Philip II and Alexander and continued to be a major tactical feature on the battlefield throughout the Hellenistic period.

In terms of unit organization, hoplites formed up with a frontage and depth of some 90cm per man, with each hoplite's right side protected by the neighbouring projecting *aspis* shield. All of the above various depths detailed were created by multiples of four-men deep, though there is little evidence of any particular sophistication here outside of the Spartan army. However, in the case of the latter we have much detail thanks to Xenephon and his *Constitution of the Lacedaemonians*, dating to the beginning of the fourth century BC. This most organised of hoplite phalanxes was divided into six *morai*, each commanded by a senior officer called a *polemarch*. Below him were various officers of decreasing seniority, starting with four *lochagai*, then eight *pentecosters* and finally sixteen *enomotarchs*, the latter commanding a platoon-sized *enomotia* of thirty-six men. These were divided into three files of 12, the *enomotarch* commanding the right-hand file with his *ouragos* second-in-command at the rear of the same file. The idea here was to ensure that every Spartan unit, no matter how small, had its own commander. The much less complicated Athenian system from the same period featured ten regiments called *taxeis* of variable size, one drawn from each of the tribes of Athens and commanded by a *taxiarch*.

The experience of battle fighting as a hoplite is vividly described by the Spartan elegiac poet Tyrtaeus who wrote in the mid-seventh century, saying (*Greek Elegiac Poetry*, 21-38 of fragment 11):

> Let each man stand firm with his feet set apart, facing up to the enemy and biting his lip, covering his thighs and shins, his chest and shoulders with the wide expanse of his shield. Let him shake his spear bravely with his right hand, his helmet's crest nodding fiercely above his head. Let him learn his warfare in the heat of battle and not stand back to shield himself from missiles, but let him move in close, using his spear, or sword, to strike his enemy down. Place feet against the enemy's feet, press shield against shield, nod helmet against helmet, so that the crests are entangled, and then fight your man standing chest to chest, your long spear or your sword in your hand.

This highly-descriptive passage provides great insight into phalanx combat as experienced by the individual hoplite, weighed down carrying their *aspis* and perhaps wearing heavy armour, with their visibility and hearing impeded by their helmet. Hoplite engagements, whether against other hoplites or opponents armed differentially, usually began with a steady advance towards the enemy line by one or both combatants. The usual practice for the citizen hoplites of most *poleis* was to advance in a fairly loose order (the actual organization dependent on the individual state and circumstances) until in missile range of the opposing army when close battle order was adopted. Crowd psychology would then take over, no matter how well-trained the warriors, with the speed of advance increasing given the desire of most hoplites to get the engagement over as quickly as possible (especially if advancing under missile fire). At this point a key feature of hoplite combat would then become evident, this a prominent drift to the right as each warrior tried to take advantage of the protection offered by the adjacent *aspis*. This was exacerbated by the normal ancient world practice of deploying the better troops on the right flank.

Unless adopting a defensive posture, for example against a cavalry opponent, at around 200m from the opposing battle line the hoplites charged, usually shouting their battle cry. If at this point there was a clear disparity between the two sides, the one with inferior morale and training might break. Assuming neither did, the primary sources then seem to indicate the hoplites would now slow down to redress their ranks, giving the better-trained troops a clear advantage from this point. Once the line was under control again, the final move to contact was then carried out and combat finally joined. Against most contemporary opponents the tactics, and weapons and armour technology of the hoplites then gave them a clear advantage unless against another hoplite force or, later, Macedonian pike-armed phalangites. In the case of the former, when two hoplite battle lines clashed, a spear-duel ensued called by contemporary commentators the *othismos* (translating literally as 'to push'). Spears were thrust, aiming for the exposed faces and arms of opponents, with swords only drawn if the *doru* shattered.

One puzzle here regarding the *othismos* and other forms of hoplite combat is how those pressing forward in the rear ranks did not asphyxiate those fighting at the front. A modern rugby scrum is only three-men deep for good reason, to preserve the physical integrity of those in the front row. Given the depth of hoplite phalanxes, some very deep in the later period as detailed, one would think that given the additional weight of amour and the press of each *aspis* into the backs of those in front, serious injury was unavoidable. The key factor here is that human beings need a minimum space around their thorax to expand their chests and breathe. To explain how the hoplite overcame this in the crush of phalanx combat, we can turn to experimental archaeology. Bardunias and Ray (2016,

131) explain that modern experimentation by re-enactors, where an increasingly deep line of 'warriors' pushes against a sports compression sensor, shows that the dome of the convex *aspis* when positioned against the back of the man in front leaves sufficient space to permit the man pushing to expand his thorax and breathe. Interestingly, the pressure sensor used in the experiments shows the extra pressure added by each new man in the file falls off sharply after eight ranks when the point of diminishing returns takes over. It is therefore probably no coincidence that eight men was the original preferred depth of a hoplite file.

At some point in the *othismos*, or other type of hoplite engagement, one side would weaken and tire, with those towards the rear stumbling into a newly exposed space in the front rank to likely be slaughtered if not fully aware of the situation to their front. Soon those at the very back, sensing the loosening cohesion at the front, would begin to flee, often discarding their weapons as they did. It is in this crucial phase of combat that the training, experience and morale of those fighting really came into play. Modern research into the behaviour of an average citizen as opposed to a professional soldier shows that most of the fighting and killing in combat is carried out by as few as 10 per cent of those engaged. Once these are thinned through natural wastage in the fighting, the outcome is increasingly inevitable. The losing side will break.

Meanwhile, light troops formed an increasingly significant component of the armies of the Greek *poleis* as the age of the hoplite progressed. These are first recorded in use in Greek armies as early as the Persian invasion of Greece in 490 BC. Later, Athens is recorded as deploying 800 archers at the Battle of Plataea in 479 BC during Xerxes' subsequent invasion.

Such troops can be categorised into two specific types, *peltasts* and *psiloi*. The former had their origins in the servants of hoplites who carried and maintained the former's panoply when on campaign, their role then evolving into also providing a light foot function armed with javelins. This troop type then continued to evolve into the classic battlefield *peltast*, these much better equipped with a wicker crescent-shaped version of the *pelte* shield (giving the troop type their common name) and sometimes a light helmet. Their primary weapon remained the javelin which could be used at ranges of up to 60m, these carried in bundles to pepper an enemy battle line. Increasingly *peltasts* were also equipped with a sidearm, such better-equipped light troops more suitable for close combat than *psiloi*. In that context, though initially used in ambushes and to drive away enemy skirmishers, by the age of Philip II and Alexander their use in the line of battle had become increasingly common. Indeed it was an upgrade of Athenian *peltasts* that gave rise to the Iphicratean hoplite.

As the Hellenistic age progressed after Alexander's death a further innovation of the *peltast* troop type was the advent of the *thureophoroi*, these named after their oval *thureos* shield, a development of the Gallic infantry shield. This was smaller and less substantial than the hoplite *aspis* but, like the Iphicratean shield, more flexible. Armed with a long thrusting spear and javelins, but unarmoured except for a helmet, *thureophoroi* were initially heavily-armed *peltasts*, better equipped for close combat. However, given their ubiquity in contemporary epigraphy and artwork they seem to have eventually become a standard line-of-battle troop type, fighting alongside the later pike phalanxes of the various Hellenistic kingdoms. They were also ideally equipped for garrison duties. In some armies *thureophoroi* were used as a transitional stage between the traditional hoplite and the pike armed phalangite, for example Boeotia which switched from hoplite to *thureophoroi* by 270 BC and then on to the pike by 245 BC. A further development of the *thureophoroi* was an armoured variant known as the *thorakitai* (cuirassier), wearing a light version of the Gallic chainmail shirt. These are mentioned by Polybius in the Achaian and Seleucid armies (*Rise of the Roman Empire*, 15.5 and 10.29.6) and were used to bolster the staying power of the less well-armoured *thureophoroi*.

Meanwhile, one specific type of *peltast* stands out above all others from both the classical Greek and Hellenistic periods, namely those recruited as allies and mercenaries from Thrace. These are most often depicted in their distinctive Thracian caps (which, as detailed above, gave rise to the Thracian style of helmet), and were renowned by contemporaries not just as expert skirmishers but also for their fierce charge, especially when armed with the vicious-looking *rhomphaia* two-handed cutting polearm.

Moving on to the *psiloi*, this was a catchall term for all other classical Greek and Hellenistic light infantry. Such troops could be armed with javelins, bows, slings and, in extremis, anything that came to hand. In the armies of Philip II and Alexander the former was the most important, with all types deployed in loose formations which could be up to eight deep and sometimes more. Such skirmishers were used for scouting and controlling rough ground, while in battle they were deployed ahead of the main battle line, phalanx or otherwise, to open the engagement. Once hand-to-hand combat was imminent they then withdrew behind the battle line. They were also used to control flanks and the rear, and occasionally to support mounted troops including elephants (see below). Some nations had an association with a particular *psiloi* type, for example Alexander's Agrianian javelinmen and Cretan archers, while Rhodian slingers had an equally high reputation among contemporaries. Tyrtaeus, in his elegiac poetry, vividly describes the role played by such light troops in battle, saying (*Greek Elegiac Poetry*, 21-38 of fragment 11): 'And you, the light armed men, hiding behind the shields, launch your sling-stones and javelins at them, giving good support to the heavy infantry.'

Turning to cavalry fighting in the age of the hoplite, these were very much an inferior component of classical Greek armies, excepting in the *poleis* in Thessaly. Thus, as detailed in Chapter 1, for much of this period the role of cavalry was largely relegated to scouting and skirmishing, though as part of the general trend towards the *poleis* fielding more balanced armies their role had increased by the beginning of the fourth century BC. For example Lazenby (1989, 71) highlights the success of the Boeotian cavalry in the Theban army at the Battle of Delium against the Athenians in 424 BC when the appearance of two squadrons from behind a hill panicked the victorious Athenian right wing, this causing their whole army to break. This indicates the Athenian hoplites expected the Boeotian horse to charge to contact.

In contemporary artwork, for example on pottery, cavalry in the early hoplite period are generally shown equipped wearing a light panoply with little armour, perhaps having helmet and shield. For offensive weaponry short spears and javelins were ubiquitous, with a sidearm if the mounted warrior could afford it. As time progressed this panoply improved, and by the beginning of the fourth century BC cavalry in a more advantageous position are shown wearing much-improved protective equipment. For example a late fifth/early-fourth century BC relief found at Thespiai in Boeotia shows a trooper in a bronze muscled cuirass (flaring at the hip to allow free hip movement in the saddle) with leather *pteruges*, Boeotian helmet and Thracian-style tall leather boots. The weapons of this much-better-protected cavalryman remained the short spear and javelin, together with a sidearm, though few are shown in artwork at this time with a shield.

The ultimate example of these better-equipped cavalry were those from Thessaly, where access to its fertile coastal plains gave rise to a significant industry breeding fine quality cavalry horses in wealthy stables. These mounts were much sought after regionally, particularly in Macedon. Given the larger horses available to the cavalry of the Thessalian *poleis*, and the greater quantity available, their mounted troops comprised a much greater component of Thessalian armies. Additionally, they were far more likely to charge to close combat with an opponent than those of other *poleis*. For example, coin evidence shows Thessalian cavalry thrusting their spears underarm in a similar manner to *xyston*-armed Macedonian companions and *prodromoi*.

These heavier cavalry in the later hoplite period were organised in a variety of ways dependent on each individual *poleis*. For example the Greek allied cavalry that accompanied Alexander on the earlier stages of his *anabasis* were formed in five *ilia* of 128 men each. These deployed on the battlefield in a square formation sixteen wide and eight deep. Given their prowess, Thessalian cavalry were noted for the more complex formations they were able to utilise on the battlefield, for example the 1,800 who accompanied Alexander often deploying in a rhomboid formation led by their *ilarch* commander at the point closest to the enemy.

Even at this later stage, lighter-armed cavalry still remained a component in the armies of the various *poleis*, either indigenous poorer troopers or allies and mercenaries. The latter two categories included specialist Thracian and Paeonian javelin and bow-armed horse, and highly-sought-after Scythians known for their prowess firing their bows from the saddle. The latter played a particularly prominent role supporting the Greek colonial *poleis* around the Black Sea, and later still in the Hellenistic period when they provided allies and mercenaries to the various eastern successor armies, much in the manner they had earlier provided vassal contingents for Achaemenid Persian armies (who called them the Saka).

The Scythians were a nomadic people comprising hundreds of different tribes who thrived in a vast territory stretching across the central Asian Steppe ranging from the northern reaches of the Black Sea through to modern Siberia and eastwards to the borders of China and Mongolia (Simpson, 2017, 14). Their success was founded on their exceptional horsemanship and the technological innovations they introduced to the manufacture of the bow. While composite bows comprising alternate layers of wood and sinew, which provided much greater springing and so penetrating power, had been in use in the Near East since the Mesopotamian Akkadian period (Elliott, 2020a, 51), the Scythians developed this technology to a new level. In particular, they were renowned for the use of the *gorytos* combined case for bow and arrows. This could carry up to 279 arrows, with experimental archaeology showing that a single mounted warrior could fire 30 arrows in three minutes while mounted, so 150 in a single 15-minute concentrated arrow shower (Simpson, 2017, 18).

Foot Troops in the Age of Philip II and Alexander

The composition of early Macedonian armies, for example those of Alexander I, Archelaus I and Amyntas III, reflected the kingdom's diverse geography and social structure. Thus, when on campaign and in battle, the principal arm comprised the king's retainer-based *hetairoi* companion cavalry and other mounted nobility. These and other Macedonian and allied mounted troops are considered later in this chapter.

In terms of the foot component of early Macedonian armies, these tended to be a fairly unorganised collection of units based on tribal structure, these comprising either lowland peasants or highland herdsman who were called to arms as required. Such troops were armed in a similar fashion to early Greek *poleis peltasts* and *psiloi*.

Alexander I created the first regular foot unit in the early fifth century BC with his *pezetairoi* foot companion guard regiment who were trained and equipped in the same manner as the city-state hoplites of the Greek *poleis*. From this point an increasing number of Macedonian foot were trained as hoplites, though they proved less capable than their *poleis* counterparts excepting the *pezetairoi*. Macedonian rulers made up for this by employing increasing numbers of experienced Greek mercenary hoplites when state finances allowed.

However, as detailed in Chapter 1, it is with the accession of Philip II in 359 BC that a true revolution occurred with the foot component of the Macedonian army, and one which played a crucial role in setting the kingdom on track to conquer the then known world. This was the advent of Macedonian *sarissa* pike-armed phalanx, with all of the pikemen now known as *pezetairoi* foot companions. Its exact origins have long been debated, with Matthew (2015, 40) and others suggesting that as a new monarch Philip would have struggled to initiate such a dramatic change so early in his reign. Not only did he have to contend with the loss of the 4,000 warriors who died with Perdiccas III fighting Bardylis and his Illyrians, but additionally the cost of replacing the hoplite *doru* with the much longer *sarissa* (on average 850g of wood compared to 4,070g) would have added to the financial strain on a Macedonian economy already struggling under the impact of war with the Illyrians. To that end Matthew believes that the switch from hoplite to phalangite began earlier, for example under Alexander II. However, others disagree. For example Sheppard (2011, 53) earlier suggested that given the parlous state of the Macedonian army and treasury that Philip inherited, his only option to remain militarily competitive was to innovate from the very beginning of his reign with new weapons and tactics. I totally agree, with his pike phalanx the ultimate example. Archaeological evidence also backs this interpretation, for example Head (2016, 218) highlighting that no *sarissa*-heads have been found at Olynthos which Philip besieged immediately after taking power, while several have been found at the 338 BC battlefield site at Chaeronea.

It was Philip who uniquely was best placed to facilitate the integration of all of the key lessons he had learned when a Theban hostage, and later from the Macedonian association with Iphicrates. Further, Philip as a ruler proved to be skilled at managing his kingdom's finances from the very beginning of his reign. I therefore think it likely he swiftly found the means to raise the revenue to implement his reforms.

A final reflection here concerns who Philip employed to advise him as he finessed what was arguably the most radical change in the nature of Greek *poleis* warfare since the advent of the hoplite. Though bright, and clearly experienced in all things military in the world in which he lived, the changes Philip initiated were so dramatic that in one generation he set the Macedonian army on a level well above any of its opponents. Indeed, this Hellenistic method of warfare went on to dominate conflict across the known world for the next 200 years. Component parts not only included his pike phalanx, but also improvements to Macedonian cavalry, and crucially the interplay between all of the arms of his military establishment. For example, note here the 'hammer and anvil' interplay between Philip and Alexander's shock cavalry and phalanx, and his army's greatly increased capability in siege warfare. These were such significant changes that I believe it must be the case the young king, with his embryonic ideas ready to come to fruition, must have gathered a brains trust around him of the leading military thinkers of the age to advise him. Sadly, the names of these unknown *strategos* and technologists are now lost to us excepting the siege specialist Poleidus of Thessaly.

Specifically on equipment, the key change in the defensive panoply of the Macedonian phalangite was with his shield. Gone was the *aspis* that prevented the use of a two-handed weapon. Its replacement was a development of the Iphicratean hoplite's *pelte* that retained the same name, though was usually faced with bronze rather than leather. Matthew (2015, 94) argues its core was most likely made from solid wood using whatever suitable type was locally available, he dismissing earlier claims that a wicker or leather core was used. This would produce a substantial shield, and indeed later examples were manufactured completely from bronze.

The Macedonian phalangite *pelte* was some 66cm in diameter based on examples found in archaeological excavations at Staro Bonce in the modern Republic of North Macedonia. Unlike the *aspis* it was rimless, though retained the slightly concave shape. It was hung on the left shoulder and held in place with a central arm-grip for the left arm and a strap around the neck given both hands were needed to wield the *sarissa*.

We can track the iconographic development of Macedonian *pelte* shield decorations from their depiction on coins. Sekunda (2012, 18) says that the early shields of Philip and Alexander and their immediate successors featured torches, thunderbolts, *gorgoneia* amulets featuring a gorgon head, the heads of Gods and heroes, and the classic Macedonian star design which radiated from the centre of the shield. It was only later that they began to feature a portrait of a given monarch, for example in the reigns of Demetrius *Poliorcetes*, Pyrrhus of Epirus and Antigonos *Gonatas*.

The armour of the Hellenistic pikeman was similar to that of the later classical hoplite, with front rank troops the most likely to wear such protection, this based on the fines levied on warriors who misplaced equipment (Sekunda, 2012, 20). This was most often of the linen variety, again sometimes reinforced with bronze or iron plates or scales. Bronze muscled cuirasses were worn by those who could afford them, usually officers. Meanwhile, very late in the Hellenistic period and well after the age of Philip and Alexander, contact with the Galatians and Rome also saw the introduction of the chainmail shirt.

The helmet of the *sarissa*-armed phalangite was again similar to those of later hoplites, with the advanced Thracian type dominating for front rankers in the armies of Philip and Alexander and the simple *pilos* helmet another popular design, especially for those at the rear of the pike phalanx. The traditional Macedonian broad-rimmed *kausia* hat was worn when on the march. Front rank troops were also the most likely to wear additional armour, for example leg greaves.

Aside from the *pelte* shield, it was the *sarissa* two-handed pike that most clearly differentiated the Macedonian pikeman from the hoplite with his *doru*. Between 4.5m and 5.5m long when first introduced, this had grown to 7.3m by the time the Romans fought the Macedonians. The pike was usually made from ash, with *sarissa* fittings from a tomb in Vergina in northern Greece indicating the shaft was made in two pieces, with an 17cm-long iron tubular sleeve locking them together. This allowed the weapon to be dismantled for ease of carrying on the march. As with the *doru*, the *sarissa* featured a leaf-shaped iron blade (usually 0.51m in length,

Devine, 1989, 106) and a slightly shorter iron butt spike, both secured with hot pitch. The latter was significantly heavier than that used on hoplite spears given the role it had in helping balance the weapon, as the pike was held using a handgrip towards the rear. The butt spike usually featured four 'wings' to steady the weapon when set in the ground. Meanwhile, again as with the hoplite, most pikemen also carried a sword, they having access to the same range as hoplites.

The original *sarissa*-armed phalanxes of Philip II were formed in files ten deep, each known as a *dekad*. However, by the time of Alexander's accession the usual file depth had increased to sixteen (despite the name's reference to a unit of ten). Alexander's expeditionary force of 12,000 Macedonian foot who accompanied him in 334 BC as he began his *anabasis* included 3,000 *hypaspist* 'shield bearer' guard troops, these covered later, and 9,000 *pezetairoi* foot companion phalangites. The latter were organised into six regionally-recruited *taxeis*, this representing around half of the overall total available in the Macedonian army. It seems likely that other *taxeis* of *pezetairoi* from Parmenion's original expeditionary force then joined Alexander after he arrived in Asia Minor, though we have no detail of their number. Any remaining *taxeis* formed the core of the home army under the command of Antipater in Pella. Later, three of Alexander's *taxeis* were honoured with the title *ashhetairoi* after showing great bravery at the Battle of Issus in late 333 BC. Then, as Alexander's campaign against Persia continued, a further *taxeis* of *pezetairoi* was added to his army in 330 BC, likely built around a core of veterans from existing units. Two further *taxeis* may have been added even later for his Indian campaign, bringing the final total of *taxeis* at the time of Alexander's death to 15, or around 22,500 *pezetairoi*.

In Alexander's army each *taxis*, of roughly 1,500 men depending on unit strength at a given time, comprised *dekads* as with Philip's original phalanx though now sixteen deep. An intermediate unit strength between *taxis* and *dekad* existed called the *lochos*, though we have no clarity as to its exact strength. Devine (1989, 105) argues that as the commander of each *lochos* was senior enough to attend Alexander's staff briefings when on campaign, a *lochos* must have been significantly larger than a *dekad*, with likely six per *taxis*.

After Alexander's death the organization of the phalanx continued to evolve, not surprising given its complexity and the numerous individuals and kingdoms vying for superiority from the Wars of the Successors onwards. This generated a true arms race that lasted through to the later second century BC. An early change was the introduction of the *speria* that featured two *taxis* in the better-trained formations. Much later, the Macedonian phalanxes of Philip V and Perseus that faced Rome in the Macedonian Wars featured four such *speiriai* that were formed into a *chiliarchia* of around 1,000 men, commanded by a *chiliarch* or *hegemon*. Four *chiliarchia* were then formed into 4,000 men-strong *strategiai* commanded by a *strategos*. While the standard deployment of this phalanx was still sixteen deep, the formation was still flexible enough to deploy in shallower or deeper formations as with those of Philip II and Alexander. Thus at Issus in 333 BC Alexander deployed the phalanx eight deep to maximize his frontage, while at the Battle of Magnesia in 190 BC Antiochus III deployed his pikes thirty-two deep, as did Philip V at the Battle of Cynoscephalae in 197 BC.

Within the phalanx of a given army different units had different standings based on their seniority. Aside from the *ashhetairoi* detailed above after Issus we have little insight here into the phalanx of Alexander. However, by way of analogy we have much more detail about the Antigonid Macedonian phalanx. Here for example, there featured the *peltastoi* who had a lighter panoply and shorter *sarissa* than their counterparts elsewhere in the phalanx. Within their ranks sat the ultimate elite among the foot troops of this later army, the *agema* guard. Meanwhile, the main body of the phalanx at this time was called the *chalkaspides*, the ratio between the senior troops and main phalanx at the Battle of Sellasia in 222 BC being 3,000 (including the *agema* guard) to 10,000. This breakdown of elite and line phalangites was common across all Hellenistic armies, though the units sometimes had different names. For example the guard phalangites in the Seleucid armies retained the *argyraspides* 'silver shields' name by which Alexander's *hypaspists* had been known from the time of the campaign against Porus (Bar-Kochva, 1976, 59, see below). Polybius (*The Rise of the Roman Empire*, 5.79.4) says these were specifically armed 'in the Macedonian manner', reflecting their principal weapon being the *sarissa*. Meanwhile, Livy details their elite nature by styling them 'regia cohors' when deployed near Antiochus III at the Battle of Magnesia (*The History of Rome*, 37.40.7).

When arrayed for combat the Macedonian *sarissa* phalanx featured the front five ranks with pikes lowered. These were held level at the waist, providing an impenetrable hedge of spear points. Those in the rear ranks then added their weight to the phalanx during the charge, replacing fallen comrades at the front just as with the earlier Greek hoplite phalanx. These rear rank troopers, with their hedge of raised pikes, also broke up the impact of missiles fired at the phalanx. It is this Macedonian pike phalanx that led Polybius to comment on its imperviousness if tackled frontally in good conditions, saying (*The Rise of the Roman Empire*, 18.28-32):

> [S]o long as the phalanx retains its characteristic form and strength nothing can withstand its charge or resist it face to face…we can easily picture the nature and the tremendous power of a charge by the whole phalanx, when it advances 16 deep with levelled pikes.

With regard to how each phalangite used his *sarissa* to its best lethal effect in such a cohesive formation, Matthew in his very useful discussion on the phalangite 'kill shot' explains that (2015, 206):

> The long sarissa, held at waist level, was primarily used to hold an opponent in place, preventing him from reaching the phalangite with a shorter weapon like a sword or spear. In engagements where a pike-phalanx fought against another pike-phalanx, these same initial principles applied to both sides using their weapons to keep their opponents at bay. During the course of the encounter the phalangite would have continued to use his weapon in the same manner – pushing forward with the weight of his body and the weapon to both hold the enemy at bay and to probe his defences by slightly adjusting the position of the pike to try and move the opponent's shield out of the way or force them back. When this occurred, certain areas of the opponent's body would become exposed for a brief moment. At this stage the phalangite could either direct an attack towards the opponent's chest… or strike at the opponent's head.

We know much more about the organization of the Macedonian pike phalanx than the Greek hoplite phalanx due to the late Hellenistic *Tactica* military manual of Asclepiodotos. Dating to the first century BC, this may actually be a reproduced long-lost work by Posidonius of whom Asclepiodotos was a pupil. The latter was a sophist and historian who Plutarch (*Life of Aemilius*, 19) says was a contemporary of the Macedonian King Perseus and who described the crucial Battle of Pydna in 168 BC. Asclepiodotos' work is particularly useful given its focus not only on the phalanx but also other ancillary arms such as cavalry, light infantry and elephants. The work was heavily utilized in later Roman military manuals.

The *Tactica* and later manuals indicate the Macedonian pike phalanx was a step-change in complexity compared to earlier classical Greek examples, featuring three densities of formation that were almost certainly extant earlier in the phalanx of Alexander. These were:

- Open order, with a frontage and depth per man of 1.8m and with no special name. This was the natural formation when deploying or manoeuvring.
- *Pyknosis*, with a frontage and depth half of that above and the usual battle formation.
- *Synaspismos*, the locked shields formation with a frontage and depth half of that used for *pyknosis*. This was a purely defensive formation, it being used for example against Darius III's scythed chariots at the Battle of Gaugamela in 331 BC and in the later stages of the Battle of the Hydaspes in 326 BC.

One key point to consider regarding the Macedonian pike phalanx was the sheer number of men required to make the formation work effectively. While this was less of an issue for Philip II and later Alexander on his *anabasis*, phalangite recruitment became increasingly problematic as the Hellenistic period progressed. This had more of an impact on Macedon than the other kingdoms, it arguably being a lack of manpower rather than inferiority in military technique that sealed Macedon's fate in the Second and Third Macedonian Wars (from 200 BC to 197 BC, and 171 BC to 168 BC respectively). Thus, by the end of Alexander's reign he could likely muster 22,500 *pezetairoi* in fifteen *taxeis* (plus his 3,000 by then pike *sarissa*-armed *hypaspist*). However, by the time of the Cynoscephalae campaign in 197 BC Macedon could raise only 18,000 phalangites (including 2,000 *peltastoi*, see above), and this by conscripting 16 year olds and retired veterans. This total had risen to a phalanx of 21,000 by the time of Perseus' Third Macedonian War, but only through an emergency socio-economic policy of requiring native Macedonian's to beget more children.

One of the reasons for this decline in the number of trained phalangites was the vast geography of the Hellenistic world following the astonishing success of Alexander's *anabasis*. The world the successors inherited from Alexander after his death in Babylon in 323 BC spread from the western Balkans to India, with his active troops, military settler veterans, mercenaries and allies spread across this huge global landscape. The biggest concentrations were in Babylonia, where the Royal army was based, and the Macedonian homeland. Once his Empire began its break up these troops were more or less locked in place unless their leader suffered a major defeat – as with the successor *strategos* Eumene's *argyraspides* at the Battle of Gabiene in 315 BC Susiana in modern Iran – or for some reason mercenaries were unable to be paid. The overall effect was to dilute this core feature of armies fighting in the Macedonian manner across all the territories of the Hellenistic world.

A number of methods were used to compensate. At first veteran troops were often 'run on' for as long as possible, with again Eumenes' *argyraspides* a good example. At the same time native troops from the conquered territories were recruited and trained to fight in the Hellenistic military tradition, for example the Persians equipped as phalangites under Alexander. Later, both Antigonus *Monophthalmus* and Eumenes used similar *pantodapoi* phalangites in their conflict, while the Ptolemies used native Egyptians trained as phalangites from the time of Ptolemy IV Philopator.

Finally focusing back on Alexander's *pezetairoi*, these showed a degree of training and flexibility perhaps lacking in those of his later successors. This is best illustrated by the fact that certainly in the later part of his *anabasis* as he campaigned in the north-eastern region of the Achaemenid Persian Empire many of his phalangites were temporarily re-equipped with short spears and javelins. Troops armed in this way, which enabled them to operate much more effectively in difficult and inhospitable terrain, were later called *euzenoi*.

Meanwhile, Alexander's elite foot companions were called *hypaspists*, the king taking 3,000 of them on his *anabasis*. The name derives from the ancient Greek for 'shield bearer'. Within the Macedonian military they were the only force not raised on a regional basis, this to ensure loyalty to the monarch given the feudal nature of the Macedonian state. Their exact origins are unknown, though it seems likely they evolved from Alexander I's original *pezetairoi* guards when the latter were greatly expanded by Philip II to become his new foot companion phalangites. A key point of difference seems to be the way they were armed, they initially retaining the *aspis* and *doru* rather than re-equipping with *pelte* and *sarissa* as did the *pezetairoi*. Meanwhile, in contemporary imagery and history they are often shown and described wearing the finest defensive panoply, with Thracian helmets and high-quality cuirasses common, together with greaves.

The *hypaspists* were organised into three units of 1,000, with Arrian saying that later in Alexander's reign these were styled *chiliarchia* (*Anabasis Alexandri*, 4.30.5 and 5.23.7), presumably the origins of this unit size in the later Antigonid, Seleucid and Ptolemaic phalanx. This corresponds with the origins of the title *chiliarch* which Curtius says came into use after 331 BC (Quintus Curtius Rufus, *The History of Alexander*, 8.1.3). One of the thousand-strong units was the senior, providing the king's bodyguards along with the seven close personal guards chosen from the companions and the royal pages. This unit of the *hypaspists* was additionally known as the *agema*, and for the early part of Alexander's *anabasis* was commanded by Hephaestion.

From 327 BC a new term comes into use in the primary sources referencing the *hypaspists*, this the *argyraspides* based on their silver-plated shields (Arrian, *Anabasis Alexandri*, 7.11.3). Under this name, after Alexander's death they then became the most sought after unit in the Macedonian army as the successors fought for control of his Empire, finally fighting for Eumenes as detailed above. Following the latter's defeat by Antigonus *Monophthalmus* and his son Demetrius at Gabiene, where they proved a two-edged sword given their own success in the battle but subsequent betrayal of Eumenes, they were broken up as a unit and sent to the furthest corners of Alexander's Empire to live out their days as out-of-favour border guards. By the time of this battle in 315 BC they were armed as elite phalangites with *sarissa* and *pelte*, and it seems likely they were also similarly equipped in the later campaigns of Alexander as his *anabasis* concluded. Given their ubiquity on many of Alexander's campaigns it also seems very likely that for much of the time they were also armed, as required, in the lighter fashion of the *euzenoi*.

Regarding other foot troops in the armies of Philip and Alexander, these very much reflected those available to the Greek *poleis* detailed above. For example when Alexander crossed into Asia to begin his *anabasis* his army included 7,000 allied Greek warriors and 5,000 Greek mercenaries (mostly hoplites though including *peltasts* and *psiloi*), 7,000 Thracian and Illyrian irregulars armed in their native fashion, and 1,000 other skirmishers. Among the *psiloi* and other skirmishers, the elite troops remained the Agrianian javelinmen, Cretan archers and Rhodian slingers. Later, as Alexander progressed on his *anabasis*, his battle line was additionally bolstered by allied and mercenary foot troops armed in their own traditional manner. This included Persians and other Iranians (though soon many of these were being equipped in the Macedonian manner), Bactrian and other Asiatic hillmen, and Indians. The extensive use of allies and mercenaries continued in the later armies of the successors, some by now settled colonists, with for example 3,000 Thracian and 5,000 Galatian troops (the latter recruited from their later homeland in central Anatolia) participating in Antiochus IV Epiphanes' famous military parade at the Games at Daphnae in 166 BC (Polybius, *The Rise of the Roman Empire*, 30.25.3-11). Meanwhile, further east indigenous Indian foot (and indeed horse) contingents continued to make up a significant proportion of the armies of the Bactrian Greek and Indo-Greek kingdoms (Nikonorov, 1997, 45).

Meanwhile, the final evolution of Hellenistic line-of-battle infantry occurred after the shock of successive defeats by the armies of Macedon and the Seleucid Empire at the hands of the manipular legions of mid-Republican Rome. By this time, with pikemen available in fewer and fewer numbers, *thureophoroi* and *thorakitai* had already begun to form a significant component of the heavy infantry complement of Hellenistic armies, rather than just playing a supporting role to the phalanx. However, after the shattering defeats at Cynoscephalae in 197 BC, Magnesia in 190 BC and Pydna in 168 BC, line-of battle troops armed and equipped as 'Romans' began to appear in Seleucid, Ptolemaic, Pontic (under Mithridates VI) and Armenian (under Tigranes the Great) armies. They are first referenced in Antiochus IV's Daphnae parade where 5,000 of the elite *argyraspides* were armed and equipped as Romans with heavy throwing javelins, stabbing swords and chainmail shirts. This amounted to 50 per cent of the guard troops in attendance. The main organizational difference between these Hellenistic 'legionaries' and their Roman progenitors was the size of the smaller units of organization of the infantry formations. The Polybian legions of Rome, with their *hastati*, *principes* and *triarii* (see Chapter 7 for full detail), had evolved from the original manipular legions instituted by the warrior statesman Marcus Furius Camillus at the beginning of the fourth century BC after the defeat of Rome by the Senones Gauls at the Battle of Allia in 390 BC and the subsequent sack of Rome. Here, the basic legionary building block was the *contubernium* of six men (this later increasing to eight men after the reforms of Gaius Marius at the end of the second century BC). However, this was at odds with the 16 man *decad* of the phalanx, and it was along the lines of the latter that the Romanised infantry of the later Hellenistic kingdoms were organised. This was less flexible than the Roman system, with Sekunda saying (1994, 10):

> One consequence of this form of (Hellenistic) organization was...that the maniples of the Seleucid army, when drawn up in a 'chequerboard' formation, could only form a double or single

line of maniples, the Roman *acies duplex* or *simplex*, and not
the standard Roman *acies triplex* or three rows of maniples.

Mounted Troops in the Army of Phillip II and Alexander

The key mounted arm in the armies of Philip II and Alexander were the
companion shock cavalry. Originally recruited from the leading aristocratic
families in Macedon and numbering around 800 horsemen, as detailed
earlier they initially fought in a similar manner to the mounted troops in
the armies of the Greek *poleis*. However, from the early fourth century BC
the primary sources indicate they had begun to charge to contact using
long *xyston* lances up to 4m in length, with the king's *hetairoi* companion
close bodyguards the first to make the change. Soon all squadrons of the
companions followed, with the weapon later giving its name to such cavalry in
the armies of Alexander's successors, these elite warriors called *xystophoroi*.

However, it was the widespread military reforms of Philip II that
really set the companions aside as a crucial battle-winning component
of Macedonian armies. His key change was to significantly expand their
number using the wealth from his reforms of the Macedonian economy,
particularly once he had regular access to the extractive resources of
Mount Pangaion. This facilitated new-found large-scale access to the finest
cavalry horses in Greece, principally from Thessaly, and also financed a
new and deliberate policy of opening up recruitment into the ranks
of the companions for anyone who could meet the wealth qualification.
As detailed in Chapter 2, this included non-aristocratic Macedonians and
even Greeks. Thus, by the time of Alexander, there were 3,300 companions,
all *xyston*-armed and organised into *ilia*. Here we are fortunate that the
primary sources provide much detail regarding Alexander's companions
as he began his *anabasis* in 334 BC. These included the king's own by now
300-strong *hetairoi* bodyguard *ile* (also now confusingly referenced as
agema), and seven other *ilia* of 200 horsemen. The remaining companions
stayed in Macedon under the command of the Antipater, presumably all
organised along the same lines (eight *ilia* of 200). Alexander's companions
were then increased in number in 329 BC following the demobilization
of his Thessalian cavalry. Then, following the 328 BC failed plot against
the king involving Parmenion's son Philotas (the commander of the
companions at the time), they were reorganised into four new *hipparchia*
squadrons with one group commanded by the ultra-loyal Hephaestion
and the other by Cleitus 'the Black', one of the army's most seasoned

leaders. The sub-divisions of these new formations are unknown, with the regiments eventually becoming part of the later Seleucid army after the end of the early Wars of the Successors. The companions of Philip and Alexander were highly disciplined on the battlefield and could adopt a number of formations, though their key shock tactic was to deploy in the *embolus* half-rhomboid wedge. It was this formation that was used to such great effect by both kings as the hammer to the phalanx's anvil.

After the death of Alexander all of the major Hellenistic kingdoms replicated his army's use of what became known as *xystophoroi*, with the elite still called *agema*. The importance of cavalry in Hellenistic armies was most manifest in the east where a few battles were actually cavalry-only affairs. The most notable example was in 208 BC at the Arios River in western Afghanistan when the Seleucid king Antiochus III defeated the Bactrian-Greek king Euthydemus I.

However, as the Hellenistic Age progressed the importance of cavalry in their armies, particularly in the west, diminished. Indeed, by the time Macedon faced the growing might of Rome, many Hellenistic line-of-battle cavalry had diminished to a skirmishing force once more as with their hoplite-era predecessors, using light spears and javelins. These only engaged enemy cavalry in hand-to-hand combat when necessary. Such a change in role is often associated with the introduction of the large cavalry shield in the third century BC. This followed Pyrrhus' campaigns in Italy where he was suitably impressed by their use. The Galatian invasion of Greece in 279 BC was another catalyst. The advent of these shields made using the long *xyston* problematic for cavalry using the saddle technology of the day.

The diminishing capability of the Hellenistic cavalryman was also matched by a decrease in their size as a percentage of the army. A key factor here was the need for mounted military settlers to have large estates. This was fine while Alexander and his immediate successors were gathering larger and larger tracts of land through Imperial expansion. However, once such opportunities became less common as the Hellenistic world began its geographic regression from the mid-third century BC, the ability of rulers to parcel out such land reduced significantly. This led to an overall reduction in available mounted troops, particularly those fighting in the Hellenistic tradition. This can be seen with Philip V's 'conscription' decree, found in the *Kassandreia* and other *diagrammata* (ordinance) documents. These recorded emergency efforts to expand his cavalry force in the context of the Second Macedonian War. However, it failed as he could only field 2,000 mounted troops against the Romans. After even more aggressive recruitment methods, his son Perseus could still only field 3,000 in the Third Macedonian War. A key outcome of this general diminishing in the quality and quantity of the Macedonian and other Hellenistic cavalry was an increasing reliance on the phalanx as the key battle-winning arm in a given army. Thus, by the time Philip V and Perseus fought the Romans, long gone was the highly successful 'hammer and anvil' companion and phalanx combination of Philip II and Alexander, with the performance of the Macedonian army diminishing accordingly. The decreasing role for cavalry continued right through to the end of the Hellenistic period, with only the eastern kingdoms bucking the trend. Here, in the armies of the Seleucid Empire and Bactrian Greek kingdoms not only did lance armed cavalry persist for longer, but the cataphract emerged. Troops equipped in this way, featuring fully-armoured horse and rider fighting in deep formations with long thrusting spears, originated among the Dahae, Massagetae and Saka central Asiatic steppe peoples, they becoming a key feature of Parthian armies (Nikonorov, 1997, 50). In the eastern successor kingdoms it was also more common to see cavalry armed in their native styles, for example Persians and Indians.

Meanwhile, Phillip II and Alexander's armies also featured one further type of indigenous Macedonian cavalry type, *prodromoi* light horse. These were also equipped with the *xyston*, and were sometimes called *sarissaphoroi*. Such cavalry wore a light and often non-existent defensive panoply, although they could take their place in the line of battle when required. However, they were mostly used to protect flanks, drive off enemy light cavalry, for scouting and to pursue a defeated enemy. Alexander's campaigning force for his *anabasis* included four small *ilia* of 150 *prodromoi* that, together with the allied and mercenary Thracian and Paeonian horse, formed the king's brigade of light cavalry.

The armies of Philip II and Alexander also featured significant numbers of Thessalian and other Greek heavy cavalry fighting as allies and mercenaries. These were armed and fought in the same manner as those detailed earlier in this chapter when discussing the hoplite era. Meanwhile, as his *anabasis* continued eastwards, Alexander also increasingly recruited Iranian cavalry into his army, especially when the steady flow of replacement troops from Macedonia and Greece began to slow due to the increasing distance. Though their numbers were marginal as the king completed his campaign against Darius, Arrian says their numbers were more significant by the time the king was leading his army into central Asia (*Anabasis Alexandri*, 4.17.3). Here they were joined by other locally-recruited cavalry including Bactrians, Sogdians and Arachosians. Some of these were later recruited into the *hipparchies* of the companions after Alexander had returned to Babylon, where he also accepted Persian nobles into his personal bodyguard cavalry, much to the consternation of many Macedonians. Prior to incorporation into Macedonian units, these native cavalry units were armed in their native manner, as were the Indian allied cavalry who served with Alexander in India. Meanwhile, just as with the Greek *poleis* around the Black Sea coast, Alexander also made use of Scythian allies and mercenaries, especially when campaigning against their neighbours.

Continuing with light cavalry, after Alexander's time skirmishing mounted troops continued to be a key component of Hellenistic armies. Again, like their foot equivalents, specialist types later emerged armed mainly with javelins and bows. As earlier, such troops were more common in the east. Meanwhile, in the west a particular light cavalry troop type emerged in the later fourth century BC whose name became synonymous with skirmishing javelin-armed cavalry at the time. These were the Tarantines, named after Taras (modern Taranto) in south-eastern Italy. Such was their ubiquity that 2,300 signed on as mercenaries to fight with Antigonus *Monophthalmus* in his conflict with Eumenes for control of Alexander's Asian territories (Fields, 2008, 26). Here they played a pivotal role in the Battle of Gabiene when they sacked Eumenes' baggage camp, bringing the battle to an end despite the success of the latter's *argyraspides* elite phalangites. As detailed, the latter then handed over Eumenes to meet his fate in exchange for the return of their worldly possessions. Such was the success of the Tarantines in the Antigonid army that they are later recorded still fighting for Antigonus' son Demetrius *Poliorcetes* at the Battle of Gaza against Ptolemy in 312 BC, and later still were part of his expeditionary force to Athens in 307 BC.

Finally I come to elephants, the most glamorous component of Alexander's army, albeit it very late on. These huge beasts made a big impression on the king and later became a key component in many Hellenistic armies given their size and shock value on the battlefield. As Murphy argues, a key factor here was the prestige an elephant corps bestowed on a respective monarch, such was their status (2020, 26).

Alexander first came across elephants at Gaugamela in 331 BC where the Persian army included fifteen, though whether they were used in the battle or not is debatable. Parmenion then captured these when sacking the Persian camp after the battle, while twelve more came into Macedonian possession when they later captured Susa (Arrian, *Anabasis Alexandri*, 3.15.5, and Quintus Curtius Rufus, *The History of Alexander*, 5.2.10). However, there is no evidence any of these were incorporated into the Macedonian army at this time.

Elephants then became a regular opponent of Alexander when campaigning in the Punjab against his various Indian opponents, for example playing a prominent role at the Battle of the Hydaspes in the army of Porus in 326 BC. By that time Alexander had already received the first elephants officially incorporated into his army, these from Porus' rival Taxiles of Taxila, though they took no part at the Hydaspes engagement. By the time the king returned to Babylon, from this small beginning a fully-fledged elephant corps had been established in the Macedonian army with 200 of the beasts. Their importance is well-illustrated by a series of large silver coins thought to have been minted in Babylon around this time which on one side feature Alexander on horseback fighting Porus and his mahout atop an elephant, and on the reverse Alexander holding a thunderbolt and spear, with Nike hovering towards him with a wreath. Alexander's early elephants retained their full Indian fighting crews, though by the time of his death the bowmen may have been replaced by a fully-armed Macedonian pikeman. This latter interpretation is based on the description by Diodorus Siculus of panels depicting Macedonian war elephants on Alexander's funeral carriage, though note others have interpreted this passage as referencing the pikemen following the elephants rather than riding atop them (*Library of History*, 18.27).

Two different elephant types were used in Hellenistic and later classical armies. The first was the Indian variety first encountered and then employed by Alexander. The Macedonian elephant corps he created used such beasts, these then distributed throughout the early successor kingdoms after his death, with those remaining in Macedonian service lasting until mid-way through the reign of Antigonus Gonatus (277 BC to 239 BC). The Seleucid Empire and those further east were more fortunate, proximity to India allowing frequent resupply of the elephants. Meanwhile, the second type was the smaller African forest elephant used by Ptolemaic Egypt, these also used in Numidian, Carthaginian and Republican Roman service. These elephants were sourced from the Horn of Africa after the Ptolemies were cut off from supplies of Indian elephants by the Syrian Wars. The third type of elephant was, and remains, the African bush elephant. This was the largest of the species, though proved impossible to train for war given its natural aggression.

We have much insight into the organization of Hellenistic elephant units thanks to contemporary commentary on the extensive Seleucid elephant corps. This was called the *elephantarchia*, commanded by an *elephantarchos* who was a key figure in the royal court. Its elephants were organised into units of one, two, four, eight, sixteen and sixty-four animals, with Antiochus I using units of four and eight when fighting the Galatians (see below for detail). Meanwhile, those in the army of Antiochus III at the Battle of Magnesia in 189 BC were organised in pairs deployed between the units of his phalanx (a unique deployment), and two larger groups of sixteen on the flanks, those on the right a reserve (Murphy, 2020, 27). By this time, given what had been over the past century an arms race between the elephant corps of the various Hellenistic kingdoms, the fighting crew of the beasts had been significantly increased, depending on their size and training. In addition to the mahout controlling the animal, a fighting tower was now added featuring up to three crew armed with pikes, bows and javelins. Such towers were first used by Antigonus *Monophthalmus* when he fought Eumenes at the Battle of Paraitacene in 317 BC in modern Iran.

In Macedonian and later Hellenistic service elephants were used in a variety of ways, they most frequently deployed in line abreast across the front of the main line of battle in the centre, flanks or both, though they could also form a very effective reserve (as on the right wing at Magnesia). Later Hellenistic elephants were often deployed with a guard of light troops to screen them from missile-equipped enemy infantry and to prevent them being hamstrung, even when wearing banded bronze and leather leg armour. Elephants are also naturally nervous, and were targeted by opponents in a variety of novel ways to make them panic. If this happened they became as much a threat to their own side as their opponents. Some went to extreme lengths here, for example the use of squealing pigs by the Romans against Pyrrhus and the Megarians against Antigonus Gonatus. In the latter example, as an added flourish, the Greeks covered their pigs with tar and set them alight. The Romans also allegedly fielded 300 'anti-elephant wagons' against Pyrrhus at the Battle of Asculum in 279 BC. These were of the larger four-wheel variety and featured poles fitted with mobile horizontal beams that were equipped with large blades, tridents and grapnels wrapped in pitch-daubed taw that was then set alight. They were initially successful in slowing an Epirote breakthrough of the Roman battle-line-led Pyrrhus' elephants, but were then overwhelmed by light infantry.

When deployed and commanded well, elephants could be very effective. In the engagement detailed above in the context of elephant unit size, those used by Antiochus I in Asia Minor against the Galatians in 273 BC were so successful that a swift victory followed an elephant charge at the Galatian chariots and cavalry. It became known as the 'Elephant Victory'. However, maintaining an effective elephant corps proved a significant logistics exercise given each beast typically eats up to 7 per cent of its own bodyweight in food per day. Therefore huge amounts of forage were needed to sustain the elephants when on campaign. Foraging on this scale proved a dangerous task in enemy territory, with the gathered elephant forage then proving the most onerous of loads to transport.

Siege Warfare in the Age of Philip II and Alexander

Though Alexander is arguably best known for his prowess in set piece battle, for example against Darius III and Porus, he spent far more time on his *anabasis* engaged in siege warfare. The best known examples are perhaps the lengthy investment of Tyre and the capture the Sogdian Rock, though over his eleven-year campaign he actually engaged in hundreds of sieges.

Expertise in the Greek world to carry out this most specialized form of warfare actually had its origins much earlier. As Connolly explained, offensive siege warfare is inextricably linked with fortifications, with each dominant in the various phases of the historical narrative (1988, 274). In the classical Greek world, until the time of Philip II and Alexander, the latter was in the ascendency.

Although highly specialized siege warfare featuring sophisticated siege engines and tactics had been a key feature in the later Biblical world, for example in the armies of the Neo-Assyrian kings (Elliott, 2020a, 266), they were later notably lacking among the Greek *poleis* of the Balkan peninsula. There, each key city featured significant wall circuits and often citadels, as with the *Cadmea* in Thebes, many based on the much older cyclopean fortifications of their Mycenaean predecessors. To counter these, aside from the traditional use of primitive rams, mining, firing or ladders, the technology available to each *poleis* was, certainly early in the hoplite era, notably lacking.

The earliest type of Greek artillery was the *gastraphetes* belly bow, a simple crossbow-like device too powerful to be drawn by hand that could fire a heavy arrow up to 250m. The military engineers of Dionysios I of Syracuse invented this at the turn of the fourth century BC, with the bow itself comprising a composite of wood and sinew. This technology proved very scalable, and soon larger versions were developed. These were mounted on stands that used a windlass to draw the bow. Named *katapeltes* in ancient Greek, they give us the word 'catapult' today. Further developments led to the specialized bolt or dart-shooting *oxybeles*, and the stone shot-firing *lithobolos* or *petrobolos*, these giving us the Latin name *ballista*. The latter stone-throwing engines tended to be larger than their bolt- and dart-firing counterparts, with a good example being that designed by Charon of Magnesia which had a 2.7m-wide bow that could throw stone shot weighing almost 3kg. It was engines of this scale that were used so successfully by the Phocians against Philip II in the Sacred War (see Chapter 2). At the larger end, Isodorus of Abydos built a very large stone thrower that featured a 4.6m bow which could fire stone shot weighing up to 18kg (Head, 2016, 340).

While such technology became increasingly available to the Greek *poleis* as the classical period progressed, the defensive-wall circuits of the key cities largely remained in the ascendency. However, this all changed with the advent of Philip II and his military reforms. Many have rightly focused here on the creation of the *sarissa*-armed Macedonian pike phalanx and the new 'hammer and anvil' tactics combining this with the king's shock cavalry. Equally important though was his revolutionary development of the Macedonian siege train that, over time, allowed both he and later Alexander to invest even the best-defended cities and fortresses with confidence.

In the first instance Philip hired Poleidus of Thessaly to take charge of greatly expanding his siege warfare capability. First he built large numbers of arrow, dart and stone throwers using existing technology. Then his engineers began to innovate, for example building the 35m-high siege towers used when besieging Perinthus in 340 BC that were higher than the defensive towers in the town wall. These, together with the use of newly developed advanced rams mounted on rollers and skilled mining, soon ensured the walls fell to the Macedonians. Siege towers of this scale later became a favourite technology used by Alexander on his *anabasis*, these often mounting artillery. The two huge towers he built at the end of his maritime mole when besieging Tyre are good examples (see Chapter 4). Later, as the Hellenistic period progressed, extreme examples of such enormous siege towers became commonplace, these best illustrated by Demetrius *Poliorcetes* ('the besieger') and his *helepolis* 40m-high iron-clad siege tower which he built to invest Rhodes in 305/304 BC.

However, Philip II's true legacy regarding siege warfare, and also the use of artillery on the battlefield, was the innovation in his reign of the torsion dart or arrow-firing catapult, and later the torsion stone thrower. Here the composite bow of the engine was replaced with two vertical springs made from sinew or horsehair set in wooden frames, with iron levers used to tighten them at the top and bottom. The springs were then further tightened as the arms were winched backwards, they springing sharply forward into their original position once the trigger was released. Overnight this technology doubled the range of existing dart- and arrow-throwers, and was soon being used with stone-shot-throwing catapults too. Such weapons proved so successful that designs on all scales were soon created for use in siege warfare and on the battlefield, and by the mid-third century Ptolemaic engineers had created a set of calibrated formulae that set out the most effective dimensions for a torsion catapult firing a given size of dart, arrow or stone, and the respective dimensions for each part of the weapon (Head, 2016, 341). By this time the acknowledged ideal size of stone ball for use against stone-built fortifications was 26kg, though the largest engines could throw a stone-shot three times this size. Weapons of this scale proved to be the elite military technology of the classical world and weren't surpassed until the Byzantine adoption of the Chinese-developed trebuchet in the sixth century AD.

Naval Warfare in the Age of Philip II and Alexander

Most campaigning theatres in the ancient Greek world were dominated by access to the sea, with control of the open ocean, coastal littoral and the riparian zone down major river systems vital to the success of military operations. Corresponding naval capability dated back to at least 2,000 BC with the Minoan civilization that flourished on Crete. Indeed Thucydides says it was the Minoans, with their principal city states at Knossos, Phaistos, Mallia, Khania and Zakro, who first mastered naval warfare, saying (*The Peloponnesian War*, 1.4):

> Minos (the mythical Minoan king) is the first to whom tradition ascribes the possession of a navy. He made himself master of a great part of what is now termed the Hellenic Sea; he conquered the Cyclades, and was the first colonizer of most of them, expelling the Carians and appointing his own sons to govern them. Lastly, it was he who, from a natural desire to protect his growing revenues, sought, as far as he was able, to clear the sea of pirates.

Thucydides here is describing the creation of the first maritime empire in the eastern Mediterranean, and although Minoan civilization had fallen to Mycenaean predation from the Peloponnese and Attica by 1,450 BC, the precedent they set of naval prowess remained a key feature of warfare across the region.

We certainly have great insight into the naval capabilities of the Mycenaean city-states through the epic Catalogue of Ships in Book 2 of Homer's *Iliad* (2.494-759). This lists the contingents of the Greek army that sailed to Troy. The list not only includes the names of the leaders of each contingent, but also the actual number of ships required to transport their men on the famous expedition. For example, Pylos under Nestor needed eighty vessels, Menelaus of Sparta fifty vessels and the Cretans under Idomeneus eighty. Given there were twenty-nine contingents in all, this implies a huge fleet was gathered. Late period Linear B tablets from Pylos specifically detail how a fleet as large as theirs (in the Catalogue of Ships it was second only in size to that of Agamemnon from Mycenae) was manned. This includes a muster of 600 rowers needed for the part of the fleet based at Navarino Bay near the city, the 20 ships there requiring 30 rowers each. Other contemporary warships needed larger crews, with for example earlier Minoan frescoes from Thera (modern Santorini) showing vessels with a complement of 42 rowers each. Meanwhile, we have further insight into the importance of naval warfare in Mycenaean culture through the naming of one of their months, namely *poroweto* which in proto-Greek means 'sailing time' (this from a Pylian Linear B tablet, Elliott, 2020a, 127). This importance continued well after the demise of the Mycenaean city-states as part of the Late Bronze Age Collapse around 1,250 BC, with the various successor cultures in the region known as the Sea Peoples. These seafaring peoples travelled far and wide in the eastern Mediterranean, seeking plunder and later settlement. In the latter context, the best known example are the group known as the Peleset who were settled by Egypt as a buffer state in the region of modern Gaza. Here they became the Philistine culture so well referenced in the Old Testament, their name then giving us today's Palestine.

The naval technology utilized by the Minoan, Mycenaean and various Sea People cultures was ubiquitous across the chronology of their existence, and geography of their maritime activities. We are fortunate here given their extensive depiction in highly-coloured contemporary frescoes, and in the archaeological record. Both show lightly-built wooden galleys that were easily launched and beached, featuring high prows and sterns that were akin to the reed-built vessels of the Egyptians. Most featured a central mainsail, with the rowing crew sat amidships on benches, and with any fighting crew based fore and aft.

However, as the Geometric or Dark Age period of ancient Greek history progressed a new maritime technology emerged that revolutionized naval warfare in the eastern and later western Mediterranean. This was the use of locked mortise and tenon plank fastenings from the beginning of the first millennium BC, originally by the Phoenicians. This enabled true Mediterranean war galleys to be built for the first time, a technology that in the much later form of galleasses lasted into the Renaissance period over 2,500 years later.

The first such war galleys were monoremes featuring a single bank of oars, these called pentaconters, featuring a ram on the waterline in the bow as the main weapon alongside its fighting crew. By the time of the Greco-Persian Wars at the beginning of the fifth century BC the principal line of battleships had grown to include biremes and triremes, the latter invented by the Corinthians around 530 BC. These were so called because they featured two and three banks of oars either side respectively, with Athenian ships standardizing on twenty-seven *thalamites*, or rowers, each side on the lower level. By this time the vessels were large enough to carry additional weaponry, for example artillery.

It was ships of this design and size that dominated the fleets used by Alexander, and indeed those of his eastern Mediterranean opponents. One should note here that the key role they played in his *anabasis* was in the early part of the campaign when he was campaigning in the littoral coastal regions of Anatolia and the Levant, particular supporting siege operations and interdicting Persian lines of supply. Indeed, a key feature of his eastern Mediterranean strategy was to increasingly deny Darius III the use of the vassal fleets the latter relied on in the region, with Alexander's strategy to capture the key regional ports one by one.

As the Hellenistic period progressed following Alexander's death, larger and larger polyremes appeared, including quadriremes (the '4', and so on), quinqueremes (first used by the Syracusian dictator Dionysius I in 399 BC), hexaremes, septiremes, octeres, enneres and deceres (Elliott, 2020b, 78). As one can see, the pattern here was for the vessels to get larger and larger, clearly a symptom of an arms race in the fairly symmetrical conflicts between the Hellenistic kingdoms and later during Rome's expansion across the western and eastern Mediterranean (especially during the Punic Wars, and the later wars with Macedon). In the case of the wars of the eastern Mediterranean in the third and second centuries BC, the successor kings Demetrius *Poliorcetes* and Ptolemy IV built even larger ships, the latter apparently a '40'. However, the larger vessels were much fewer in number serving principally as flagships and platforms for heavy artillery, with the main line of battleships at the time of the Second Punic War being the quinquereme, and the main scout ship the trireme.

In terms of the naming of the vessel types by size, the larger polyremes derived their names not from the number of banks of oars but from the number of men rowing on each over and above the third bank of the trireme. In this context, a quinquereme would be a feature a trireme arrangement but with two oarsmen rowing the top two tiers of oars.

Whatever their size, the vessels also came with various degrees of protection. These were aphract (with the oarsmen unprotected by deck planking, as with the Athenian-led fleet that defeated the Persians at the crucial Battle of Salamis in 480 BC), semi-cataphract (oarsmen partially protected) and cataphract (oarsmen fully protected), with the larger line of battleships in the Hellenistic period usually being the cataphract type.

Chapter 4

On Campaign and In Battle: Alexander

Alexander the Great has often been referenced as the greatest conqueror and military leader in world history, certainly until the mid-twentieth century when serious academic rigour was adopted to consider for the first time the scale of his success, both at a strategic and tactical level. In terms of his conquests, the bare facts still support his reputation in that he conquered much of his known world in just eleven years, this a geographically vast area which included his destruction of the greatest empire of his age. Critiques here have therefore concentrated on the moral aspects of these conquests, and his lack of planning to secure his legacy after his untimely death. However, in specific aspects of his campaigns and battles, much more debate has taken place that focuses on the scale of his prowess. This will be the focus of this chapter, where I detail the five key engagements of his career once king (as I determine them), namely the Battle of the Granicus River, Battle of Issus, Siege of Tyre, Battle of Gaugamela and Battle of the Hydaspes River.

It should be noted that all of these engagements are difficult to recreate in print, especially that at the Hydaspes River, given the multiple accounts in the primary sources which are often contradictory. Further, subsequent attempts to recreate them in contemporary history have often become accepted as a true version of events, even when not firmly embedded in the (as noted contradictory) primary sources. To that end, wherever possible I have reverted to the original histories to take my own view on which are likely the most accurate. Consequently, what you read here are my own personal views, which often include new interpretations printed here for the first time.

Battle of the Granicus River

As detailed in Chapter 2, large-scale Achaemenid Persian military activity operated on two levels, satrapal and royal. In the first instance the force was regional in nature, led by one or more of the king's satraps. In the latter, usually in wars of conquest or to tackle existential threats, an army was gathered from across the wider Empire and led by the king in person. In 334 BC, as Alexander crossed into Asia, Darius' initial response was to rely on his local satraps in Anatolia to deal with the upstart Macedonian king. Only if they failed, which he thought highly unlikely, would he then become directly involved.

Here, having been caught out by Parmenion's earlier Macedonian expedition, Darius now moved with unusual speed (Pietrykowski, 2009, 35). Using the Empire's sophisticated system of Royal trunk roads, the king's royal couriers swiftly delivered his orders to the satraps ranged across Anatolia. By early May these and their military commanders had gathered to consider their campaigning strategy at Zeleia, the Homeric town in the Troad at the foot of Mount Ida. Goldsworthy suggests Darius placed the local regional governor in charge of the gathering, and also the subsequent campaign, this being Arsites who was the long-standing satrap of Hellespontine Phrygia (2020, 247). This region covered the north-western coast of Anatolia where Parmenion's expedition had earlier campaigned, and where many of the latter's troops still remained. Arsites was already known to Alexander as the satrap who had earlier been the first Persian leader to send aid to Perinthus when Philip II had besieged the city in 340 BC.

Arsites was joined at Zeleia by the leading nobles from the Persian west, all keen to show their metal against Alexander and impress Darius. Foremost were two more key satraps, Arsames of Cilicia and Spithridates of Lydia and Ionia. The latter had a particular interest in stopping the Macedonian advance at the earliest opportunity given it was in his satrapy where resided many of the leading Ionian Greek cities that Alexander was hoping to liberate. These included Ephesus, Miletus and Priene. This key satrapy also included Sardis, Darius' regional capital where the king had an Imperial palace and treasury. Meanwhile, other key noblemen arriving at Zeleia included Spithridates' brother Rhoesaces, Darius son-in-law Mithridates, Rheomithres whose son Phrasaortes was later appointed satrap of Persis by Alexander, and the cavalry commanders Petenes and Niphates.

However, the key figure attending the gathering at Zeleia was Memnon of Rhodes, the mercenary Greek *strategos* who had earlier defeated Parmenion and his expeditionary force near Magnesia. We know far more about him than any of the other leaders at Zeleia, not surprising given all of our primary sources are Greek. Born around 380 BC, he had served the Persian Empire for most of his life, alongside his brother Mentor. Indeed, their sister had married the Phrygian satrap Artabazos II. Memnon knew the Macedonians well, having accompanied Artabazos into exile in Philip II's court at Pella after the satrap's failed rebellion against Artaxerxes III in 352 BC (the two taking their eleven sons and daughters with them). However, Mentor had stayed loyal to the then Persian king, later distinguishing himself in Persian service fighting the last native Egyptian pharaoh Nectanebo II, the Greek playing a key leadership role in the decisive Battle of Pelusium in 343 BC.

Eventually Mentor persuaded Memnon to return to Persian service after four years in Macedon. Mentor died in 340 BC, after which Memnon married his brother's wife Barsine (a daughter of Artabazos), she later becoming the lover of Alexander the Great and mother of Hercules, the Macedonian king's supposed illegitimate son.

In 339 BC Memnon helped the city of Byzantium defend itself against Philip's siege (see Chapter 2 for detail), and subsequently led the Persian campaign against Parmenion's expeditionary force. Then, when the Macedonian king was assassinated Memnon urged Darius to foment a rebellion against Macedonian hegemony in Greece, knowing the difficulty Alexander faced in securing his hold on the throne. Now, as the Persians gathered at Zeleia to tackle the new king's invasion, Memnon became one of the leading commanders of the combined satrapal army.

The speedy response of Darius to Alexander's invasion wrong-footed the young king who quickly changed his invasion strategy. Instead of heading southwards along the western coastline of Anatolia where he had planned to quickly liberate the Greek cities one by one, he now headed north-west along the coast of the Hellespont and Phrygia to meet the Persian challenge. To ensure a speedy advance he left much of his invasion force behind, taking just 18,000 troops overall. This included most of the cavalry including the companions and *prodromoi*, all of the *hypaspists* and available phalanx, and his Agrianian javelinmen and archers, the latter including the highly-experienced Cretans. At this point Memnon advised a scorched earth policy to buy time for a royal army to be gathered under Darius which he felt would guarantee victory. However, the Persians were reluctant to further damage the regional economy given the severe disruption caused by Parmenion's earlier campaign. They therefore decided to challenge Alexander directly instead.

Having been forewarned by Memnon, and then fought Parmenion, the Persians were keenly aware of the Macedonian pike phalanx's fearsome reputation. Therefore, they now moved their army away from the open plains around Zeleia where the terrain was more suitable for Alexander's army. Heading westward, soon the Persians found themselves among the hills and streams on Mount Ida's western slopes. There they built a large camp on the eastern side of the Granicus River. They then prepared to defend the waterway against any attempt by Alexander to cross. This river gently meanders north-east to the Sea of Marmara through the plains of Phrygia, and while not a significant waterway at the time of year (at its deepest it was only 1m in depth), the Granicus did feature steep muddy banks, making it eminently defendable.

Soon Alexander's scouting *prodromoi* and light foot arrived at the river. Here they found the Persians arrayed for battle on the far bank. Informed an engagement was imminent, the king first consulted his senior officers, with Parmenion advising he wait until the following morning before engaging given their lengthy march that morning. Alexander, eager for the first victory of his crusade against the Persians, rejected the advice and swiftly deployed his column on the west bank where they prepared for battle.

Confusion surrounds the size of the Persian army, with some ancient historians giving even more improbable numbers than usual. For example Diodorus Siculus talks of 100,000 foot and 10,000 cavalry (*Library of History*, 17.19, the former clearly incredible, though the latter is oddly more believable). The most commonly accepted figures are those detailed by Arrian who speaks of 20,000 cavalry (these comprising most the retinues of the various satraps and nobles in attendance, so with an unusual preponderance of high-class troops) and 20,000 foot, the latter mostly mercenary Greek hoplites (*Anabasis Alexandri*, 1.14.4). I use Arrian's figures here.

Further confusion relates to the actual events of the Granicus River battle given there are two very different descriptions by the ancient sources. In the first instance both Arrian and Plutarch say Alexander, eager for battle, attacked directly across the Granicus (*Anabasis Alexandri*, 1.13, and *Lives*, Alexander, 16). Meanwhile, Diodorus Siculus (*Library of History*, 17.19.3) says the Macedonians crossed the Granicus during the night and attacked the Persians before dawn the following morning on the flat ground beyond the river. Given the Persians usually sacrificed before sunrise, this sounds a good stratagem as they would have been unprepared and off guard. However, most commentators then and now follow the first narrative, with Arrian providing a little more insight in saying Alexander scouted the safe fordable crossings of the river first (*Anabasis Alexandri*, 1.13). I therefore, broadly, follow that description of the engagement here.

In terms of deployment, Alexander positioned six *ilia* of the companions on the extreme right under Philotas, including his own 300-strong *hetairoi* guard *ile*, with Agrianian javelinmen and archers in support. Next in line came the *prodromoi*, now taking their place in the line of battle, the Paeonian light horse and the remaining single *ile* of companions, all under the command of Amyntas, son of Arrabaeus. Hard against these in the right centre were the *hypaspist*, then the phalanx, and finally on the left wing the Thessalian and Greek allied heavy cavalry and the Thracian light horse (Goldsworthy, 2020, 253). Alexander took command of the Macedonian right wing and right centre, Parmenion the left centre and left wing.

Arrayed against them on the eastern bank the Persians deployed in an unusual formation given their plan was to defend the steep-sided riverbank. Most contemporary sources suggest that instead of positioning their heavy infantry atop the steep riverbank, as one would expect, they instead deployed the entirety of their cavalry across the front of their battle line, with the hoplite foot relegated to a position atop a hill to the rear. Many have speculated one reason for this might be the Persians being wary of the Greek mercenaries' loyalty, especially when fighting compatriots (this certainly being the case with Alexander's Greek allied cavalry). However, another reason was the desire of the various foremost Persian noblemen leading their regional retinues to achieve glory on the battlefield. Certainly, their disposition indicates this all played a prominent role in the ensuing battle, leading from the front and with many seeking to confront Alexander in person. In that regard, facing Alexander on the Persian left were Memnon with his sons and Arsames, each with their own cavalry contingent. Next, moving left to right, were Arsites with his Paphlagonian horsemen and Spithridates with his elite Hyrcanian guard cavalry who together commanded the Persian centre. Finally, on the right wing Rheomithres led a large contingent of Median and Bactrian horse.

As Alexander looked across the Granicus it quickly became clear the Persians were refusing to advance. Diodorus Siculus describes the scene, saying (*Library of History*, 17.19):

> The Persians, resting on high ground, made no move, intending to fall upon their foe as he crossed the river, for they supposed they could easily carry the day when the Macedonian phalanx was divided (the last a reference to the expected disruption as it crossed the river).

By now it was late afternoon and Alexander decided to take the offensive. First he ordered the *prodromoi*, Paeonian light horse, their supporting companions and a unit of *hypaspists* to force the river under Amyntas, they targeting the extreme left of the Persian line. By this time, having ridden up and down the Macedonian line making final dispositions, Alexander had arrived back to take his position on the extreme right wing with the remaining companions alongside Philotas. Positioned at the apex of the wedge of his own 300-strong *hetairoi* guard *ilia*, he now gave the command for a general advance, the primary sources saying he plunged into the water first.

Meanwhile, his lighter horse spearhead, targeting Memnon and Arsames, had already waded through the river and reached the far bank where they were targeted by the javelins and bows of the Persian horse. Many unarmoured *prodromoi* and Paeonians were cut down, and the Macedonian advance quickly wavered. Sensing an easy victory, the Persians on the left wing now surged forward down the muddy bank, including Memnon himself, with more and more drawn into the engagement from the centre. Soon, with weight of numbers increasingly in their favour, the Persians began to push the Macedonians back over the river, leaving twenty-five companions dead on the eastern riverbank.

However, urgent help was on the way. Alexander now unveiled a tactical masterstroke from the extreme right flank. Having led the majority of the companions into the Granicus, these now passed behind the initial spearhead, crossing right to left where they then charged at full speed up the eastern riverbank into Memnon and Arsames' surging Persian left wing cavalry. This positioned them at the juncture of the Persian left and centre. A desperate melee ensued, with the Macedonians having the advantage given their long *xyston* lances. Soon the Persian cavalry in the river and atop the bank broke, with the companions then forcing the eastern shore of the Granicus to pursue into the flank of the Persian centre. The primary sources now focus entirely on Alexander as he led his companions from the front. Arrian says the king deliberately made himself as conspicuous as possible through the 'brightness of his arms' and the brilliant white plume atop his helmet (*Anabasis Alexandri*, 1.13). This certainly attracted the attention of the Persians, many of who now sought to engage Alexander directly. This included Mithridates who was in Arsites' command in the Persian centre. Darius' son-in-law headed directly for Alexander who, seeing the danger, countercharged with his close guard. A desperate fight ensued, with the Macedonian king shattering his own *xyston* and borrowing another from Demaratas of Corinth, a Greek companion recruited by Philip. With this he impaled Mithridates in the face, killing him instantly. However, there was no respite for the Macedonian king, with another Persian nobleman charging into the melee. This was Mithradates' brother Rhoesaces who aimed a blow at Alexander's head, the king dodging the blow just in time, with the Persian's sword slicing off part of his plume and cracking his helmet. Alexander ran him through with the same *xyston*. By this time Spithridates had closed on the king with his Hyrcanian guard, the Lydian satrap aiming another blow at Alexander's head. However, Cleitus the Black, Alexander's close bodyguard in the battle, attacked the Persian first and severed his arm, saving Alexander's life.

By this time Alexander's centre and left had begun to surge across the eastern bank of the Granicus. Seeing this, especially after the loss of so many leaders in the savage cavalry fight, the Persians began to fall back. Then, when Parmenion charged the Persian right wing with his Thessalians and Thracians, the Persian cavalry broke and began to flee the battlefield, along with any of the surviving Persian leaders. This left just the Greek hoplite mercenaries on the hill at the rear, no doubt bemused at the sudden change in Persian fortunes.

Alexander now rallied his troops to prevent a headlong pursuit of the Persian cavalry. He then turned his attention to the Greek heavy foot. Their leaders first tried to negotiate a truce with Alexander and when this was turned down, begged for mercy. However, the Macedonian king was infuriated by what he saw as their treachery fighting with the Persians and ordered a general attack. First Parmenion with the Thessalians and Thracians circled to the left of the Greek line. Then Alexander with the companions positioned himself on the right. Finally, the phalanx drew up to pin the Greeks in place to their front. When all was in place the Macedonian king ordered a general assault, and a terrible slaughter began. Though the Greeks fought desperately with nothing to lose, the engagement was short and one sided. Plutarch has Alexander leading the way and charging headlong into the fray, with his charger (not Bucephalus) killed from under him when a *doru* spearhead was driven into the horse's ribs (*Lives*, Alexander, 16.14). However, the end was never in doubt and soon 18,000 hoplites were slain, with the surviving 2,000 sent back to Macedon in chains where a short future working as slaves in the mines awaited (as detailed in Chapter 2). As to other casualties, if one takes the primary sources at face value, 2,500 Persian cavalry were slain, while the Macedonians lost 85 cavalry and 30 infantry, most when fighting the doomed Greek foot. Though the latter figures for Alexander's losses are improbable, they do show the scale of his victory. Meanwhile, of the surviving

Persian leaders Arsites made good his escape though later committed suicide, while Memnon chose not to fall with his Greek compatriots but also fled (Goldsworthy, 2020, 258). Shortly afterwards Darius made him the governor of all of the western satrapies, he later leading the failed defence of Halicarnassus and finally being killed during the siege of Mytilene.

Though the Granicus River engagement was a small battle by the later standards of Alexander's *anabasis*, it was a crucial victory as it set the tone for his later campaign. Darius now knew he was facing the kind of existential threat that required his own presence with the royal army and started planning accordingly. Meanwhile, seeing the Macedonian victory and Alexander's harsh treatment of the Greek mercenaries in Persian employ, many of the cities in western Anatolia now opened their gates to the king as he arrived, for example Sardis and Ephesus. In short order all of the Anatolian satrapies fell to Alexander, and the scene was set for his next great battle.

The Battle of Issus

Many view the later Battle of Gaugamela as the crucial engagement in Alexander's *anabasis*. However, that near Issus in the northern Levant in November 333 BC is to my mind equally, if not more, important. Here, for the first time, Alexander and the Macedonians fought the King of Kings in person, the latter commanding a full-scale royal army. Yet, despite facing a huge disparity in numbers and relying on highly vulnerable lines of supply, the Macedonian victory was so total that from that point Alexander's eventual victory seemed the most likely outcome of his campaign.

The Macedonian king had spent much of early 333 BC pacifying Anatolia, this including his famous visit to Gordium. By the early summer he had passed through Cappadocia and the Cilician Gates, the latter the crucial pass through the Taurus Mountains that provided access from the Anatolian plateau to the coastal lowlands of the Levant.

Following the failure of Arsites and his fellow satraps at the Granicus River, and the subsequent collapse of any resistance to the steady Macedonian advance through the cities of Anatolia, Darius determined to stop Alexander once and for all. Gathering a huge royal army, he manoeuvred the vast force behind Alexander's lines of supply to their north. This was a shrewd move, as with his earlier swift response to Alexander's initial invasion across the Hellespont. In particular, given the Persians still

Right: Thracian-style helmet, a later style of head protection worn by the pikemen and hoplites and in Alexander's army. (*Apostoloff via Wikicommons*)

Below left: Fragments of a fine-quality Macedonian *pelte* shield, found in Bonce, North Macedonia. (*Beat of the tapan via Wikicommons*)

Below right: Fine-quality Macedonian pikemen depicted on a wall painting from a tomb in Agios Athanasios near Pella, Greece. (*Public domain*)

Above: Hellenistic cavalryman depicted on the 'Alexander Sarcophagus', Istanbul Archaeological Museum. (*Wikicommons*)

Left: Macedonian *hypaspist* foot companion fighting a Persian *kardakes*, 'Alexander Sarcophagus', Istanbul Archaeological Museum. (*Wikicommons*)

Alexander the Great slaying a Persian cavalryman, 'Alexander Sarcophagus', Istanbul Archaeological Museum. (*Wikicommons*)

Achaemenid Persian coin of Darius III, minted around 331 BC. (*Classical Numismatic Group*)

Detail of the 'Alexander Mosaic' from the House of the Faun in Pompeii, now on display in the *Museo Archeologico Nazionale di Napoli*. Dating to around 100 BC, it depicts either the Battle of Issus or Gaugamela.

Artist's interpretation of the 'Alexander Mosaic' from the House of the Faun. (*Public domain*)

Detail of Darius III on the 'Alexander Mosaic' from the House of the Faun. Note the fear depicted by the artist as the king flees Alexander. (*Wikicommons*)

Alexander's opponent in Anatolia, Memnon of Rhodes. (*Classical Numismatic Group*)

Alexander's father, Philip II of Macedon. (*Ancient Coin Traders via Wikicommons*)

Bronze greaves from the tomb thought to belong to Philip II of Macedon, Aigai, Vergina Greece. (*Mary Harrsch via Wikicommons*)

Later *hypaspist* officer, equipped as an *argyraspides* silver shield guardsman. Note the high-quality muscled cuirass.

Hellenistic war elephant. Alexander established the first Macedonian elephant corps after his Indian campaign. (*Robert Raynor*)

Hoplite musician, showing detail of the bell cuirass, a common earlier design.

Right: Wall painting of a classical scene from Pompeii showing hoplites with equipment typical of that worn by Alexander's mercenaries and allies.

Below: Wall painting relief of a *trireme* war galley, Pompeii.

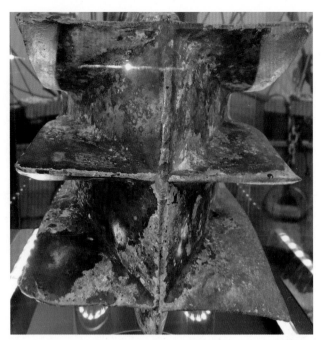

The business end
of a classical war
galley, the ram,
designed to smash
through an enemy
vessel's hull.

Late Republican legionary
equipped with *lorica hamata*
chainmail hauberk and *scutum*
shield.

The theatre in Ephesus, key city on the western coast of Anatolia in both the Hellenistic and Roman periods.

Temple of Mars Ultor, Forum of Augustus, Rome, built alongside the Forum of Caesar.

Roman merchant vessel bringing grain to Rome from North Africa, Ostia Antica.

Forum Romanum, Rome. Political heart of the Roman Republic and later Empire.

Parthenon, Athens. The leading city of Greece played a key role in the careers of both Alexander and Caesar.

Theatre, Butrint in modern Albania. Originally a Hellenistic city, this is where Caesar settled his veterans after the Battle of Pharsalus in 48 BC.

Above: Forum, Pompeii with Vesuvius brooding menacingly in the background. The Roman upper-classes in Republic and Empire travelled each year to the Bay of Naples to spend time in the region's fine villas along the coast.

Left: Caesar as a young boy. (*Museo Archeologico Nazionale di Napoli*)

Right: Caesar, the great statesman. (*Museo Archeologico Nazionale di Napoli*)

Below: The island of Farmakonisi (Roman *Pharmacussa*) off the southwestern Anatolian coast where Caesar was held by Cilician pirates.

Above: Temple of Apollo, Didyma in modern Turkey. When kidnapped by Cilician pirates, Caesar raised money from across the region to pay his ransom.

Left: The price for standing up to the might of Rome. Badly damaged *pilos* helmet.

controlled much of the eastern Mediterranean through the fleets of their regional vassals, this threatened to cut the Macedonians off from their route home. Once more, at a strategic level, Alexander was now forced to respond to Darius, turning back and immediately seeking a decisive meeting engagement. This he got in the narrow coastal plain between the sea and mountains near the key regional port of Issus (Goldsworthy, 2020, 283).

This was a true epic battle in every sense of the word, and one we know much more about than the Granicus River battle given the primary sources go into much more detail. Sadly for Darius, the high point of his engagement was the pre-battle strategic manoeuvring detailed above, as he then made three tactical errors to confound his earlier seizing of the strategic initiative. First he killed his best general. This was the Greek *strategos* Charidamus who, on learning of the Macedonian countermarch to intercept the royal army, advised the king to divide his army in two. One, under the Greek general, would tackle Alexander directly, while the other under Darius would be held in reserve. However, with his prestige at stake after the Persian defeat at Granicus River, Darius ignored the advice and determined to continue onwards to fight the Macedonians with his entire force. Unfortunately Charidamus then made the mistake of saying a few ill-chosen words in Greek about the Persians while in Darius' presence. The king, who spoke Greek perfectly, was instantly offended and had the general executed out of hand. In the long run this clearly proved a major error as with Memnon already dead, the King of Kings was running out of reliable military advisers.

Then, as his enormous army meandered towards the Macedonians, Darius made his second error. At one point, still some distance from Alexander, he called a halt near a badly-positioned Macedonian camp his Bactrian scouts had found. However, far from it being Alexander's main base, it turned out to be a field hospital for those Macedonians still wounded from the Anatolian campaign or suffering from illness. Darius showed no mercy, ordering the execution of many recuperating soldiers, with any allowed to live having their right hand severed. Alexander, already determined to defeat the Persians in a winner-takes-all battle, was infuriated and vowed revenge.

Darius' final error was his choice of battlefield. Faced with Alexander's advance northwards to force an engagement, he chose a defensive position similar to the satrap's failed defence of the Granicus. This time Darius arrayed his huge army along the Pinarus River, which bisected the coastal plain near Issus. This was a small stream running from the mountains to the north before turning west-east as it met the coastal plain, its route broadly tracking the border today between Turkey and Syria.

At first glance defending the bank of a waterway, however small, against an aggressing opponent certainly gave the Persians a defensive advantage. However, Darius should already have been aware that the Granicus had proved no real obstacle in that engagement given the determination and training of the Macedonians. Further, his key advantage at Issus was weight of numbers, and here the waterway was naturally bounded by the sea to the west and the coastal mountains to the east. Therefore an envelopment of the Macedonians was not an option, and the battle would become a straight fight based on the quality of the various troop types in each army. That gave Alexander an enormous advantage, with Plutarch saying 'Fortune certainly presented Alexander with the ideal terrain for the battle….' (*Lives*, Alexander, 20).

When Alexander's scouts found the Persians ready for battle, the Macedonian king immediately moved to deploy his army out of its marching column into battle array. By this time he had his full campaigning force with him, totalling over 40,000 men. However, when considering the size of the Persian army, we are again faced with incredulous numbers as detailed by the primary sources. For example, Arrian says Darius fielded 600,000 men (*Anabasis Alexandri*, 2.8.6). Meanwhile, Diodorus Siculus opts for an equally outrageous 400,000 (*Library of History*, 17.19). However, most modern commentators opt for between 60,000 and 120,000. For example Goldsworthy (2020, 248) argues for the presence of up to 30,000 heavy and lighter cavalry, 30,000 Greek mercenaries (many of whom had formerly served as marines in a Greek vassal fleet under the now late Memnon), and a large contingent of *kardakes* line-of-battle foot (many equipped to fight as hoplites, *peltasts* and *psiloi*, see Chapter 2). Whatever the actual Persian numbers, Alexander was certainly heavily outnumbered. This engagement is also notable for the late time of year in which it was fought, reflecting Alexander's propensity for campaigning out of season. In that regard, conditions were notably cold and wet.

In terms of deployment Alexander followed his by now standard pattern, with himself on the right with the *ilia* of companions deployed in their *embolus* wedge formations, then moving right to left the *hypaspists*, then the phalanx (at least partially under the command of Craterus, promoted after his success commanding a *taxis* of *pezetairoi* at the Granicus River), and finally Parmenion on the left with the Thessalian and Thracian horse. Light troops, including Thracians, Agrianians and Cretans, supported both flanks, while the Macedonian centre was bolstered by allied and mercenary Greek, Illyrian and more Thracian foot. The Macedonian phalanx deployment here is particularly interesting. As Alexander approached the Pinarus River it was thirty-two deep, but the king then reduced it to eight deep on arrival at the waterway as he sought to extend his centre so as not to leave the extreme flank of the companions on the right exposed. This meant the bristling deployment of the *pezetairoi* and heavy foot alone stretched for over 1.6km.

Meanwhile, Darius deployed his heavy cavalry next to the coast on his right flank where they could make best use of the broad expanses of flat beach next to the Gulf of Issus, then *kardakes* Hellenised Persian foot, next the Greek mercenaries deployed in two large bodies of 15,000 men (both commanded by the *strategos* Thymondas), and finally more *kardakes* and a small number of Median and Hyrcanian cavalry extending the Persian line to the high ground on its extreme left. There Darius stretched his line even further, with (despite Alexander's best efforts to extend his own line) some *kardakes* wrapping around the Macedonian extreme right flank in the foothills. This forced Alexander to match them there in the rough terrain with some of his own elite Agrianian javelinmen. The Persians then deployed a second line of levies behind those deployed along the riverbank, Pietrykowski (2009, 68) describing them as a '…disorganised throng'. Finally, Darius positioned himself with his elite guard cavalry between the two bodies of Greek mercenaries to the front. It is noteworthy here that a number of the surviving Persian nobles who had fought at the Granicus River were also present. These included the former Cilician satrap Arsames and also Rheomithres, both deployed with Darius and his guard, and both falling in the ensuing battle. Meanwhile, as a final comment on the Persian deployment at Issus, Arrian adds that the foot across the centre (presumably both the Greeks and *kardakes*) reinforced their riverbank defence with '…stockades…' where the shoreline was particularly gentle, which he describes elsewhere as '…precipitous…' (*Anabasis Alexandri*, 2.10). Polybius describes the same defended riverbank as covered in thorny bushes (*The Rise of the Roman Empire*, 12.22). Clearly we are talking here about a significant natural and, with the stockades, man-made obstacle.

Both armies now faced off across the Pinarus River. Here Arrian makes a further interesting observation, saying the security of the Persian position actually counted against Darius' army psychologically, with Alexander believing it indicated inaction, and that therefore Darius was already '...in spirit a beaten man...' (*Anabasis Alexandri*, 2.10.2). This seems harsh, given as Goldworthy observes this was a battle Darius in reality simply needed not to lose, rather than achieve a crushing victory (2020, 288). The Macedonians were already cut off from their lines of supply to the north, and a loss at Issus would have forced Alexander to effect a maritime evacuation across the eastern Mediterranean in waters under Persian control, or head inland or south even further away from safety.

However, Alexander was clearly emboldened by Darius' reticence to engage as he now ordered a general attack across his entire line. One factor here may have been the Macedonian line coming under missile fire from the Persians as soon as it came into range while deploying along the southern riverbank. Again Alexander led the way, either at the head of a thunderous charge across the Pinarus with his companions on the right wing, or dismounting with his close guard and leading the *hypaspists*. Goldsworthy has a useful discussion in this regard, noting the word used by Arrian to describe Alexander's initial advance is *dromo*, meaning 'at a run'. This might suggest he was on foot (2020, 289). However, this seems unlikely to me given Alexander's swift success on the right, where he quickly broke through the *kardakes* to threaten the Persian centre. The primary sources certainly indicate Darius' left wing was terrified by the speed of Alexander's advance, especially after his Agrianian javelinmen moved to prevent any envelopment by the *kardakes* on the Persian hanging left flank.

However, elsewhere things did not go as well for the Macedonians, with the phalanx unsurprisingly struggling to keep its formation as it crossed the river and navigated the far bank which, as detailed, had been fortified where not steep. Here Arrian describes gaps forming between individual phalanx units (*Anabasis Alexandri*, 2.10.1), presumably the 1,500 strong *taxeis*, with the eight-deep *pezetairoi* suffering at the hands of the Greek mercenary hoplites and Hellenised *kardakes* atop their bank. Indeed, Matthew argues it was only the length of the Macedonian *sarissas* that allowed the pikemen to engage the enemy at all (2015, 337). Soon Arrian says 120 Macedonians 'of note' had been slain, this usually interpreted as officers (*Anabasis Alexandri*, 2.10.3).

Meanwhile, any Persian troops armed with missile weapons continued to pour fire into the Macedonian phalanx at point-blank range and, denied the almost unstoppable impetus they enjoyed when on open ground, the *pezetairoi* began to fall back slowly over the Pinarus. Diodorus Siculus says this initial phase of the infantry encounter only lasted a short time (*Library of History*, 17.33), with one interpretation being the Macedonian foot now began the difficult manoeuvre of disengaging from an enemy to their front. The likelihood of this increases when one considers that the Greek mercenaries and *kardakes* defending their bank were unlikely to pursue given the security of their position, especially with stockades deployed in places across their front.

Meanwhile, on the Macedonian left Parmenion was faring little better, his outnumbered Thessalian and Greek cavalry rebuffed time and again as they tried to counter Darius' main body of horse. Soon their casualties began to mount and the Persian cavalry began to press them back, Parmenion's horsemen only just holding their line.

However, swift and brutal relief for the Macedonian centre and left was at hand as just when momentum had been lost there Alexander smashed through the *kardakes* to his front with the companions and *hypaspists* and, again showing true leadership on the battlefield, instead of pursuing his beaten foe turned left to hammer the now exposed left flank of the Greek mercenaries. Little resistance was offered given the latter were engaged to their front with the *pezetairoi*, and soon individual men and then small groups of hoplites broke and ran to the rear. Once the integrity of the Greek phalanx was lost it quickly folded under the combined assault of Alexander's troops and now resurgent pikemen. A savage slaughter ensued, with Alexander then spying Darius and his close guards. Knowing this was his chance to bring the campaign to a swift end, he immediately charged the Persian king. This is the scene some believe is shown in the Alexander Mosaic from the House of the Faun in Pompeii and detailed in Chapter 3, where the Macedonian king thunders towards Darius in his chariot, *xyston* leveled at the Persian king, the whole montage set against a hedge-like backdrop of waving *sarissas*. However Darius' brother Oxyathres now intervened, with Quintus Curtius Rufus saying (*The History of Alexander*, 3.11.8):

> Oxyathres saw Alexander charging Darius and moved his own cavalry right in front of the king's chariot. Oxyathres far surpassed his comrades in the splendour of his arms and in physical strength, and very few could match his courage and devotion to Darius. In that engagement especially he won distinction by cutting down some Macedonians who were recklessly thrusting ahead and putting others to flight.

This bought time for Darius to flee the battlefield with his bodyguard, leaving the Persian army to its fate. This now quickly disintegrated, the better troops to the front hampered in their escape by the levies to their rear. Alexander and the Macedonians pursued until nightfall, with the Persians massacred wherever they were found and little quarter given. Plutarch says that at one point Alexander himself captured Darius' chariot and bow, though the king himself made good his escape on horse with around 4,000 cavalry including Oxyathres (*Lives*, Alexander, 20.2). The primary sources indicate that the Persians lost up to 100,000 men killed in the battle (an unlikely figure given the overall size of the army, though certainly Persian losses were very high), with some 8,000 Greek survivors escaping by ship. Meanwhile, Alexander lost 450 dead with around 5,000 wounded. This was a stupendous victory indeed that, as detailed in Chapter 2, set the tone for Alexander's forthcoming conquest of Darius' empire. Highlights in the aftermath included his capture of Darius' camp, which included the royal family, with Plutarch enigmatically describing the scene (*Lives*, Alexander, 20.2):

> Darius's tent, which was full of splendid furniture and quantities of gold and silver, they (his soldiers) reserved for Alexander himself, who, after he had put off his arms, went to bathe himself saying, 'Let us now cleanse ourselves from the toils of war in the bath of Darius.'

Later Parmenion secured the regional satrapal capital of Damascus with its huge treasury, the enormous wealth there adding to that captured in Sardis. However, despite the scale of his defeat, Darius was still abroad with the vast resources of his remaining Empire to call upon. He now resolved to fight on, this time through his surrogates, with Alexander's next major engagement taking place on the Levantine coast.

The Siege of Tyre

After his flight from the battlefield at Issus Darius continued east, withdrawing beyond the Euphrates to consolidate in the heart of his kingdom. This left Alexander free rein to continue his campaign along the eastern Mediterranean coastline, and soon he was marching south again through Syria and Phoenicia. His primary aim was to isolate the Persian fleet from its bases there, given Darius' vassal navies still controlled the sea lanes and coastal littoral despite his defeats ashore.

As earlier detailed, the cities of Arados and Marathos quickly submitted to the Macedonians, which led to the Persian king's first peace offer.

Alexander swiftly rejected this, after which Biblos and then Sidon fell as Alexander continued his victorious march south. However, much to his consternation, when he reached the key port of Tyre in early 332 BC the city chose to bar its gates to him and resist any attempt to capture it by force, its leaders claiming neutrality. At the time Tyre was the largest and most important city in Phoenicia, with a population of over 40,000. Its main metropolis was built on an offshore island almost 1km off the coast which featured two natural harbours and defensive walls 46m high. The latter were at their most formidable on the landward-facing side.

At first Alexander tried to negotiate the city's surrender, suggesting that if its leaders allowed him to worship at the Temple of Melqart (identified by the Greeks with the demi-God Hercules) then he would accept this as their submission and leave the city alone. However, the Tyrians, for unknown reasons given the campaign momentum was clearly with the Macedonians and not Darius, overplayed their hand and suggested that Alexander instead worship in an old temple ashore in the abandoned original settlement. They had some reason to believe they could withstand a lengthy siege if needed, given the city had successfully held out for thirteen years against the Assyrians centuries earlier. Further, they were also expecting a relief fleet from their key North African colony of Carthage, though in the event this never arrived (Heckel, 2002, 44).

Rebuffed in his first attempt to negotiate, Alexander tried again. However, this time though Tyrians were even more intractable, casting the king's heralds from the high walls of the city to their deaths in the sea. Unsurprisingly, Alexander was enraged and soon the investment of Tyre began.

By this time the Macedonians had the finest siege train in their known world. However, this was no ordinary siege given Tyre's offshore location. Undeterred, the determined Alexander ordered a stone-built causeway be constructed to bridge the waterway separating Tyre from the coast. The key aim here was to provide a man-made platform for his siege engines. Such was the scale of the mole he built that it remains the foundation of the land bridge linking the old island with the coastline to this day.

At first work to build the causeway progressed at speed given the shallow coastal water. However, as it approached the island city's walls the water became much deeper, with repeated attacks by the Tyrian fleet then making the mole's continued construction next to impossible. Alexander therefore ordered the construction of two 50m-tall siege towers that were then positioned at the end of the causeway. These featured artillery platforms on top, allowing catapults and *ballista* to target any Tyrian ships sent out to harry Alexander's engineers building the causeway. Soon the construction process was on track again. The Macedonians were aware their wood-built towers were vulnerable to fire and covered them in rawhide to minimise the danger from Tyrian artillery and fire-arrows trying to set them alight. However, the defenders countered Alexander's ingenuity with a stratagem of their own, commandeering an old horse-transport merchant ship which they filled with sulphur, pitch, dried branches and other combustibles. They then hung cauldrons of oil from the ship's masts and weighed down the rear of the vessel so that its bow was proud of the water. Setting their fire ship ablaze, they then waited for the tide to turn towards the towers before setting it on course to ram them. The towers caught alight immediately with the fire quickly engulfing both, and also destroying any other siege engines on the causeway. The Tyrians then assaulted the mole nearest the walls to drive off any remaining Macedonians.

Alexander now switched strategy, realising any attempt to rebuild the towers would meet the same response from the Tyrians. He therefore looked to his new-found fleet of 223 ships, these comprising 80 ships from Arados, Marathos, Byblus and Sidon, 120 from Cyprus and 23 ships from the Greek *poleis* along the Ionian coast of Anatolia. In the first instance the king blockaded the city, then fitting some of the war galleys with cranes and other engineering equipment to remove huge underwater blocks of stone that the Tyrians had set in place on the seaward side of the walls to prevent the Macedonians closing on the weaker fortifications there. Once the way to the walls was open other galleys were then fitted with battering rams that Alexander set against the fortifications. The Tyrians again countered, this time sending out ships with rudimentary deck armour and divers to cut the anchor cables of the ram-equipped galleys. The Macedonians responded by replacing the cable ropes with chains, and soon the battering rams were at work again. The defenders then mounted one final sortie; this time targeting the ram ships at noon when they had noticed Alexander always went ashore for lunch. However, on this occasion they were unlucky as the Macedonian king had broken with his usual routine to remain with his assault force. The Tyrian attack was quickly defeated with heavy losses. Then, after prolonged attacks across the breadth of the seaward walls, in early July the Macedonian rams eventually opened a small breach in the circuit at the south end of the island. Alexander now concentrated all of his efforts here, with a massed artillery bombardment from catapult and *ballista*-equipped vessels providing cover for an assault involving siege towers, the latter also built atop war galleys. Plutarch adds that at this point the greater part of the Macedonian army, which had been resting after the strenuous Issus campaign, were called in to help with the final onslaught (*Lives*, Alexander, 307). Eventually the Macedonians forced their way into Tyre, with Alexander in the lead as always, after which any determined resistance was crushed, with 8,000 defenders slain.

With the fall of Tyre the survivors now sought terms, with the king and any fugitives found seeking sanctuary in the Temple of Melqart spared. However, 2,000 more were crucified on the sea front, while a further 30,000 were enslaved. With the fall of the city any Persian-inspired resistance in the Levant ended, with Alexander leaving Parmenion to mop up resistance in Syria while he continued south, eventually reaching Egypt after a second long siege at Gaza.

The Battle of Gaugamela

Having conquered Egypt, where he had been hailed a liberator, Alexander returned to Tyre in early summer 331 BC. By now the whole eastern Mediterranean was under his control. To celebrate he sacrificed to Melqart in the city and then hosted a spectacular theatre festival and sporting contest, funded by the enormous wealth available after the capture of the Persian treasuries in Sidon and Damascus. Alexander then decided to wait in Tyre for 15,000 fresh troops to arrive from home. However, when these failed to appear (the regent Antipater keeping them in Macedon given his struggle with Agis III of Sparta), Alexander decided to seek out Darius and finish matters once and for all.

The Persian king had been biding his time in the east, slowly gathering another vast army in the heartland of his remaining Empire. With his second peace offer rejected by Alexander (see Chapter 2 for detail), he now knew that at some stage there would be a climactic battle with the Macedonians. He therefore chose his campaigning theatre very carefully. Taking advice from whichever Greek *strategos* and Persian military advisors were still available to give counsel, the King of Kings decided not to move directly against Alexander, but rather draw the Macedonians as far inland as he could, well away from any key urban centres and other means of supply. He knew if he could then force a successful meeting engagement far from the Mediterranean coast, the Macedonians would have to withdraw through hostile and unforgiving territory, harried by the Persians the whole way as they attempted to reach the sea.

Back in Tyre Alexander appointed a Macedonian satrap in Syria to secure his rear, and then replaced the officer he had initially appointed to gather provisions for the next phase of his *anabasis* with someone more capable (Goldsworthy, 2020, 324). It is unclear if the last minute change marked an unrecorded setback, but soon the Macedonians set out eastwards and the *anabasis* was underway again.

An advance force had already set out under Hephaestion to Thapsacus, the ancient town on the western bank of the River Euphrates, today located in eastern Syria. By mid-summer they had built two pontoon bridges across the huge waterway, though they had also drawn the unwelcome attention of a large Persian mounted force on the northern bank of the river under Mazaeus, the satrap of Babylonia. However, the latter left the Macedonian pioneers unmolested, their orders to shadow them rather than force an engagement, with the ultimate aim being to draw them towards Darius.

Soon Alexander arrived with the main Macedonian army. By this time other fresh troops had also arrived from Greece (though not the 15,000 originally expected in Tyre), giving the king a main field force of some 40,000 foot and 7,000 horse. This proved too much for Mazaeus who withdrew his cavalry from the northern bank, the satrap then disappearing from the narrative until he reappears to play a key role at Gaugamela.

Alexander now faced two choices of route to take. He knew that Darius was somewhere to his east, and that the Macedonians needed to force a meeting engagement as quickly as possible, given the vulnerability of their lines of supply. The quickest route to get to Babylon, capital of the satrapy and one of the great cities of the ancient world (and where the Macedonians knew more untold wealth awaited in Darius' treasury there), was to follow the Euphrates as it meandered slowly through its enormous flood plain towards the Persian Gulf. This route would also greatly ease Alexander's logistics operation since the river itself could be fully utilized to transport the huge amounts of material needed to keep his army in the field. However, that route also meant his troops would have to endure the intense summer and autumn heat in the riparian lowlands of modern Syria and Iraq, with daytime temperatures in the region of 49°C and over. Further, many of the key cities in the region were threaded along the Euphrates, and each would have to be invested along the way to ensure there were no remaining threats to the rear of the Macedonian advance. Given the time lost the previous year besieging the likes of Tyre and Gaza, Alexander knew this would further delay his advance and allow Darius time to gather even more troops from the east.

Alexander's second option was to follow a much longer route through northern Mesopotamia. This was north up the valley of the Balikh River, and then eastwards through the headwaters of the Little Khabur River before finally arriving at the upper Tigris. From there the Macedonians could then loop back south-east towards Babylon once the temperatures were more agreeable later in the year. Although Alexander knew this route would present real challenges for his baggage train and lines of supply, Arrian says it was this route he eventually chose given the respite it would give his men in the sweltering heat of high summer (*Anabasis Alexandri*, 3.7.4). Travelling over 400km in forced marches the Macedonians soon reached the Tigris, travelling via Harran (Roman Carrhae, site of the later disastrous defeat of Marcus Licinius Crassus by the Parthians, see Chapter 5 for detail) and Nisibis (modern Nusaybin in south-eastern Turkey). However, unbeknown to Alexander his northern route was also steadily drawing him directly towards Darius. This was because, having belatedly received intelligence that Alexander had chosen not to follow the Euphrates route, the Persian king had moved northwards himself travelling 480km up the Tigris to Gaugamela, a vast dusty plain between Arbela (modern Irbil) and the old Assyrian capital of Nineveh in the upper Tigris valley. Having learned his lesson at Issus, the Persian king chose this as his likely future battlefield site because he knew it would allow his vast army the chance to envelope the Macedonians. The location was named after the Semitic word *gammalu* meaning dromedary, given it sat below a large low hill shaped like a camel's hump.

With his army camped at Gaugamela, Darius set up his command centre in Arbela 75km away, which was a regional stronghold famous across the region as home to the fertility goddess Istar. Given the Persian name for the city meant 'city of four gods', it was also clearly home to a number of other religious cults. Much more importantly, it was also here the royal trunk roads from Armenia in the north and the eastern satrapies converged.

At this point neither Alexander nor Darius knew the other was close, the only tell-tale sign of any Persian activity the crops in the fields on the far bank of the Tigris being torched each day as the Macedonians progressed to prevent their use by Alexander. By September the Macedonians had reached a suitable fording point on the river and crossed over, entering the satrapy of Assyria on the far shore where they met little Persian resistance. Alexander now gave his men two days to rest and recover from their exhausting march, though all were troubled by a lunar eclipse on the night of 20/21 September. The king promptly offered sacrifices to the sun, moon and earth, with his diviner Aristander declaring the omens were only bad for Darius.

With no real opposition to impede their movement, the Macedonians now continued their advance down the line of the Tigris. Soon, the *prodromoi* at the head of the column encountered Persian cavalry to their front. Thinking this was the whole Persian army Alexander began to deploy for battle. However, reinforced with the Thracian and Paeonian light cavalry, the *prodromoi* determined there were only 1,000 Persian horse blocking their advance. Alexander then joined his light-horse brigade, reinforcing them with an *ila* of companions, and together they drove off the Persians. Crucially, they captured some stragglers who revealed that Darius' main force was nearby at Gaugamela.

Alexander now halted, knowing the crucial battle would take place shortly. That evening he gathered his army and built a substantial fortified marching camp, wary of any surprise night attacks by Darius. Meanwhile, the Persian king had travelled to join his own army from Arbela, and on the 24th sent a messenger to Alexander with a third peace offer. This included proposals to grant the Macedonians all of the land to the west of the Euphrates, and also the hand of one of his daughters who had been captured by Alexander at Issus in marriage. The primary sources say that once more Alexander rejected the offer, and that the Persian heralds then returned to Darius not only with this bad news, but also details of Alexander's army.

A few days now passed while both armies gathered themselves for what all knew would be a titanic struggle. However, by the evening of 30 September all was ready in both camps, with Darius keeping his troops awake into the early hours of 1 October, reviewing them by torchlight. Meanwhile, the primary sources say Alexander was far more relaxed in his camp, allowing the Macedonian troops to rest, though he himself spent much of the night outside his campaign tent with Aristander performing religious rights and making offerings. Here Plutarch then has the king disagreeing with his senior officers and advisors on the means of engaging Darius and his vast army. This is an important passage given the light it casts on Alexander as a military leader, and also on Parmenion, and therefore deserves reporting in full. To that end, Plutarch says (*Lives*, Alexander, 31.1):

> Meanwhile, some of the older of his companions and Parmenion
> in particular looked out over the plain between the River Niphates
> and Gordyaean mountains and saw the entire plain agleam with
> the watch-fires of the barbarians, while from their (Persian) camp

there arose the confused...murmur of myriads of voices, like the distant roar of a vast ocean. They were filled with amazement at the sight and remarked to one another that it would be an overwhelmingly difficult task to defeat an enemy of such strength by engaging them that day. They therefore went to Alexander... and tried to persuade him to attack at night, so as to conceal from his men the most terrifying element of the coming struggle... the odds against them. It was then that Alexander gave them his celebrated answer, 'I will not steal my victory.' Some thought this an immature and empty boast on the part of a young man who was merely joking in the presence of danger. But others interpreted it as meaning that he had confidence in his present situation and that he had correctly judged the future. In other words, he was determined that if Darius were defeated he should have no cause to summon up courage for another attempt; he was not to be allowed to blame darkness and night for his failure on this occasion, as at Issus he had blamed the narrow mountain passes and the sea.

In modern popular culture it is this debate that features prominently in the 2004 Oliver Stone movie *Alexander*.

With Alexander's response to Parmenion and the other senior leaders given, all was now set for the final encounter between Alexander and Darius, which took place on 1 October. In terms of the armies engaged, Alexander fielded the full 47,000 available to him, this proportionally similar to his earlier though smaller armies at the Granicus River and Issus, with his companions, *prodromoi*, Thessalian and Greek heavy horse, Thracian and Paeonian light horse, *hypaspists*, *pezetairoi*, Greek allied and mercenary foot, Thracians, Illyrians, Agrianians and Cretans.

However, as usual there is far more debate about the size of Darius' army among the primary sources, and subsequently (as already referenced in Chapter 2). For example Arrian says that it comprised 40,000 cavalry and 1,000,000 foot (*Anabasis Alexandri*, 3.8), Plutarch gives an unspecified 1,000,000 (*Lives*, Alexander, 31) and Diodorus Siculus 200,000 cavalry and 800,000 foot (*Library of History*, 17.53). Meanwhile, at the other extreme Quintus Curtius Rufus says the Persian army comprised 45,000 cavalry and 200,000 infantry (*The History of Alexander*, 4.12.13). Arrian, Diodorus Siculus and Quintus Curtius Rufus also add colour in their descriptions of the size of Darius' army, for example saying it included the 200 scythed chariots detailed in Chapter 3, while it is Arrian who talks of the 15 elephants among the Indian and eastern contingent commanded by the Bactrian satrap Bessus. It is also he who says Darius was only able to field 2,000 Greek hoplite and *peltast* mercenaries, with the vast majority of his foot most likely *kardakes* (some Hellenised, though this far east most probably not) and levies. In terms of the actual size of Darius' force, in reality we will never know, though it was certainly far larger than Alexander's army, even more so than at Issus. In particular, given much of it was recruited and conscripted in the east, Darius had a huge advantage in the number of cavalry. This disparity in mounted troops certainly precluded a Macedonian disengagement once battle was joined, a fact which clearly influenced Alexander's approach to the engagement.

In terms of the Macedonian order of battle, Lane Fox has the Macedonian king at the height of his tactical genius here (1986, 234), he ordering a particularly complex deployment which to my mind would only be possible for the most disciplined and motivated of armies. His centre was deployed in echelon in two lines to prevent an encirclement, the Macedonian phalanx to the fore under Crateros, with the *hypaspists* the furthest forward on their right under Parmenion's son Nicanor, with the Greek allies and mercenaries then deployed to the rear. The latter were positioned to allow an about-face if the army was enveloped. Alexander once more commanded his own shock cavalry to the right of the *hypaspists*, including all six *ilia* of the companions in their wedge formations. Parmenion again commanded the left. His wing, deployed furthest from the Persians in the oblique set up, included the Thessalian and Thracian cavalry, and more heavy foot. Additionally, floating units of cavalry and light troops covered the flanks and rear of both wings, with the *prodromoi* on the extreme right.

The exact deployment of Darius' vast army eludes us today, though it likely comprised a rolling front of various types of cavalry stretching from horizon to horizon, intermingled with the better foot, and with the huge numbers of levies to the rear. Once more, as the battle unfolded the latter's main role would be to obstruct Darius' better troops once his army broke.

We do have some detail here and there from the primary sources that give a flavour of the colourful composition of the King of King's army. For example, Darius positioned himself in his accustomed position in the exact centre, with his close relatives, royal guard cavalry and 'apple bearer' royal foot guards in attendance. Either side were the Greek mercenaries, with 100 of the scythed chariots deployed across their front. Nearby were some of the Indian contingent (thought to include the 15 elephants), Carians (presumably refugees from the region in Anatolia) and Iranian cavalry. Meanwhile, behind Darius in a hollow could be found the Babylonian and Red Sea contingents, these most likely levy foot given their position to the rear. Mazaeus, the former satrap of Cilicia, commanded the right-wing cavalry, including large contingents of Syrians, Mesopotamians, Medes, Parthians, Saka, Tapurians, Hyrcanians, Albanians (from the Caucasus), Sacasinians, Cappadocians, Armenians and fifty scythed chariots. Meanwhile, Bessus commanded the Persian left wing facing Alexander on the Macedonian right, his force including more members of the royal family, Bactrians, Dahae and more Saka, together with fifty more scythed chariots.

Less is known about the actual battle, though most primary sources suggest Alexander opened the engagement with a general advance which maintained his oblique formation, with the centre still deployed in its two lines. This placed the *hypaspists* and companions furthest forward on the right, with the king to the fore.

This makes sense given the huge disparity in numbers, with Alexander knowing time was against him and that his quickest route to victory was to target Darius directly. It also replicated his success at Issus, with his plan to use the best troops under his own leadership to punch through the enemy battle line while the latter was pinned by the *pezetairoi* in true later Argead 'hammer and anvil' fashion. One can envisage the Macedonians here advancing in an offset rhomboid, with the front right corner furthest forward, moving at speed towards a seemingly endless line of Persians to their front.

Darius responded quickly, matching Alexander's aggression with a general advance of his own. This meant that soon both of his wings easily overlapped the Macedonian formation. However, he quickly realised that the companions and *hypaspists* were moving so quickly that they would likely impact his battle line near his own position before his army could effect the planned envelopment. He therefore ordered Bessus and his eastern horsemen on the left wing to speed their own advance so as to wrap around the Macedonian right wing to slow them. This managed to push back the Macedonian right wing flank cover, with more and more Persian cavalry then joining Bessus to reinforce his initial success.

Meanwhile, in the centre Darius now launched his scythed chariots against the *pezetairoi*, hoping to at least disrupt the Macedonian pikemen before they could impact the Persian battle line. However, as usual the chariots proved a spectacular failure, with most shot down by Alexander's skirmishers and those reaching the phalanx refusing to charge the hedge of pikes but instead being driven down lanes deliberately opened between the units of *pezetairoi* to their doom. Soon the phalanx resumed its advance and began pressing the hoplites and 'apple bearers' to Darius' front. The 'anvil' was now in position.

On the Macedonian right wing Alexander noted the thinning of the Persian left wing as more and more of Bessus' cavalry, and now mounted troops from the Persian centre, began to lap around his extreme right wing. Soon a gap had opened up in the Persian line and Alexander pounced, the 'hammer' charging through at full pelt with the king at the head of the companions, supported by those units of the *hypaspists* who could keep up and unengaged units of the phalanx. This attack punched through the Persian royal guard cavalry, exposing Darius himself. The King of Kings then fled again, rather than stand and fight. Alexander pursued vigorously, wanting to finish things there and then. However, on the Macedonian left Parmenion had been under pressure for some time with Mazaeus' huge cavalry wing attacking in repeating waves. Indeed some Persian cavalry had actually reached the Macedonian baggage camp where they killed the camp guard and freed a large number of Persian prisoners. The *strategos* now sent word to Alexander requesting support to prevent his wing being overrun. The primary sources differ here on the Macedonian king's response, with Diodorus Siculus saying the courier could not find Alexander who was too far ahead in his pursuit of Darius (*Library of History*, 17.53). However, Arrian says Alexander received the report and, hugely frustrated, broke off his pursuit and headed back to help Parmenion (*Anabasis Alexandri*, 3.8). On the way though his force met some returning Persian cavalry including Parthians and Saka, and a desperate melee ensued. According to Arrian this was some of the heaviest fighting Alexander experienced in the entire battle, with sixty companions killed and many more wounded including Hephaestion. Anticlimactically, by the time they reached Parmenion his left wing had been secured, and it seems likely the cavalry Alexander met if Arrian is correct were Mazaeus' troops withdrawing after word reached them of Darius' wretched escape.

By this time the Macedonian success on the right had enabled the rest of the army to roll up all that remained of the demoralised Persian centre. The vast army now finally broke, with Alexander again in the van leading a vigorous pursuit. Once more a huge slaughter ensued, with Head summarizing the various reports of casualties, saying the Persians lost between 40,000–300,000 dead depending on the source, and the Macedonians an unlikely 100–500 (2016, 151).

Sadly for Alexander, Darius escaped with some Bactrian cavalry and Greek mercenaries, fleeing north-east to Media. The Macedonians pursued for a number of days until they lost contact. Alexander then occupied Babylonia and reinstalled Mazaeus as the regional satrap in Babylon (alongside a Macedonian commander), recognising the Persian's leadership and bravery at Gaugamela. Thus ended Alexander's greatest battle, and soon his *anabasis* was underway once more, with India beckoning after the later death of Darius.

The Battle of the Hydaspes

By early 326 BC Alexander had forced a route through the Punjab to the Indus, where on arrival he then stormed the supposedly unassailable mountaintop fortress of Aornos. This was within a day's march of the river itself, which he crossed in the spring of 326 BC near Attock. His army then entered Taxila. Here the ruler Taxiles gave the king elephants and Indian troops in return for support against his great rival Porus, the king of Paurava. This set in train the events leading to Alexander's last great victory, fought on the southern bank of the Hydaspes River (the modern Jhelum River, a tributary of the Indus).

Porus swiftly responded to Alexander's support for Taxiles and moved against the Macedonians. In typical fashion Alexander immediately countered, seeking a meeting engagement as soon as possible. He built a fortified camp near a local town, thought to be modern Jhelum, as his base of operations. Then, in the spring he learned that Porus had drawn up his army on the south bank of the nearby Hydaspes to counter any crossing by the Macedonians. This was a significant waterway, deep and fast enough to prevent any crossing attempt except by a significant ford. Arriving at the river, Alexander began to scout the north bank each night with his mounted troops, looking for a suitable ford. However, every time they found a candidate site to cross, Porus arrived to deter them. Finally, in early May the Macedonians found a suitable crossing 27 km downstream of their camp where a forest-covered island (some sources call this Admana island) sat in the middle of a meandering bend in the river. The current here was unusually sluggish, allowing Alexander to use the transport vessels his pioneers had ready to assemble to ferry his army across when all was ready. However, he knew that transporting such a huge force across the river would quickly draw Porus' attention. Then, if the Indian army arrived before he could get his army across to the southern bank, he had be forced to fight a defended river-crossing battle yet again. This would most likely spell disaster given the Hydaspes, even here at the island meander, was a far more significant waterway than either the Granicus or Pinarus. Alexander now employed a stratagem to put Porus off his guard. Instead of crossing directly, he noisily paraded mounted troops up and down the northern bank of the Hydaspes each evening within earshot of Porus' troops. The Indian king took the bait, on successive nights deploying for battle much of his army including his elephants in case the Macedonians really did cross. Eventually, after repeated night-time false alarms, Porus relaxed his guard and stopped responding to the Macedonian cavalry on the far bank given, as Arrian details, he was 'no longer expecting a sudden attempt under cover of darkness, and was lulled into a sense of security' (*Anabasis Alexandri*, 5.15). Then Alexander pounced.

On the appointed night the assembled ferrying fleet was readied on the northern bank of the Hydaspes by the engineers, this comprising thirty oared galleys, smaller vessels 'cut in half' and skins filled with hay (Arrian, *Anabasis Alexandri*, 5.18). Alexander was now faced with a dilemma, knowing he could not ferry his entire army over in one night, and that the following morning Porus would quickly become aware of the crossing and counter it. The Macedonian king therefore devised a classic pincer tactic strategy, with he first leading much of his cavalry and some foot across to pin the Indians in place while, later, the rest of his army would cross to effect the victory. The latter were split into two divisions. The first, under Craterus, featured two *taxeis* of *pezetairoi*, 5,000 Indian allies and some allied cavalry. These initially stayed in the Macedonian camp. Meanwhile, the second division under Meleager featured three *taxeis* of the phalanx and some mercenaries. Deployed a few kilometres upstream from Alexander, but short of the camp and Crateros, Meleager's command had orders to cross the Hydaspes first when the king sent word, with Crateros to follow after. Attalus and Gorgias acted as the key subordinates (Head, 2016, 152).

Alexander's assault force comprised 5,000 horse and 6,000 foot. The former included the *agema* royal guard and a further three *hipparchies* of companions (note the change in their unit title by this time), plus newly recruited allied and mercenary cavalry from Bactria, Sogdiana, the Saka and the Dahae. Meanwhile, his foot comprised the *argyraspides* (as the *hypaspists* were now known), two *taxeis* of the phalanx, his Cretans and the Agrianians (Goldsworthy, 2020, 429).

Alexander now began his crossing to the south bank of the Hydaspes, bypassing the island to his immediate west, with the cavalry mounts on the galleys and boats, while many of his foot waded across. The king himself led the way standing in the prow of a *triaconter*, the smallest class of war galley though the largest vessel available. Plutarch here makes reference to the atrocious night-time conditions of the crossing, saying (*Lives*, Alexander, 60):

> Here he was overtaken by tremendous bursts of thunder and lightning. Although he saw that a number of his men were struck dead by the lightning, he continued the advance and made for the opposite bank. After the storm, the Hydaspes, which was roaring down in high flood, had scooped out a deep channel, so that much of the stream was diverted to this direction and the ground between the two currents had become broken and slippery and made it impossible for his men to gain a firm footing. It was on this occasion that Alexander is said to have exclaimed, 'O Athenians, will you ever believe what risks I am running just to earn your praise.'

However, on landing on the opposite shore the Macedonians realised they had made a mistake, because far from landing on the southern shore they found that instead they had arrived on the banks of a smaller, though still treacherous branch of the Hydaspes (Pietrykowski, 2009, 75, this error showing how heavily wooded the banks actually were). This meant yet another crossing to actually reach Porus' side of the river. This Alexander achieved, though not without a huge amount of effort, and by the time he had gathered his crossing force ready for action the sun was high in the sky and Porus had had time to respond. This was in the form of an armed reconnaissance comprising 120 heavy chariots and 4,000 cavalry under the command of his son. However, as they approached Alexander they came under sustained mounted bow fire from the Bactrians, Sogdians, Saka and Dahae light horse, followed by a headlong charge by Alexander leading the *agema* and other companions (Arrian, *Anabasis Alexandri*, 5.15). The Indian force was completely routed, with many of the chariots abandoned in the soft mud along the shoreline. Plutarch says they left 400 dead behind, including the king's son (*Lives*, Alexander, 60).

Soon news reached Porus of the death of his son and the failure of the chariots and cavalry to push Alexander back over the Hydaspes. Aware the main engagement was now imminent, he deployed his army accordingly.

This followed the standard practice as detailed in the *Arthaśāstra* treatise on military strategy, with the Indian cavalry on the wings, fronted by heavy chariots, and the infantry in the centre with the elephants stretched across their front. The Indian king, clad in chainmail and riding his tallest war elephant (described by Plutarch as highly intelligent and paying great attention to Porus' safety, *Lives*, Alexander, 60), chose a broad riparian plain for the engagement to allow his chariots the best chance of success given their earlier issues facing Alexander's crossing force. He also left behind a small force of elephants and poor quality infantry to face Craterus if he attempted to cross the Hydaspes from the Macedonian camp. Finally, it seems Porus also had to his rear a reserve of poor-quality foot, most likely local levies. The primary sources all detail the bright spectacle on display across the ranks of the Indian front line troops, with multi-coloured shields, hauberks, cloaks and scarves, the bowmen poised with long iron-tipped arrows at the ready. One can also imagine the cacophony of noise from the elephants, and the trumpets and bells used to signal Indian troop movements across the battlefield.

As detailed in Chapter 3, the primary sources all emphasise the smaller scale of Porus' army at the Hydaspes compared to the enormous forces earlier deployed by Darius. Arrian says his army included 200 elephants, 300 chariots, 4,000 cavalry and 30,000 foot (*Anabasis Alexandri*, 5.15.4), while Diodorus Siculus says 130 elephants, 1,000 chariots (highly unlikely) and 50,000 foot (*Library of History*, 17.87.2). Meanwhile, Plutarch details 2,000 mounted troops and 20,000 foot (*Lives*, Alexander, 62.2). It is unclear if these numbers include the younger Porus' earlier blocking force or that left to counter Crateros. Indeed, given the wide range of numbers the primary sources detail for the Indian army, and the various options regarding their actual deployment, Pietrykowski argues that trying to determine the true size of force Porus fielded is an exercise in futility (2009, 76).

We have more insight into the size of the army Alexander fielded in the main engagement, if only because we have detail about individual unit sizes in the Macedonian army. This included the troops Alexander had initially led across the river and Meleager's force that had by this time crossed the Hydaspes, most likely after the king had engaged Porus the younger's blocking force, though it is unclear where the crossing was actually made. Crateros' troops in the Macedonian camp set out to join Alexander when battle was about to be joined but arrived too late to participate, later joining in the pursuit of the Indian army. Pietrykowski estimates Alexander's overall force for the main engagement was at least 18,000 strong

(2009, 76), though given Head estimates the king's total force for his invasion of the Punjab numbered 52,000 (2016, 152), his army at the Hydaspes was probably considerably larger, and certainly bigger than that of Porus.

Piecing together the various isolated details of Alexander's deployment at the Hydaspes in the primary sources, a reasonable recreation places the king with the companions, allied and mercenary cavalry on the right wing, then the *argyraspides*, phalanx and Greek allies and mercenaries in the centre (in that order right to left) and the Thracian and Paeonian light horse on the left wing. A cloud of light foot, including the Cretans (to the right) and Agrianians (to the right centre) were deployed across the front of the army. It is unclear where the *prodromoi* were positioned, though most likely they were with Alexander and the companions. Finally, in the last minutes before battle commenced, the king detached a unit of companions under Coenus (it is unclear how many, though no more than a *hipparchia*) from his right wing to support his left-wing light-horse, having seen more Indian cavalry arrive opposite them at the last minute.

Battle commenced in the sweltering Indian afternoon with Alexander ordering his allied cavalry on the right, led by the Dahae, to harass the Indians to their front. A thundering charge by the companions led by Alexander himself then followed, which left the Indian left-wing chariots and cavalry on the point of breaking. Seeing this, Porus countered by sending some of his right-wing chariots and horse to support his left wing. However, as they arrived, the recently arrived Coenus on the Macedonian left spurred his companions to follow the departing Indians opposite and soon the reinforced Indian mounted troops on the left found themselves fighting Alexander to their front and Coenus to their rear. The Indian horse tried to form a double-facing line to tackle the dual threat but lacked the training and soon the whole left wing broke under the Macedonian onslaught.

Some of the Indian horse fled to the safety of the elephants deployed across the front of the Indian centre. Seeing this, Alexander ordered the *argyraspides*, phalanx and Greek allies and mercenaries in the centre to advance, aiming to taken advantage of the state of confusion to their front, this caused by the retreating Indian cavalry as they mingled with the elephants and Indian foot. Porus then ordered his elephants to charge en masse though the milling Indian cavalry, and soon a titanic clash ensued as they smashed into the Macedonian heavy foot in the centre. At first the powerful beasts caused heavy losses among the pikemen and spearmen, their armour-clad tusks impaling many men while others were tossed into the air before being crushed under foot by the elephants. However, under great duress, the Macedonian centre held and soon their pikes and spears were causing heavy casualties among the Indian elephants' crews. Meanwhile, the Cretan, Agrianian and other Macedonian skirmishers began harassing the beasts with their bows, javelins and slings, aiming at the eyes of the elephant, and again their crew. Then re-armed *pezetairoi* emerged from the ranks of the heavy infantry equipped with heavy axes, bravely weaving in and out of the stamping elephant feet to chop at their hamstrings. Soon many of the wounded and crewless beasts were panicking, with one after another fleeing back towards their own lines. There, chaos ensued as the elephants ran amok among their own cavalry and infantry. The Macedonian heavy foot now reformed, with the *argyraspides* and *pezetairoi* adopting the *synaspismos* locked-shield formation and advancing on the confused, thrashing mass of elephants, horses and men to their front. Once more the 'anvil' was set in place as they drove all before them backwards, advancing step by advancing step. Meanwhile, Alexander led the companions and other Macedonian cavalry in a devastating charge into the rear on the Indian centre, with the 'hammer' once again winning the battle. The Indian army quickly broke, with Crateros and his men then arriving to join the pursuit.

Porus himself was soon captured, though he only agreed to surrender when overcome by thirst, with Alexander riding out to meet him and treating him as a celebrated and worthy foe (as detailed in Chapter 3). In terms of losses, Arrian says the Indians lost around 23,000 men (*Anabasis Alexandri*, 5.18), while Diodorus Siculus details 12,000 dead and 9,000 captured (*Library of History*, 17.89.1). Porus also lost another son, while his ally Spitakes was also killed, and most of his nobles. Alexander also captured eighty elephants on the battlefield, and also intercepted seventy more as they arrived to reinforce Porus' now-defeated army.

Arrian assesses Macedonian losses to have amounted to 80 infantry, 20 companions, 10 allied horse archers and 200 other horse (*Anabasis Alexandri*, 5.18). Diodorus Siculus gives a more reasonable 1,000 Macedonian dead, this easily believable after the initial clash between Porus' elephants and the Macedonian centre (*Library of History*, 17.89.1). Thus ended Alexander's last great victory in set piece battle, a spectacular affair which even if smaller in scale than the engagements at Issus and Gaugamela, made up for it in its setting and splendour. The battle at the Hydaspes River also marked the high point in his campaign in the Punjab, and soon he would begin his fraught march back to Babylon, there to meet his destiny in June 323 BC.

Chapter 5

The Roman Republic

In exactly the same way that, as a son of the Macedonian Argead dynasty, Alexander the Great's life was shaped from birth, so too was Julius Caesar's as a product of the later Roman Republic. Its traditions and institutions defined his life, no matter how hard he tried to free himself from those he found most onerous to his unbounded ambitions. Therefore, a chronological knowledge of the Republic is very useful in providing context for the events of his own time.

Rome before the Republic

The origins of the Roman Republic are shrouded in myth, with the most familiar founding myth that concerning Romulus and Remus. In the tale the twins were born in the key regional Latin town of Alba Longa to the vestal virgin Rhea Silvia, the daughter of a former king called Numitor who had been usurped and then imprisoned by his brother Amulius. The latter forced Rhea Silvia to become a Vestal Virgin after seizing the crown, she then conceiving twins after a clandestine visit by Mars in a sacred grove dedicated to the Roman pantheon's God of war. Hearing of their birth, Amulius ordered the twins killed. Their mother then abandoned them on the banks of the River Tiber where they were saved by the river God Tiberinus. The twins were then suckled by a she-wolf in a cave which was later called the Lupercal.

A shepherd called Faustulus later adopted Romulus and Remus. They grew to manhood unaware of their noble origins. Eventually though, their natural leadership qualities became evident and through a series of adventures they eventually became aware of their own identities, later helping their grandfather regain his throne. The twins then decided to build their own settlement on the banks of the Tiber, choosing the site that later became Rome. However, they fell out over which of the seven hills they should build the new town on, with Romulus preferring the Palatine Hill and Remus the Aventine Hill. When Romulus claimed divine support for his choice, violence broke out between the two and Remus was killed. Romulus then founded Rome on the Palatine Hill, with 21 April 753 BC eventually set by Roman annalists as the date for this seminal event (Elliott, 2020b, 27).

Problematically for Roman historians, this dramatic legend had to be reconciled with yet another great founding myth of Rome. This was set much earlier in the context of the Trojan War, featuring the Trojan refugee Aeneas who escaped to Italy following the fall of Troy. Landing near Anzio south of Rome with his followers after a series of exploits across the Mediterranean, Aeneas established a settlement after defeating the local opposition. However, it was his son Iulus, namesake of the later Julio-Claudian family, who founded Alba Longa, there establishing the line of kings that bridged the gap between the Trojan Wars and Rome's ultimate founding. It later took the great Roman poet Virgil to finally merge both foundation stories in his first century BC epic *The Aeneid*, one of Rome's greatest literary works.

Rome's location was central to its later rise to global dominance. The original settlement was one of a number that were built on the hilltops spread along the left bank of the Tiber at its lowest crossing point. This major waterway is one of two rising in the Apennine Mountains that bisect Italy, the river flowing south into the Tyrrhenian Sea. The other is the Arno flowing west into the same sea. The region between the two was called Etruria, ranging from Pisa in the north to Ostia (originally a fort, later the port of Rome) in the south. This was home to the Villanovan Iron Age culture from around 900 BC that, by the early seventh century BC, had evolved into the Etruscan culture centred on a number of powerful city-states. Key examples included Veii, Caere and Tarquinii.

The influence of the Etruscans spread rapidly across the region, mainly because of their seafaring skills. Soon a mercantile empire had been established in the western Mediterranean. Through this they came into contact with the Greek colonies of Magna Graecia in southern Italy and eastern Sicily, and also the Phoenicians of the Punic Empire in North Africa. It is from the former that they adopted the Greek hoplite phalanx (see Chapter 3) as their principal line-of-battle formation. This gave the Etruscans a crucial advantage as they cast their gaze south to the settlements on the banks of the Tiber, including Rome. This was a region called Latium, it soon falling under Etruscan control.

From that point Rome was governed by an Etrusco-Roman king. It was under Servius Tullius, the second of these who reigned from 575 BC to

535 BC, that the town really began to grow in size. Livy for example says it was at this time the dense urban sprawl on the Palatine Hill grew to encompass the Quirinal Hill to its north (*The History of Rome*, 1.44). However, Tullius is best known for the Servian Constitution he instituted. This created Rome's first formalized military system and is fully detailed in Chapter 7.

By the mid-sixth century BC Etruscan power had reached its height, with much of Campania below Latium, including many of the Greek settlements of Magna Graecia, conquered. Crucially though, they failed to capture the Greek regional capital at Cumae with its fortified *acropolis*. This went on to form the centre of regional resistance to the Etruscans, who were finally defeated in battle in 524 BC. This emboldened the other conquered settlements, and soon those in Latium formed the Latin League that, fighting alongside the free Greek settlements of Magna Graecia, began to drive the Etruscans back northwards to their home territory in Etruria.

Rome's rise to prominence in Latium happened at this time, the settlement soon becoming the principal town there under the usurper Tarquin the Proud, king from 534 BC to 509 BC. However, towards the end of his reign he became increasingly autocratic, with Livy saying he resorted to ruling by fear, and in 509 BC the aristocracy rebelled and expelled him (1.49). Thus was born the Roman Republic. It is in the context of this dramatic event that we have the famous tale of Horatio and his two companions holding the last bridge over the Tiber against Etruscan hoplites trying to fight their way back into Rome to help put Tarquin back on the throne. Their sacrifice proved worthwhile, with Tarquin the last Roman king, the bitter old man living out his remaining years in exile in the Latin city of Tusculum in the Alban Hills (Matyszak, 2003, 42).

Birth of the Roman Republic

Kingless, the new Republic now came under the control of the great families of Rome. These were called patricians after the Latin word *patres*, meaning father. Only members of these great houses could hold religious or political office, particularly in the Senate where the wealthiest nobles processed legislation under the authority of two annually-elected consuls. This Senatorial class made up the top tier of the three aristocratic 'leisure classes' in Rome, these being endowed with 'moral excellence', wealth and high birth. The Senators displayed this by wearing the broad purple stripe on their togas. Next were the equestrian class, with slightly less wealth but still with a reputable lineage, these wearing the narrow purple stripe on their togas. Finally there was the curial class, again with the bar set slightly lower. The latter were largely mid-level merchants and landowners.

Below the Senatorial class all Roman citizens, including the equestrian and curial nobility, were called plebeians. They had no political authority, even though many were wealthy. Tensions between the two classes grew quickly in the early years of the Republic. Matters came to a head in 494 BC when the plebeians went on strike, gathering outside Rome and refusing to move until granted representation. This famous event was called the first *secessio plebis* (First Secession of the Plebs). Against the odds, the risky move worked, and the plebeians were rewarded with an assembly of their own called the *concillium plebis* (Council of the Plebs). This body was granted a degree of oversight of the legislation proposed by the consuls and enacted by the Senate. In this way, while the government of the Republic was certainly not democratic (for example, women were excluded from public office), it was more so than the hated monarchy that preceded it. Indeed, it was an important aspect of the Republican self-image that votes by those eligible for key magisterial positions really did matter, even in the most clear-cut situations (this often the case with Caesar, see Chapter 6). As the great scholar, lawyer and statesman Marcus Tullius Cicero later said (*In Defence of Plancius*, 11): 'It is the privilege of a few free people, and particularly of this great free people of Rome... that it can give or withhold its vote for anyone, standing for any office.'

The early Republic spent much of the fifth century BC battling external threats. First up was the Latin War where Rome fought its erstwhile Latin League partners from 498 BC – 493 BC. Though Rome was victorious in the main engagement at the Battle of Lake Regillus in 496 BC, it had to acknowledge its Latin neighbours as equals in the Cassian Treaty that brought the conflict to an end.

With Etruscan power waning, the Latin League then spent the next fifty years repelling repeated raiding by a variety of hill tribes from the Apennines. These included the Aequi, Sabini, Umbri and Volsci. Increasingly squeezed out of their own lands and onto the coastal plains of Latium by the expanding Samnites of south-central Italy, in the mid-fifth century BC the hill tribes burst into southern Italy and conquered Campania, Apulia and Lucania. The fight back was led by the Latin towns, with the Aequi being defeated in 431 BC and the Volsci driven back into the Apennines. Peace then descended on the region, with the Latin League consolidating its control over central and western Italy.

Conflict with the Etruscans and Gauls

This amity across the region was not to last. In the north the Etruscans remained a threat, and soon another war broke out, with Rome investing the key Etruscan city of Veii some 15km to the north of Rome in 404 BC. So began the long eight-year siege which led to Camillus paying his legionaries for the first time (as detailed below). Veii finally fell in 396 BC, thanks to the use of a 'divinely inspired' tunnel that ended in the Temple of Juno, giving access to the heart of the city (Hall, 2020, 24). This proved to be the high point of Roman foreign policy in the first half of the fourth century BC, largely because their next opponents were the Senones Gauls of Brennus from northern Italy, one of the toughest opponents ever faced by Rome.

Gauls from central Europe had been settling in the Po valley in northern Italy for over a century, challenging Etruscan power there. The latter had established Bologna (Etruscan *Felsina*) as their principal city in the region. However, the riches of Etruria proved too big a draw for the Gauls and soon they marched south, sweeping all before them. Brennus, his warriors enriched with plunder, then targeted Latium. Rome deployed its Tullian legions, expecting a quick victory, but its army was annihilated at the Battle of Allia in 390 BC. Rome was then sacked, a truly shocking event which prompted the building of the city's first defensive circuit in the form of the 11km Servian Wall after the Gauls were paid to leave.

It was earlier, in the midst of the grinding siege of Veii, that Rome's then leading patrician Camillus was appointed in 401 BC as consular tribune to command the army. He was the first Roman leader to raise taxation as a means of paying his troops; given at the time they were citizen soldiers recruited as necessary in time of war (see Chapter 7 for detail). It was also he, in the wake of the stunning defeat at the hands of the Gauls, who introduced the legionary manipular system (Fields, 2012, 11). This is a supreme example of the grit displayed on frequent occasions by Rome, responding to catastrophic defeat by innovating a new military system fit for purpose in the expanding world the city now found itself at the centre of.

The new Camillan military system was soon tested against the Etruscans to the north. Throughout the mid-fourth century BC, at the same time as Philip II was consolidating his grip on the Macedonian throne across the Adriatic Sea, Rome and the Latin League fought a series of increasingly brutal wars against the Etrurian city-states who were now fighting for survival. The final assault took place in

351 BC when Etruscan resistance in southern Etruria was finally broken, with Bologna in the north then falling to the Gauls in 350 BC. With its common enemy defeated, the Latin League now turned on itself and a final struggle for dominance soon began. Rome again emerged as the victor, the city on the Tiber now controlling all of western Italy from northern Campania to southern Etruria.

The Samnite Wars

Rome's next opponents were the Samnites. These were an Oscan-speaking people well used to fighting in the rough terrain of their homelands in the central-southern Apennine Mountains. They were arguably the first major confederation in central Italy to wake up to the fact that, in Rome, the region suddenly had a powerful predator in their midst (Holland, 2003, 6). The Samnites had initially been an ally of the Latin League against the hill tribes there, but in 343 BC a long series of wars broke out with Rome that lasted for over fifty years. This included the famous Roman defeat at the Battle of the Caudine Forks in 321 BC. Here, in a pass near Caudium (the capital of the Samnite Caudini tribe) both Roman consuls led their combined armies into a trap where their whole force was captured. Every man was forced to pass under a 'yoke' formed from three spears. A peace favourable to the Samnites followed (Fields, 2012, 4).

Typically, Rome never forgave the Samnites for this humiliation and moved to exact revenge at the first opportunity. Within five years the 'Caudine Peace' had broken down and hostilities were again renewed. For the most part the Samnites were once more victorious. However, the Romans again showed their true grit and refused to accept defeat, fighting back every time. The Samnites finally sued for peace in 304 BC, but again this was short-lived, only lasting six years.

The Samnites then launched a full-out assault on Rome in 296 BC, their aim to settle matters once and for all. To achieve this they gathered a coalition of allies including the remaining Etruscan city-states, Umbrian hill tribesmen and Gauls. Once more they were initially successful, but ultimately lost the crucial Battle at Sentinum in 295 BC. Here, only the Gauls turned up to support them and though initially a close-run thing, their eventual crushing defeat marked the end of Samnite resistance to Rome's southward expansion (Fields, 2012, 45). It was also the death knell for the Etruscans, with all of their remaining city-states now falling under Roman control.

Rome's regional dominance continued to grow, and the city next turned its attention to northern Italy where the Gauls were still dominant in the Po valley. Population pressure here was causing friction with Rome on its northern border. This was because in the early 280s BC a large-scale migration had begun of the Gallic peoples of central Europe. Soon huge tribal groupings were on the move, one eastwards to ultimately found the Galatian kingdoms of central Anatolia after ravaging Greece (and the source of the Galatian mercenaries in later Hellenistic armies, see Chapter 5), and another south into Italy. The Senate decided to tackle this new threat to the north head on before a full invasion of Roman territory took place, and in 284 BC a 13,000-strong Roman army marched north to challenge the Gauls. Disaster again followed, the legions being massacred at the Battle of Arretium. Their commander, Lucius Caecilius Metellus Denter, was among the dead. However, as usual the Romans once more refused to admit defeat and launched a massive counterstrike into the heart of Gallic territory. This time they were successful, smashing the power of the Senones tribe and evicting them out of Italy. Another Gallic tribe, the Boii, then started raiding into Roman-controlled Etruria but were fought to a standstill. Eventually they too sued for peace. This broke effective Gallic resistance in the north of Italy which now gradually came under Roman control, with a final Gallic coalition defeated in 225 BC at the Battle of Telamon.

Pyrrhus and Hannibal

Rome now controlled most of the Italian peninsula, excepting the Greek *poleis* to the south in Magna Graecia. They now became the next target of Roman attention when the Senate tried to force them into an alliance. This was quickly rebuffed, with Taranto (the leading naval power on the peninsula) appealing for help from the Hellenistic king Pyrrhus of Epirus on the western coast of the Balkans. A relation of Alexander the Great, and earlier briefly king of Macedon, he responded by crossing the Adriatic in 280 BC with an army 25,000 strong. These were crack troops who fought in the Hellenistic military tradition detailed in Chapter 3. His force included phalangites with six-metre long pikes, shock cavalry armed with *xyston* lances and, most shockingly for the Romans, war elephants (again, see Chapter 3).

When word reached Rome that Pyrrhus was recruiting allies from its enemies across the Italian peninsula the legions marched south to intercept. The first of three major battles followed at Heraclea, this proving a bruising experience for the Romans. Pyrrhus won, though at great loss, hence the phrase 'Pyrrhic victory' (Sekunda, 2019, 14). Two further battles occurred at Asculum in 279 BC and Beneventum in 275 BC, the first another narrow Epirot victory and the second an equally close Roman success. Pyrrhus left Italy soon after. One result of this conflict was the evolution of the Camillan manipular system into the Polybian system, this change detailed in Chapter 7.

Roman expansion now began to take on an international flavour. In 272 BC Taranto was captured, providing Rome with its first effective maritime capability. This led to an inevitable clash with Carthage, the regional superpower in the western Mediterranean. The First Punic War started in 264 BC, the trigger an argument over control of the key Sicilian city of Messina. The war lasted through to 241 BC and included the Battle of Agrigentum on the south coast of Sicily in 261 BC where Rome defeated the Carthaginians for the first time in battle. However, the conflict was largely naval in nature and here the Romans displayed their innate skill at adopting the tactics and technology of their opponents. They started the conflict as maritime underdogs but copied the Carthaginian's expertise at sea to the extent that they ultimately won the naval war and thus the whole conflict. Under the peace treaty Carthage evacuated Sicily and also paid a huge indemnity to Rome.

Peace was again short-lived, with the Second Punic War breaking out in 218 BC and lasting seventeen years. This seminal conflict tested Rome's powers of endurance to its very limit. At the outset the Roman fleet cut off the Punic North African homeland from its key colonies in Spain, a major source of Punic wealth. The Carthaginians were led this time by the brilliant general Hannibal who responded with an audacious plan to invade Italy itself from Spain through southern Gaul and the Alps. This lightning campaign, one of the most famous in the history of warfare, caught the Romans completely off guard. Hannibal soon defeated the legions three times at the Trebia in 218 BC, Lake Trasimene in 217 BC and Cannae in 216 BC. The latter was a battle of immense scale with 50,000 Carthaginians facing 86,000 Romans. Hannibal here completed his famous double envelopment of the Roman battle line, slaughtering 50,000 legionaries and allied troops. After such an immense disaster many opponents would have ended the conflict. Indeed, as Craven said in his highly influential history of the Punic Wars (1980, 140): 'Cannae was in itself a major disaster for Rome. Few ancient states could have taken it in their stride...'

However, by straining every sinew of Roman grit and determination, the city on the Tiber did. New legions were soon raised, two comprised of freed slaves. Crucially, Hannibal failed to capture Rome itself and was ultimately pinned down in southern Italy where attempts to re-supply him from North Africa and Spain failed, again largely due to Roman naval power. Then in 204 BC Rome went on the offensive, with the consul Publius Cornelius Scipio (later Africanus) landing in the Carthaginian heartland near Tunis with a large force of 25,000. These legions and their Numidian allies decisively defeated Hannibal at the Battle of Zama in 202 BC, with peace soon following under the most onerous terms for the Carthaginians (Elliott, 2020b, 36).

Peace again did not last, mainly because the Roman political classes viewed their encounters with Carthage as unfinished business. By this time the Senate had grand designs on new foreign territories in Spain and Africa, and the Third Punic War broke out in 146 BC. Here Carthage, effectively disarmed after defeat in the Second Punic War, was backed into a corner by the escalating demands of its conqueror. This third conflict was a very one-sided affair, with Carthage quickly succumbing. The city itself was destroyed, with 50,000 of its citizens being sold into slavery. Rome was now master of the western Mediterranean, with Sicily, Sardinia and Corsica, the Balearic Islands, Spain and a significant part of North Africa all under its direct control.

Wars with the Hellenistic Kingdoms

Roman attention now turned to the eastern Mediterranean and the kingdoms created when Alexander's Empire fragmented after his death in 323 BC. There, after the end of the Wars of the Successors, three main kingdoms had arisen. These were Antigonid Macedon, the Seleucid Empire and Ptolemaic Egypt. All soon found themselves the subject of unwelcome Roman attention (Elliott, 2020b, 36).

First, the Macedonian King Philip V had unwisely been caught trying to make an alliance with Hannibal when the latter was still in Italy at the height of his success in the Second Punic War. Soon the First Macedonian War began, which was followed by three more that finally saw Macedonia become a Roman province in 146 BC. Rome was also victorious fighting the over-confident Seleucid monarch Antiochus III in the Seleucid-Rome War. These conflicts featured several enormous set piece battles between legion and phalanx. The most significant ones were

Cynoscephalae in 197 BC where Philip V was defeated during the Second Macedonian War, Magnesia in 190 BC when Antiochus III was defeated in western Anatolia, and Pydna in 168 BC when the Macedonian king Perseus was defeated.

The final resistance to Roman hegemony in Greece came in 146 BC when the Achaean League in the northern and central Peloponnese unwisely declared war on Rome (Cassius Dio, *Roman History*, 21.31). The ensuing Achaean War was a short-lived affair, the Achaeans being totally defeated and leading city Corinth sacked and raized to the ground at the same time, and in the same manner, as Carthage at the end of the Third Punic War.

Rome was now the undoubted superpower in the Mediterranean, with its legions triumphant across the region. One result of its spectacular success against the Hellenistic kingdoms was the fabulous amounts of loot and plunder now making their back way to Rome, there to enrich army commanders and troops alike. It should be remembered that when Alexander finally defeated the Achaemenid Persian in the later fourth century BC, as detailed in Chapter 2, the Macedonian conquerors inherited the vast wealth of Darius III's huge empire. Following the Wars of the Successors after his death, this was distributed among the various successor states. This is what fell into Rome's lap, dwarfing the riches amassed after the defeat of Carthage. The aristocracy back in Rome could now see fortunes were to be made in the east through military conquest, which from this point proved an enormous draw to any ambitious senator. This soon caused friction among the patricians as they vied for control of the campaigning forces in the east, and a new type of military leader quickly emerged which I style in my analysis of Caesar's military career the late Republican warlords (Elliott, 2019, 11). It was this development more than anything that set the Republic on the path to its demise a century later.

The Gracchi Brothers

The Roman Republic was now wealthy and victorious, the master of all it surveyed. Its consuls and Senate controlled the fate of nearly all the peoples across the wide breadth of the Mediterranean Sea. The natural thing to do at this point was to consolidate this power, yet that was not the Roman way. The new warlords were about to make their presence felt.

The first sign of trouble in Rome occurred in 133 BC. By this time friction was rising between the patricians and plebeians over the distribution of the new wealth pouring into the Republic. Then the tribune Tiberius Sempronius Gracchus, the grandson of Scipio Africanus, made a dramatic proposal. He suggested that large stretches of the *ager publicus* state-owned land in Italy, often illegally occupied by the rich, be given to the poor. However, instead of following the standard practice of consulting the Senate, he presented the idea directly to an assembly of the people. Pandemonium erupted, and when a fellow tribune tried to oppose him the latter was hounded from office. Tiberius argued that his populist reforms should be funded by the Republic's new-found wealth from the conquests in the eastern Mediterranean. His new land bill passed, but when he tried to stand for election again he was assassinated by a group of senators. This was a truly dramatic development that sent shock waves through the Roman world, setting the tone for a century of violent political turbulence. As Matyszak says (2003, 131): 'After hundreds of years of settling internal disputes by negotiation and debate, the Romans settled this one with blood.'

Next, in 123 BC Tiberius's brother Gaius Gracchus was elected as a tribune. He realised his brother's weakness was a lack of support at the top of Roman society, and knew the senatorial class would always be opposed to any suggestions that would threaten their own wealth. He therefore cleverly reached out to the equestrian and curial aristocracy, securing their backing and then using this support to build a truly populist movement across the Republic. His aim was to carry out a total reorganization of the Roman state, this designed to make it much more balanced in terms of power and wealth. First he avenged his brother by making it illegal for a Roman citizen to be put to death without a trial before the people of the city. He then ensured the law was retrospective, enabling him to target Publius Popillius Laenas who, as consul in 132 BC, had led the investigations into his brother. The latter was forced into exile.

However, Gaius' most controversial reform was with regard to the *cura annonae* grain supply in Rome. Due to the city's rapid growth it was increasingly reliant on grain imports from Sicily and North Africa. This meant that the price of grain could fluctuate wildly, influenced by factors as diverse as slave revolts, plagues of locusts or simply the size of the annual harvest each year. This fluctuation exposed the citizens of Rome to occasional food shortages when the price was too high or the amount of grain available too low. Gaius therefore stabilized the price of grain at a sustainable level, and introduced a state subsidy to pay for it. To raise the funds for the subsidy, he introduced a system of tax farming in Rome's newly conquered territories in the eastern Mediterranean where huge corporations publicly bid for the right to collect the taxes for a percentage of profit. Despite the system being open to huge levels of corruption, which in some cases beggared the new provinces, the people of Rome did not care. They now had regular distributions of cheap grain, with this basic system lasting into the late Republic. It also illustrated the Roman attitude to public administration, with only a small core of officials managing the Republic's vast territory by sub-contracting responsibility out to private business and individual *publicani* administrators.

Gaius was now getting into his stride, but realised he would need another term as tribune to complete his reforming ambitions. He did not want to stand for election himself again, but put forward his closest supporter Fulvius Flaccus to take his place. Such was his popularity that he was re-elected anyway, alongside his friend. Their manifesto was even more radical than that for Gaius' first term of office. It included a plan to enfranchise all Italian citizens, and for a major Roman colony to be built on the site of Carthage, the Punic capital laid waste by Rome at the end of the Third Punic War. Gaius himself travelled to North Africa to see the latter founded. Both policies caused even more friction with the Senate and their supporters, and when Gaius and Flaccus failed to be re-elected in 121 BC they knew they were exposed to retribution. An attempt to drag them before the Senate failed when they refused to attend, Flaccus convincing Gaius that it was a trap, and so it proved. Bloodshed soon followed, with Gaius fleeing and eventually taking his own life with the help of a servant in a sacred grove. Some 250 of his supporters also died, fighting a rearguard action to buy him time to escape, ironically on the same bridge held by Horatio and his companions 400 years earlier. Retribution against Gaius, Flaccus and their families was particularly brutal, with Plutarch saying (*Lives*, Gaius Gracchus, 17):

> Someone cut off the head of Gaius and was carrying it along, but was robbed of it by a certain friend of the consul Opimius called Septimuleius; for proclamation had been made at the beginning of the conflict that an equal weight of gold would be paid the men who brought the head of Gaius or Flaccus. So Septimuleius stuck the head of Gaius on a spear and brought it to Opimius, and when it was placed in a balance it weighed seventeen pounds and two thirds, since Septimuleius, besides showing himself to be a scoundrel, had also perpetrated a fraud; for he had taken out the

brain and poured melted lead in its place. But those who brought
the head of Flaccus were of the more obscure sort, and therefore
got nothing. The bodies of Gaius and Flaccus and of the other slain
were thrown into the Tiber, and they eventually numbered three
thousand (after a tribunal condemned their supporters after their
deaths); their property was sold and the proceeds paid into the
public treasury. Moreover, their wives were forbidden to go into
mourning, and Licinia, the wife of Gaius, was also deprived of her
marriage portion. Most cruel of all, however, was the treatment of
the younger son of Flaccus, who had neither lifted a hand against
the nobles nor been present at the fighting, but had come to effect
a truce before the battle and had been arrested; after the battle he
was slain.

Such was the price of challenging the propertied aristocracy in Rome.
In what Matyszak describes as a travesty of restoring social order, the
Senate then rebuilt the Temple of Concord that had originally been built
by Camillus at the beginning of the fourth century BC to celebrate the
ending of strife between the social classes (2003, 138).

The Cimbrian War and the Rise of Marius

The next threat to the Republic was external, in the form of the Cimbri.
These were a Germanic people who originated from Jutland in modern
Denmark. In the second century BC they, along with neighbouring tribes
such as the Teutons and Ambrones, migrated south into Gaul where
they fought a series of wars with the Gallic tribes there. In 113 BC they
invaded the lands of the Taurisci, a confederation of Gallic tribes in
Noricum (modern Austria and part of Slovenia). These were Roman allies
and the Senate decided to send an army to their aid. The Roman force
was commanded by the consul Gnaeus Papirius Carbo who requested
the Cimbri retreat. They did so but were deceived by the Romans who
set an ambush for them. The Cimbri found out and attacked the Romans
first at the Battle of Noreia. Carbo's treachery backfired spectacularly
with the Romans suffering a huge defeat. They were only saved
from complete annihilation by a storm, with Carbo lucky to escape.

This engagement marked the beginning of the Cimbrian War that
lasted until 101 BC. The Cimbri could have attacked Italy at this point but
chose instead to head west to Gaul where they invaded Roman Transalpine

Gaul in 109 BC. This was the name initially used by the Romans to detail all the lands of Gaul north and west of the Alps. However, after the Roman conquest of Mediterranean Gaul in the 120s BC, the name became synonymous with the new Roman province there. The region was also known as *provincia nostra*, translating as 'our Province', the root of today's Provence.

Next, a Roman army under Marcus Junius Silanus was sent to intercept the Germans, but again the legions were comprehensively defeated in 109 BC, with the consul put on trial for his failure. Then in 107 BC, the Romans were again defeated, this time by the Gallic Tigurini tribe who were allies of the Cimbri. The name of this battle is unrecorded, but shortly afterwards the Romans again engaged the Tigurini, this time at the Battle of Burdigala (modern Bordeaux). The result was the same, total defeat, with the consul Lucius Cassius Longinus Ravalla killed.

Much worse was to follow. In 105 BC the Romans resolved to settle matters with the Cimbri once and for all. The new consul Gnaeus Mallius Maximus gathered a huge force of 80,000 legionaries and allies. It was so large that part had to be commanded by Quintus Servilius Caepio, his fellow consul and the governor of Cisalpine Gaul. The two disliked each other intensely so they set off in two separate columns, both arriving at the River Rhône near modern Orange at the same time. Distrusting each other, they camped on opposite sides of the river. Caepio then attacked the nearby Cimbri and their Teuton and Ambrones allies on his own, trying to steal the glory, but his legions were soon crushed. Maximus and his troops saw all this from their camp and became demoralised. Soon they were attacked by the Germans and quickly broke. Many Romans tried to flee but were slaughtered, including Maximus' own sons. Altogether the Romans lost 60,000 men, the largest number since the disaster at Cannae. Only Maximus, Caepio and a few horsemen escaped the engagement, later named the Battle of Arausio, with the Rhône choked with dead legionaries for many days afterwards.

Panic now gripped Rome, with the phrase *terror cimbricus* describing the mood of the people. Roman grit showed through again however, this time in the form of the great political and military leader Gaius Marius. He was born in 157 BC, though not to an aristocratic family. Through sheer hard work and ambition he rose to become a *quaestor* in 123 BC, then tribune of the plebs in 119 BC and *praetor* in 115 BC. Though no great administrator, he proved to be a supreme soldier. His first command was in Spain where he earned fame by defeating a bandit uprising and then setting Rome's silver-mining interests there on a firm footing. Then in 109 BC he travelled to Numidia to serve as the *legate* under the consul Quintus Metellus Numidicus. Here the Romans were engaged in the Jugurthine War against the rogue Numidian king Jugurtha. This had broken out in 112 BC and was proving difficult for Rome to conclude satisfactorily. Marius and Metellus soon fell out, especially when the latter's troops began supporting Marius' own claim to take over complete command of the legions there. Marius then returned to Rome in 107 BC to stand for consul, succeeding and then initiating the reforms of the Roman military detailed in Chapter 7. He was then granted Numidia as his own province where he returned with fresh troops, officially taking control of the campaign from Metellus.

His first act was to send his *quaestor* and future enemy Sulla to nearby Mauretania to negotiate the kingdom withdrawing its support for Jugurtha. Then, with the help of its king Bocchus I, Sulla captured Jugurtha and the war ended. Marius was wildly popular among the plebeian classes in Rome and despite Sulla's key role in Jugurtha's demise he was acclaimed the hero of the hour, being granted a triumph where Jugurtha was paraded through the streets of Rome, his royal robes and earrings ripped off by the mob. Thrown into the Tullianum prison, he died of starvation there in 104 BC. Marius was particularly proud of his rise to prominence in the context of this conflict, with the first century BC historian Gaius Sallustius Crispus having him say afterwards (*War with Jugurtha*, 85.28):

> If they look down on me they do the same to their own ancestors, for they, like me, had no nobility – until we earned it. And if they envy my honours, they should envy the labour, and the danger, by which I earned those honours.

After the shattering defeat of the legions at the Battle of Arausio the Roman people now turned to Marius for salvation. He was elected consul once more in 104 BC, even though he was still in Numidia concluding matters there. Arriving back in Rome for his triumph, he took up his consulship immediately by entering the Senate after the victory parade still wearing his triumphator's robes. This did not impress the conservative Senate, but the people loved it.

Marius now gathered together an army to counter any Cimbri invasion, basing it in southern Gaul. There he waited, training new legions and being elected consul again in 103 BC and 102 BC. In the latter year he finally confronted the Cimbris' allies who had started to move south. At the Battle of Aquae Sextiae in Aix-en-Provence he destroyed a combined force of Teutons and Ambrones, inflicting 90,000 casualties on the Germans and capturing 20,000. This included the Teuton king Teutobod, the defeat of his people so total they now disappear from history, while the king was sent back to Rome for ritual execution after a triumph.

Marius was elected consul again in 101 BC and in that year was able to tackle the Cimbri head on. The enormous tribe had begun to move south and for the first time penetrated the Alpine passes, entering Cisalpine Gaul. The Roman force there of 20,000 withdrew behind the River Po, allowing the Cimbri to devastate the fertile countryside to its north. This gave Marius time to arrive with his legions from southern Gaul, his army now totalling 32,000 men. He then led the combined Roman army to an immense victory at the Battle of Vercellae near to the confluence of the Po and the Sesia River. Here his newly reformed legions proved to be superior to the Cimbri warriors, though credit was also given at the time to Sulla who led the Roman and allied cavalry that also played a key role in the battle. Defeat for the Cimbri was total, they losing up to 160,000 men including Boiorix and Lugius, two of their key leaders. Meanwhile, a further 60,000 were captured, including two other leaders called Caesorix and Claodicus, and a large number of camp followers. Soon the slave markets of Rome were overflowing.

Marius was once again the hero of the hour, though the successful conclusion of the Cimbrian War marked the beginning of the long enmity between Marius and Sulla as the latter felt that, certainly in the Jugerthine War, the consul had not given him the credit for his actions. Marius then further alienated himself with the patricians by granting full Roman citizenship to the allied Italian soldiers who had served him so faithfully in the Cimbrian Wars, without asking permission from the Senate. This was to have unforeseen consequences and caused the next great crisis to face the Republic.

The Social War

By now domestic Roman politics was divided between two distinct factions called the *optimates* and the *populares*. The terms, popularized from the later second century BC, referred to the political leanings of their followers. The former were the conservative defenders of the upper classes and Senate, while the latter advocated reform in favour of the plebeians and popular assemblies as earlier championed by the Gracchi brothers. By this time Sulla was the darling of the former, Marius the latter.

Such disagreements were set aside for a short period in the early 90s BC when Rome was rocked by a conflict that caught many by surprise. This was the Social War, a vicious struggle when some of Rome's erstwhile Italian *socii* allies in the Apennines rose in revolt. There, troops from the Italian legions armed in the Roman fashion had frequently fought alongside Rome's own legions. They had proved so valuable to Marius that, as detailed above, he had granted Roman citizenship to his Italian troops after the Battle of Vercellae. However, this gave a new-found sense of power to the Italian political classes who now demanded a greater say in Roman foreign policy. After all, it was their soldiers who were fighting and dying alongside those of Rome. With trouble brewing, in 91 BC the tribune Marcus Livius Drusus proposed new legislation in Rome to try to avert a crisis developing. This would have admitted all Italians to citizenship. However, it provoked a huge backlash in the Senate, with Drusus earning the hatred of the *optimates* and eventually being assassinated (Appian, *Roman History*, 1.36). This was the last straw for the Italians and many now rose in revolt.

The specific peoples who challenged Rome were the Marsi in the northern Apennines and the Samnites, once one of Rome's most feared enemies, to their south. The two formed their own confederation with its headquarters in the city of Corfinium, due east of Rome across the Apennines. To mark their new alliance they renamed the town Italia and created their own Senate and army. It should be noted that many Italians, for example the Etrurians and Umbrians, did not join the insurrection. They wisely sat on the side lines to see how things developed, eventually siding with the Romans.

The rebels were initially successful, the Marsi inflicting defeats on Roman armies in the north and the Samnites bursting onto the Campanian coastal plain in the south. There, the rich cities along the Bay of Naples, for example Surrentum, Strabiae, Herculaneum and Nola, fell one by one. Pompeii was spared a siege given it supported the rebellion from early on.

Marius was in charge of the Roman forces in the northern sector. Now 67, he was far less energetic than previously and viewed as slower on campaign by the *optimates* than his rival Sulla. The Senate accused him of staying in his military camp in the region for too long, though when he did emerge he did inflict two defeats on the Marsi. He then waited to be appointed supreme commander of all the Roman forces in the field, but when this did not happen he retired to Rome, taking no further part in the war.

The Senate realised this revolt needed to be brought to a halt as quickly as possible and decided to offer the rebels concessions, with the consul Lucius Julius Caesar helping to pass a law which granted Roman citizenship to any Italians who had not participated in the uprising. This may have been extended to those still fighting but who agreed to immediately put down their weapons. The move proved decisive and soon the rebellion began to falter and wane. The Senate then appointed new military commanders tasked with bringing the war to a conclusion. Consul Gnaeus Pompeius Strabo was placed in charge of the three legions in the north, while Sulla was given command of those in the south. Victory followed victory for the Romans, and the war was over by 89 BC.

To cement the peace more new laws were now passed favourable to the Italians. A key one facilitated the formal inclusion of all Italians south of the River Po into the Roman state as full citizens, such that from this time all of Italy south of this line was now a single Roman nation. All seemed set for a period of peace after the dramas of the Jugurthine, Cimbrian and Social Wars. However, this proved a false hope because, in 88 BC, a full civil war broke out. This time the protagonists were none other than Rome's two leading warlords, Marius at the head of *populares* and Sulla leading the *optimates*.

Full Civil War

Sulla's First Civil War lasted from 88 BC to 87 BC and occurred in the context of the First Mithridatic War, Rome's first conflict with Mithridates VI of Pontus, the last great Hellenistic monarch. This began in 89 BC when Sulla was given command of the campaigning army in his capacity as one of the two consuls. This was a plum command for the ambitious warlord as he knew there was fabulous wealth to be gained by conquering Mithridates' empire in Anatolia, around the Black Sea and in Greece. Some of this territory comprised Roman provinces seized by the Pontic king, so there was also glory to be had restoring Roman rule. However, Marius also wanted the post. Having encountered Mithridates on an earlier tour to the east, when he had warned the king not to fight with Rome, he thought himself an expert on the region. Relations between Sulla and Marius, already poor, became increasingly strained and in 88 BC open conflict broke out.

The flashpoint occurred when one of the tribunes of the plebs, Sulpicius, suggested that the votes of the recently enfranchised Italians be evenly split among the existing Roman voting tribes. The *optimates* in the Senate blocked the move, so he turned to Marius for support, then putting forward a long list of proposals to the popular assembly designed to bypass the Senate. One of his suggestions was to take command of the army away from Sulla, the *optimates'* champion. This was a real threat to the consul and he played for time by retiring to examine the heavens for omens. This was one of his rights as a consul and meant that all public business in Rome had to cease until Sulla had completed his task. Sulpicius now overreacted, bringing his *populares* supporters onto the streets of the capital. Violence between the *optimates* and *populares* ensued, with Sulla having to flee and seek shelter with Marius. The latter saw his opportunity and made a number of demands of the consul who agreed to allow public business to return to normal. In short order Sulla was stripped of his command, with Marius now put in charge of the army to fight Mithridates.

Sulla knew his days would be numbered if he stayed in Rome and fled. He headed south, reaching an army of six veteran legions at Nola in Campania who he had commanded in the Social War. He convinced them to support him before Marius's own tribunes arrived, they then being killed when they tried to take control of the force. The importance of this cannot be underestimated, this being the first time the legions had chosen to side with a warlord against the Republic itself. Sulla now marched on Rome, joined by his fellow consul Quintus Pompeius Rufus. The pair fought their way into the city and a pitched battle ensued in the Esquiline Forum between the *optimates* and *populares*. There, after a promising start, Marius and Sulpicius suffered a resounding defeated. The latter was betrayed and executed, with Marius fleeing to Africa.

Sulla now took control of the city, posting troops throughout the capital to ensure order. He then addressed the popular assemblies to defend his own actions, before taking away their powers to legislate unless on a law already passed by the Senate. He then added 300 new members to the chamber to ensure its support. The power of the various public tribunes was also reduced. With peace restored in Rome, at least for now, he then sent his army back to Campania and resumed his post as consul.

However, all was not well. Another Roman army was at large in Italy under Gnaeus Pompeius Strabo, the father of Caesar's later rival Pompey. Sulla gave command of the force to his own ally Rufus, but when the latter arrived to take command he was killed by Pompey Strabo's loyal legionaries. This was only the first of a number of setbacks for Sulla, the most important being the failure of his candidates to replace himself and Rufus as consul for 87 BC. The winners were Lucius Cornelius Cinna and

Gnaeus Octavius, the former a well-known opponent of his. To counter this Sulla forced Cinna to vow to support him. However, once in office Cinna immediately broke the oath. He tried to impeach Sulla, but the warlord ignored him. He took command of the army once more and marched east to fight Mithridates.

With Sulla gone Cinna tried to revive Sulpicius's voting plans for the Italians, with his fellow consul Octavius leading the opposition. On the day of the vote the tribunes vetoed the law and rioting ensued in the *Forum Romanum*, with Octavius' supporters chasing Cinna's men away. Cinna fled the pandemonium and headed for Capua in Campania where he won over the loyalty of a Roman force there (Sulla's troops there had already left), additionally recruiting Italians to swell his numbers. The old warrior Marius now returned from Africa to join him and together they besieged Octavius in Rome. The latter secured the backing of Pompey Strabo and his troops, but he died soon after helping repel a Marian assault on the city. Marius then cut off the food supply to the capital.

The armies of the two factions now confronted each other near the Alban Hills south-east of Rome, but before an engagement could occur the Senate turned on Octavius and entered into negotiations with Marius and Cinna. The pair then took control of Rome without a fight, with Octavius beheaded. In a sign of things to come, his head was then displayed in the *Forum Romanum*. A massacre followed of Marius' and Cinna's opponents, with Sulla declared a public enemy. His house was burnt down and property confiscated, his laws repealed, and Marius (for the seventh and final time) and Cinna became the consuls for 86 BC. It was into this maelstrom of political turmoil that Gaius Julius Caesar now came of age, beginning his path along the *cursus honorum* for the first time as the political classes of Rome turned on themselves.

Chapter 6

Gaius Julius Caesar: A Biography

G aius Julius Caesar was the greatest figure to emerge from the Roman Republic. As with Alexander, he had a very keen sense of his own destiny from a young age, with a subsequent career that more than lived up to his early expectations. In this chapter I provide a brief biography, examining his family background, childhood, early political and military career, and his later dramatic rise and fall.

Caesar's Clan

Caesar belonged to the Julia clan. The Julii were one of Rome's oldest patrician *gentes*, the phrase referring to a group of related families who found common cause on the great issues of the day. They originated in Alba Longa, the Latin town 19km south-east of Rome founded by Aeneas' son Iulus in Virgil's Roman origins tale. Later in the Republic, when it became fashionable for each clan to associate themselves with a divine origin, the Julii aligned themselves with Iulus, claiming him as their clan founder. Additionally, in *The Aeneid* Aeneas himself claimed to be the son of Venus, an association also embraced by the Julii. Caesar himself used both mythical connections wholeheartedly whenever it provided a political advantage.

The Julii moved to Rome with many other patrician clans after Alba Longa's destruction by Rome under its third king Tullus Hostilius in the mid-seventh century BC. The clan are also referenced in contemporary epigraphy settled at the Alban colony of Bovillae, 11km south-east of Rome.

The Julii were an unremarkable *gentes* for most of its existence before the time of Caesar. Little is known about the twelve clan members who were elected as magistrates in the first two centuries of the Republic, excepting Gaius Julius Iulus who became consul in 489 BC. For some reason the clan was not as keen to promote the achievements of its illustrious forebears as were other rival *gentes*, for example the Manlii and Fabrii.

One of the first members to rise to prominence was a Julius Caesar who reached the praetorship during the Second Punic War. He was the first in the family to receive the *cognomen* Caesar, he later claiming this derived from the Punic word for elephant (*caesai*) after he killed one in battle, though Pliny the Elder later suggested the name derived from a Julii who had been delivered by Caesarean section (*Natural History*, 2.15). Given Caesar himself issued coins featuring elephants, he seems to have favoured the martial explanation.

Shortly afterwards the clan split into two distinct lines, each registered to different tribes in the Roman voting census. Caesar's direct family sat within the less successful branch. The next clan member to rise to prominence was Lucius Julius Caesar who reached the consulship in 157 BC. He came from the more successful branch. Next, one Sextus Julius Caesar became consul in 91 BC, while another Lucius Julius Caesar became consul in 90 BC, he playing a key role in bringing the Social War to an end as detailed in Chapter 5. In the same year the latter's younger brother Gaius Julius Caesar Strabo (the last a nickname meaning 'squinty') became an *aedil*. Lucius and Gaius were from Caesar's branch of the clan and distant cousins of Caesar's father, though it is unknown from which branch Sextus originated (Goldsworthy, 2006, 32).

Little is known of Caesar's grandfather, Gaius Julius Caesar, other than his wife's name, Marcia. She was the daughter of Quintus Marcius Rex who had been *praetor* in 144 BC. The couple had at least two children that we know of, Caesar's father Gaius and a daughter called Julia. Gaius embarked on a public service career from an early age, following the *cursus honorum* set career path for aristocratic Roman men of the Senatorial class. During the last two centuries of the Republic, this was generally as follows (Elliott, 2020b, 3):

- Military service.
- *Quaestor*, the lowest-ranked magistrate – minimum age 30 years old.
- *Aedile* or *Tribune*, a mid-ranking magistrate, for example those responsible for public buildings/festivals – minimum age 37 years old.
- *Praetor*, a senior elected magistrate – minimum age 40 years old.
- Consulship, one of the two senior magistrates in Rome. Once at this level the noble could be considered for a provincial governorship – minimum age 43 years old.

By law there were minimum intervals between holding successive offices, and it was forbidden to repeat an office. However, the rules were frequently ignored, particularly in times of crisis, with Marius' seven consulships being a prime example of this.

Gaius married Aurelia, daughter of either Lucius Aurelius Cotta or his brother Marcus Aurelius Cotta. They came from a leading family of plebian nobles called the Aurelii Cottae. The former was consul in 119 BC, following Aurelia's paternal grandfather who had been consul in 144 BC. Three of her brothers also became consuls, Gaius Aurelius Cotta in 75 BC, Marcus Aurelius Cotta in 74 BC and Lucius Aurelius Cotta in 65 BC.

Gaius' prospects in traversing the *cursus honorum* were certainly boosted by association with the Aurelii Cottae, though it was patronage through his sister's marriage that played the biggest role in his political career. That was because Julia married Marius, with the benefits of this family connection soon evident. For example Gaius was nominated as one of the ten commissioners tasked with overseeing the settlement of Marius' veterans after the Cimbrian War. He then became a military tribune before being elected *praetor* around 92 BC. Next, in 91 BC, he became the governor of the province of Asia in western Anatolia, unusually before he had been a consul. However, his career was dramatically cut short before he could actually stand for consul as in 85 BC he died suddenly, allegedly while putting on his shoes one morning in Rome. Thus at the age of 16 Caesar, his only son, suddenly became the head of his family (Goldsworthy, 2007, 48).

Caesar's Early Life and Career

Gaius Julius Caesar was born on 13 July 100 BC, which in his own time would have been recorded as the third day before the Ides of Quinctilis in the consulship of Marius and Lucius Valerius Flaccus, in the 654th year after the foundation of Rome. He was the youngest of Gaius and Aurelia's three known children, with two elder sisters, both called Julia. Caesar is often associated with having a Caesarean section birth, though there is no contemporary evidence of this. The procedure was only used at the time as a last resort to save the baby if the mother was dying in childbirth. His mother actually lived a long life afterwards and Caesar's birth appears to have been normal, with no mention of any complications.

The boy was named with the full *tria nomina* of the elite Roman upper classes. He received the standard education for aristocratic children, which was arduous and repetitive and taught seven days a week. No doubt the young Caesar would have been delighted when his schooling ended with his graduation at the age of 15. He then underwent a ritual that transitioned him to manhood. This was a ceremony, carried out in the presence of his father and male relatives, which involved the removal of the *bulla* charm he had been given at birth and the replacement of his child's tunic with the toga of an aristocratic man (Holland, 2003, 116).

Throughout his childhood years Caesar was raised to think he was special. Though his clan lacked an illustrious past in comparison with many others, he was the only boy in his family and knew from an early age he would inherit the mantle of *pater familias* as head of the family. Further, his father and mother were highly thought of in contemporary Roman high society. Thus when his father died so unexpectedly, Caesar was already aware of his duties given he had spent a significant amount of time with him while growing up, learning at first hand the responsibilities he would inherit later in life. He also learned who his father's patrons were, and who owed Gaius patronage. This was a system that facilitated much of the political activity in Rome and one Caesar would make much use of later.

Caesar's coming of age was well-timed given the opportunities it presented. This was because it occurred at the height of the civil war between the *optimates* and *populares*. Though Marius had died in January 86 BC aged 71, a year later the *populares* were still ascendant in Rome. Caesar was soon nominated as the new *Flamen Dialis* high priest of Jupiter, an astonishing move given his youth. He then quickly married Cornelia, daughter of the leading *populares* politician Cinna.

It is unclear if Caesar was officially appointed the *Flamen Dialis*, but even if he did take up the post he did not stay there for long as political turmoil soon returned to Rome. This was because in 83 BC Sulla returned to Italy victorious after the First Mithridatic War. His arrival began Sulla's Second Civil War that concluded with another victory when he successfully stormed Rome in 82 BC. Rapidly seizing political control, he then declared himself dictator before turning on the leading *populares* with a savage vengeance. This included having Marius' body exhumed and thrown into the River Tiber, and destroying all of his statues. He then initiated his infamous proscriptions that saw thousands of political opponents killed or exiled, turning Rome into a bloodbath.

Caesar was 18 by this time and though Sulla did not see the Julii as a threat, the young man was quickly targeted given his wife was the daughter of Cinna, and Marius had been his uncle-in-law. In the first instance Sulla ordered Caesar to divorce Cornelia (Plutarch, *Lives*, Julius Caesar, 1). The young man showed great personal bravery here, a trait evident throughout his life, repeatedly refusing to obey. Sulla then targeted Caesar's finances, stripping away Cornelia's dowry and nominating another to become the *Flamen Dialis*. Finally he confiscated Caesar's family inheritance, and soon afterwards the inevitable order was given for his arrest. This was a sure sign execution was to follow.

Caesar wisely went on the run in the Sabine Hills, talking his way out of trouble when finally arrested. He was eventually saved by his mother who convinced two of her Aurelii Cottae cousins, leading *optimates*, to plead with Sulla for her son's life. The strategy worked better than expected as Sulla not only relented but also allowed Caesar to resume his public career. However, Suetonius provides a sting in the tail, having Sulla say the following (Suetonius, *The Twelve Caesars*, Julius Caesar, 1):

> Very well then, you win! Take him! But never forget that the man you want me to spare will one day prove the ruin of the party (the *optimates*) which you want and I have so long defended. There are many Mariuses in this fellow.

Despite the pardon, Caesar decided caution was the best path to take. Fearful Sulla would change his mind, he left for Anatolia to join the military. In his first post he served as a *contubernales* (literally, 'tent companion') aide-de-camp to Marcus Minucius Thermus, the governor of Asia and a leading supporter of Sulla. Here he learned his trade as a junior officer, observing the *legates*, centurions, and legionaries as they performed their various tasks on campaign. Caesar served on the front line with great distinction, particularly when the town of Mitylene on the island of Lesbos was stormed. For his bravery here he was given Rome's highest award for gallantry, the *corona civica* crown of oak leaves. Traditionally this was given when the recipient had saved the life of another Roman citizen. A great honour, Caesar was able to wear the crown both in military parades and also in civilian ceremonies back in Rome.

Caesar then campaigned in Cilicia on the south coast of Anatolia under Publius Servilius Vatia Isauricus, fighting against the Cilician pirates who were endemic there. It was here that dramatic news reached him in 78 BC. Sulla was dead. Caesar now felt secure enough to return home, trying his hand at a legal career. In this he was again successful, though perhaps too much so as word reached him he was making enemies in high places. Once more he decided caution was the best route to take and again left the capital for the east, this time aiming to study in Rhodes (Plutarch, *Lives*, Julius Caesar, 4).

The Cilician Pirates

On his way there the first famous event in Caesar's life occurred. This was his capture by Cilician pirates near the island of Farmakonisi (Roman *Pharmacussa*) off the cost of south-western Anatolia. Piracy was endemic in the region, and actually the result of Roman military success there during the past few decades. This was because there was now no major regional power left, other than Rome, to police the littoral zone around the coast and the sea-lanes. As Roman interests here were primarily the extraction of wealth back to the Republican capital, the pirates were left to their own devices. Many of them were actually the former crews who had manned the warships of the Hellenistic navies before their defeat by Rome, and so skilled professional sailors and marines.

Once in captivity Caesar quickly sent the retainers who had travelled with him to the nearby cities on the Anatolian mainland, for example Miletus, Ephesus, Priene and the religious site at Didyma to raise loans to pay the ransom of 20 talents of silver demanded by the pirates. He passed the time with the only two companions he kept with him, his doctor and a valet. Plutarch indicates Caesar showed bravado here in the face of this very real danger. He says (*Lives*, Julius Caesar, 2):

> He showed such contempt for the Cilicians that whenever he laid
> down to sleep he would send word to them, ordering them to keep
> quiet. For thirty-eight days, without a care in the world, he would
> join in their games and exercises as if they were not his captors
> but his bodyguard. Writing poems and speeches, he treated them
> as his audience, and those who did not admire them he called
> to their faces illiterate barbarians, and would often, as a joke,
> threaten to hang them.

Suetonius (*The Twelve Caesars*, Julius Caesar, 1) suggests this latter threat was actually crucifixion, and Caesar was as good as his word. Soon the ransom arrived and the 25 year old was released. He headed straight for nearby Miletus where much of the money had been raised. Showing good leadership skills for one who had never held public office, he convinced the local provincial leadership to help him raise and crew a small fleet. He then headed back to Farmakonisi where he rounded up all of his previous captors. They were then sent to Pergamum in chains and imprisoned. Caesar asked for them to be executed. However, the regional governor Marcus Junctus showed no interest as he was in the process of converting Bithynia into a new Roman province following the death of its king, Nicomedes IV. It is likely he actually saw an opportunity to sell the pirates into slavery, or even accept a bribe to release them. Caesar would have none of this and promptly headed back to Pergamum where he had the captive pirates crucified. However, he had clearly developed some respect for them when a captive as he had their throats cut before the gruesome procedure began.

After this dramatic interlude Caesar then resumed his journey and headed on to Rhodes where he studied under the renowned rhetorician Apollonius Molon, Cicero's former teacher. He was clearly a good pupil as many thought him the best orator of his day, with a finely tuned use of rhetoric using a simple yet effective style. However, his schooling was cut short by another opportunity for military adventure. This featured Mithridates again who had reneged on his agreement with Rome and sent a raiding party along the coast of Anatolia where it was plundering the territory of Rome's allies. Sensing these might defect to the Pontic king without a show of Roman force, Caesar took a ship to the region and raised a force of local auxiliaries. They engaged the Pontic force which promptly withdrew, and the situation was stabilized. We see here a confident young man, ready to take the initiative when he saw Rome's interests threatened, even when not officially sanctioned.

In 74 BC Caesar received another religious appointment back in Rome, this time to become one of the fifteen pontiffs who served the *Pontifex Maximus*, the chief priest of the state religion. Returning home once more, he took up his legal career again, then being elected to his first political post as one of the twenty-four military tribunes in 72 BC. In this capacity he may have fought against the famous slave revolt of Spartacus, known as the Third Servile War.

Caesar's star was now beginning to rise, with his rhetorical skills and legal expertise widely acknowledged. He was also now a father as Cornelia had given birth to their daughter Julia in 76 BC. He then began his first term as *quaestor* in early AD 69, this one of the junior magisterial posts in Rome. Shortly after the appointment, Cornelia died. Caesar was then attached to the staff of the governor of Hispania Ulterior (Further Spain), Antistius Vetus. This was one of two Spanish provinces formed following Rome's victory in the Second Punic War. While here two events occurred that were to resonate as his career progressed. The initial one was his first epileptic fit, a condition that he suffered from for the rest of his life.

The second was his encounter with a statue of Alexander the Great when visiting the Temple of Hercules in Cadiz (Roman *Gades*). Suetonius says this reduced him to tears, reminding him of how little he had accomplished by a similar age (*The Twelve Caesars*, Julius Caesar, 7).

When he again returned to Rome Caesar remarried, his second wife being a granddaughter of Sulla called Pompeia who was distantly related to his later great rival Gnaeus Pompey. The match showed an impressive degree of *realpolitik* on his part given he was marrying into one of the leading *optimates* families in Rome. Continuing his progression along the *cursus honorum*, Caesar was next elected to the post of *curule aedile* in 65 BC. His rise to the top of Roman political society now seemed well on track, though he was beginning to attract unwelcome attention from political opponents who now, for the first time, began to take him seriously (Elliott, 2019, 84).

The Catiline Conspiracy

In 63 BC Caesar ran for the post of *Pontifex Maximus*, as noted earlier the chief priest of the state religion in Rome. Running against powerful senatorial rivals, he was again successful. This was a spectacular triumph, though his campaign was marred by accusations of bribery on all sides. More drama was to follow, as in the same year the consul and leading *optimates*' champion Cicero exposed the Catiline conspiracy.

Lucius Sergius Catilina was an aristocrat born in 108 BC. He served under Pompey during the Social War, and later gained an infamous reputation as a zealous supporter of Sulla during his proscriptions when he even killed his own brother-in-law. Despite being charged with fornication with a vestal virgin in 73 BC, for which he was acquitted, he progressed along the *cursus honorum* and became a *praetor* in 68 BC. By 66 BC he was the proconsul in Africa, but his bad reputation continued to follow him and a charge of extortion prevented him from standing for consul in either 65 BC or 64 BC. There is then some speculation that, frustrated at some stage during this period, he planned to murder the existing consuls and assume power. Called the 'first Catiline conspiracy', there is little evidence this was true. However, later in 64 BC, when Cicero defeated Catiline to be elected consul for the following year, Catiline started to systematically enlist a large body of his supporters with the aim of staging an armed insurrection. Their plan was to seize control of the government (Matyszak, 2003, 203). His proposals, once in power, were an extreme form of the *populares'* platform, including the proscription of wealthy patricians and cancelling debt. This appealed to a wide variety of discontents, for example on the one hand now destitute Sullan veterans and on the other victims of Sulla's own proscriptions who had been dispossessed of their property.

Cicero, who had a well-established network of spies across Rome, was kept fully up to speed of developments with Catiline's plans. On 21 October 63 BC the consul made his move, denouncing Catiline to the Senate in a passionate speech. He charged him with treason and was awarded the 'ultimate decree' by the Senate. This allowed him to enact martial law. Catiline fled Rome on 8 November, joining his followers at Faesulae in Etruria, including the veterans who had been organizing themselves into an effective fighting force. On 3 December a group of envoys from the Allobroges Gallic tribe arrived in Rome and provided Cicero with evidence they had been approached to support Catiline. This was all Cicero needed to make his final move to extinguish the 'second Catiline conspiracy', he quickly rounding up any of the latter's supporters still left in Rome and executing them. The Senate then dispatched an army under Gaius Antonius Hybrida to destroy Catiline, who moved north-east in an attempt to cross the Apennines. Here he was confronted and, despite battling bravely against the odds, soundly defeated. Catiline was killed along with most of his supporters.

With the threat of rebellion removed, accusations now began among both *optimates* and *populares* about who had supported Catiline. Caesar himself was not immune from the charges, with one of his defeated opponents for the post of *Pontifex Maximus* trying to convince Cicero of his guilt. Fortunately the consul rebuffed the man, with Caesar emerging from the turmoil with his reputation intact.

Caesar was then appointed *praetor*, obtaining his first governorship in 62 BC and returning to Hispania Ulterior as proconsul. This proved timely as it allowed him to escape the clutches of the increasing number of creditors who had financed his rise to power. While in the new post he was immune from prosecution, including from the creditors, and this set a pattern for the rest of his life with Caesar securing increasingly high political offices to stay one step ahead of those chasing him for repayment.

Caesar excelled in his new position. Ever mindful of the never-ending threats of raiding into his province from unconquered parts of Spain, he raised ten new cohorts of legionaries. These were formed into his new *legio X*, this elite unit to become his own personal legion. He then destroyed two Lusitanian tribes challenging the authority of Rome. The victories were so total that his troops hailed him *imperator*, allowing Caesar to formally claim his first triumph on his return to Rome.

When back in the Republican capital in 61 BC he divorced Pompeia in the context of unfounded accusations of infidelity while the latter had hosted the festival of *Bona Dea* in 62 BC. Despite her protestations of innocence, Plutarch quotes Caesar as saying 'I thought my wife should be above suspicion' (*Lives*, Julius Caesar, 9).

Caesar next had a difficult choice to make regarding his career. Now 40, he planned to stand for the consulship for 59 BC. Yet he also wanted to celebrate the triumph he was due following his acclamation as *imperator* in Spain. He could only do this if still serving in the army, yet he could only stand for consul if he laid aside his military post. Forced to choose, he opted for the consulship and was duly elected. Once in power he introduced a bill to the Senate that he hoped would make him the leading politician in Rome. This was the controversial Land Bill, aimed at redistributing publicly-owned land to Pompey's veteran troops and the many urban poor in Rome. The move was to be financed by the fabulous wealth Pompey had brought back from his campaigns in the east. The passing of this legislation became a grinding battle of wills between the *optimates*, now led by Cato, and the *populares* for whom Caesar was increasingly the champion. He was greatly helped here by a new realignment in Roman politics, the formation of the First Triumvirate between the three leading men of Rome. These were the immensely wealthy Crassus, Pompey and the newly arriviste Caesar. Each pledged to support the others in the Senate, with many in Rome unaware of the development until Caesar started to overtly promote Pompey through the proposed resettlement of his veterans. In short order the Land Bill passed after a show of force by Pompey's men in the Senate chamber.

With this humiliation of the *optimates* Caesar was now ascendant. Suetonius says a popular joke in Rome described the consuls for the year 59 BC as Julius and Caesar, rather than Caesar and his fellow consul Bibulus, the *optimates*' candidate who had retired from public life after an unwise run in with the *populares* (*The Twelve Caesars*, Julius Caesar, 20). Next he married again, this time to Calpurnia, the daughter of Lucius Piso who had been elected to replace him as consul the following year. Caesar now looked to his fortunes beyond his year as consul, knowing once out of office he would be targeted by the *optimates* and his creditors in court. His solution was again to take an office that would make him immune from prosecution, namely another governorship. While consul he had had himself appointed as the proconsul in Cisalpine Gaul, the former Gallic lands in northern Italy, and Illyricum. He later added Transalpine Gaul along the Mediterranean coast to his Gallic responsibilities after the death of its governor. These Gallic territories gave him four legions, including his own founding *legio X* which had moved north from Hispania Ulterior. He set his tenure in post for five years from 58 BC and then quickly left for Cisalpine Gaul to take up his post, leaving his creditors once more out of pocket. This set the scene for the Gallic Wars, within which sat his two invasions of far-off Britain.

Caesar in Gaul

When Caesar set out from Rome for his new province of Gaul he was 41 and already had his eyes on the Gallic territories north of the Alps and Transalpine Gaul. He knew conquest there would grant the two things he craved most, money and glory. The former would help pay off his debts, while the latter would place him on an equal footing with his Triumvirate partners Crassus and Pompey. Back in Cadiz when he looked on the statue of Alexander the Great he had felt inferior. He was now determined to catch up.

To the north of Caesar in Gaul and beyond were six broad tribal regions (Haywood, 2009, 55). These were:

- Gallia Aquitania in the south-west.
- Armorica in the west.
- Gallia Celtica in central Gaul.
- Gallia Belgica to its north.
- Germania across the River Rhine to the north and east.
- Britain across *Oceanus* (as the Romans styled northern European waters) to the far off north-west, a comparatively unknown entity.

In Gaul, the most southerly tribes were already coming under Roman cultural influence by this time. Roman merchants were embedded across the region, the River Rhone providing a ready means of accessing the lands north of the Alps and central Gaul. The region was relatively peaceful, though soon the Helvetti provided Caesar with his first opportunity for adventure. This confederation comprised five inter-related tribes living on the Swiss plateau. Here the Alps and the Rhone and Rhine rivers penned them in. Coming under increasing pressure from the

German tribes expanding from the north and east, they began to plan a mass migration west (Caesar, *The Conquest of Gaul*, 2.1).

Once ready the confederation set off in a massive population shift comprising 368,000 migrants, including 92,000 warriors. Caesar, newly arrived in Transalpine Gaul with only *legio X*, was caught off guard. Rome had already tried to discourage the Helvetti from leaving their homelands given the disruption this would cause to the Roman trade routes north into Gaul. Faced with a huge disparity in numbers if conflict broke out, Caesar decided to act quickly to nip things in the bud. Heading north with his legion and some rapidly recruited Gallic allies, he soon reached the Rhone ahead of the Helvetti. There he burned the only substantial bridge across the river. He then arrayed his troops along the western bank as a blocking force. When the Helvetti arrived they realised their path was barred and sent a delegation to meet Caesar. He stalled them for fifteen days, fortifying his position with a 30km-long ditch, rampart and palisade. Then, when he felt secure enough to defend the line of the river, he finally allowed the delegation of Helvetti nobles across to meet him. They asked for permission to pass peacefully through Transalpine Gaul but Caesar refused, adding that any attempt to cross the river would be met with force. Soon small groups of Helvetti tried to ford the river but were easily beaten back by the Romans. Any that reached the western shore were quickly dispatched by the legionaries positioned there.

The Helvetti leadership now decided to head north-west, aiming to travel around the Roman fortifications. Aware of their full strength now, Caesar left his legion in place under the *legate* Titus Labienus and headed for Cisalpine Gaul to gather his other three legions, the VIIth, VIIIth and IXth. He also recruited two more from the Italicised Gauls there, naming them *legios* XI and XII. When ready he then headed back north with 27,500 legionaries and 4,000 more allied Gallic cavalry.

By this time the Helvetti had already moved through the Pas de l'Ecluse between the Rhone and the Jura mountains, and were now skirting the territory of the Aedui and their Ambarri and Allobroges neighbours in Gallia Celtica (Haywood, 2009, 55). Given the size of the Helvetti migration they had no choice but to plunder the land they were passing through, and the suffering Gallic tribes sent embassies to Caesar to ask for help. He responded quickly, staging a series of forced marches which soon caught up with the Helvetti column on Saône river, this a right hand tributary of the Rhone. When he arrived, three quarters of the Helvetti had already crossed. However, a clan called the Tigurini were still waiting on the shore for their turn to cross. Caesar wasted no time, deploying his legions in the standard *acies triplex* battle formation of three lines and launching a brutal surprise attack that pinned the Gauls against the river. The engagement, later called the Battle of Arar, was very one-sided, with any Tigurini survivors fleeing into nearby woodland where they were hunted down by Caesar's headhunting allied cavalry (see Chapter 7).

Caesar quickly re-gathered his army and set off again after the remaining Helvetti, building a wooden military bridge across the Saône and crossing his whole force in a single day. The Helvetti realised they were unable to shake their pursuer and halted, sending a delegation to Caesar to try to agree terms and offering to settle wherever the Romans suggested. However, they overplayed their hand through overconfidence in their martial prowess. Caesar was having none of this and warned he would only agree terms if they agreed to provide hostages and pay reparations to the Gallic tribes they had plundered. The Helvetti recoiled at this and stormed off.

The migrants set off yet again, this time heading south-west towards Gallia Aquitania. Caesar followed close on their heels, his cavalry snapping at the rear of the Gallic column, though on one occasion a mounted force got too close to the Gauls who about-turned and ambushed them, leading to a rare Roman defeat. This emboldened the Helvetti, whose rearguard now began to offer battle whenever the Romans approached. Caesar refused to engage at this point, staying just close enough to prevent the migrants from raiding the surrounding countryside. However, his hand was forced when supplies promised by his Gallic allies failed to arrive to feed his six legions. He then tried, though failed, to engage the Helvetti in a decisive encounter.

Caesar now realised his shortage of supplies set him at a disadvantage for the first time and he decided to break off his pursuit, reversing his course back south. Here he hoped to link up with his supply train. However, some of his Gallic allies then deserted and told the Helvetti of his plight. Soon the hunter had become the hunted, with the Helvetti reversing course to pursue the Romans. Caesar now knew he would have to give battle and chose a steep hillside for the engagement. He then drew up *legio*s VII, VIII, IX and X in the *acies triplex*, placing his cavalry and light troops on the flanks. The raw *legio*s XI and XII were positioned at the rear as a reserve, Caesar hoping not to have to use them given their lack of experience. In the ensuing Battle of Bibracte the Helvetti charged headlong uphill into the Roman legionaries but, despite initial gains, were steadily defeated even though their force was three times larger than Caesar's (Caesar, *The Conquest of Gaul*, 2.1). The fighting was most brutal around the Helvetti wagon laager as the Romans counter-attacked downhill, but Caesar's victory was soon complete. The defeated Helvetii then surrendered, with 110,000 survivors ordered back to their homeland. Only the 6,000 strong Verbigeni tribe refused, fleeing north. There they were captured by Rome's Gallic allies and returned to Caesar who executed every man, woman and child.

Caesar was now well positioned in central Gaul with six legions. There was still time left in the campaigning season for more action. He had tasted victory and wanted more. Casting around for a new target of opportunity, he alighted on the German Suebi. This was an enormous confederation of tribes to the north and east of the Rhine, 120,000 of who were now camped across the river in eastern Gaul. Here they were exacting tribute and taking hostages from the regional tribes. The Gallic leaders there asked for his help to expel them, and Caesar was more than happy to assist.

The Suebi were led by their king Ariovistus and comprised a large number of Germanic tribes including those later called the Quadi, Hermunduri, Marcomanni, Semnones and Lombards. Caesar realised he was once again heavily outnumbered. He first tried to resolve matters through dialogue, hoping the threat of Roman intervention would be enough to convince the Suebi to head home. However, he was quickly rebuffed, with Ariovistus asking why the Romans felt they could intervene in events in this part of Gaul, so far from Cisalpine and Transalpine Gaul. Caesar then ordered the Germans to refrain from any further raiding, and to return the Gallic hostages to their tribes, overtly threatening to use force if his demands were not met. Unsurprisingly, Ariovistus refused again. To prove his point the Germans then set off westwards and raided the territory of the Aeudi. Further, Caesar received word that thousands more Suebi were now massing across the Rhine, waiting to join the Germans already in Gaul. He decided to act immediately, marching his whole force westwards at a rapid pace in a series of day and night marches to catch the huge Suebi column as it ground through eastern Gaul.

Within a week Caesar's allied cavalry found the enormous German army. Ariovistus now reached out, agreeing to a meeting with Caesar. However, he insisted both parties only brought mounted warriors with them. Caesar did not trust his Gallic horse for this delicate encounter and therefore mounted as many of the Xth legion as possible on their horses, hence the legion being named *legio X equestris* from this point. The meeting was a failure though and the Romans withdrew in good order to their camp, despite German attempts at provocation.

Battle was now inevitable and, having secured his lines of supply, Caesar deployed his army in the *acies triplex* ready for battle. On the first day the Germans declined to engage, and so the following day Caesar forced the hand of Ariovistus by advancing so close to his camp that the Suebi king would have to engage or lose face. The Battle of Vosges followed, a huge engagement easily won by the Romans. No quarter was given and the German army massacred, Ariovistus one of the few to escape, only to disappear from history.

Caesar was well satisfied with his year-long campaign, first defeating the Helvetti and then Suebi. He called on his scribes to narrate his exploits as a set of commentaries that he then sent to Rome. This was the first instalment of what became *The Conquest of Gaul*. Specifically, he boasted that he had 'completed two important campaigns in a single summer' (Caesar, *The Conquest of Gaul*, 2.2).

While in Cisapline Gaul during the winter of 58 and 57 BC Caesar recruited two more new legions, *legio XIII* and *legio XIV*. There he received reports that the Belgae tribes in Gallia Belgica in the far north of Gaul were conspiring against Roman interests and immediately sent word to his Gallic allies there that he was on his way to deal with the situation. He then headed north with his two new legions, joining the existing six in the lands of the Sequani where he learned troubling news. The combined Belgae tribes were massing an enormous force of 289,000 warriors against him.

Caesar was unperturbed, ordering a general advance into the heartland of the Nervii tribe who he determined would be the most troublesome. He forced a meeting engagement at the Battle of the Sabis (the modern River Sambre) where the speed of the Belgae attack almost caught the Romans by surprise. This was another savage battle, the outcome not clear until near the end when Roman discipline won the day, with Caesar fighting in the front rank twice. Pockets of Nervii put up a dogged last stand, only to be massacred. Finally the battle was over with another great Roman victory. Belgae resistance to the Roman advance was broken, with all but one of the remaining tribes now submitting to Caesar. This was the Atuatuci who Caesar eventually defeated, he then placing their entire remaining population of 53,000 into slavery.

After the distraction of renewing his triumvirate with Crassus and Pompey at the Conference of Luca in 56 BC, Caesar again looked back to

Gaul for more glory. This time his targets were the tribes along the Atlantic freeboard who had seized the Roman officers collecting provisions for the eight legions based further south. This sparked a full rebellion along the coast, with Caesar again acting swiftly. His main target was the Veneti tribe, a seafaring people based in Armorica with strong maritime links to Britain.

For this campaign Caesar raised a fleet of quinquireme and trireme war galleys from the Mediterranean, deploying them to the north-west European coast. Here they overcame the Veneti fleet at the Battle of Morbihan Gulf in the late summer of 56 BC, with Caesar having to innovate given the Veneti vessels were more suited to northern waters than the Mediterranean-built galleys used by Romans. Caesar himself provides a detailed description of the Gallic ships, saying (*The Conquest of Gaul*, 3.1).

> The Gaul's own ships were built and rigged in a different manner from ours. They were made with a much flatter bottom, to help them ride shallow water caused by shoals or ebb tides. These had exceptionally high bows and sterns fitted for use in heavy seas and violent gales, and the hulls were made entirely of oak, to enable them to stand any amount of shocks and rough usage. The cross-timbers, which consisted of beams a foot wide, were fastened with iron bolts as thick as a man's thumb. The anchors were secured with iron chains instead of ropes. They used sails made of raw hides or thin leather, either because they had no flax and were ignorant of its use, or more probably because they thought ordinary sails would not stand the violent storms and squalls of the Atlantic and were not suitable for such heavy vessels.

Caesar's innovation to tackle this new maritime threat took the form of sickle-shaped hooks on the end of long poles which the Romans used to cut the rigging of the Veneti vessels, making them more vulnerable to boarding where the Roman marines were far better equipped than their opponents. With the destruction of their fleet the Veneti sued for peace, though Caesar as usual dealt with the rebellion harshly. The entire Veneti ruling council were beheaded. Soon only the Morini tribe around modern Boulogne and the Menapii to their north, the tribes closest to mysterious Britain across terrifying *Oceanus*, were left refusing to submit to Rome. The region was broadly at peace again (Haywood, 2009, 55).

Caesar again wintered in Cisalpine Gaul, hoping his work in the north was now over. However, in the spring of 55 BC word reached him that a new German migration was underway. This comprised the Usipetes and Tencteri tribes from the eastern bank of the River Rhine, with some 430,000 crossing into Gaul to flee the predations of the Suebi. Caesar headed north yet again. On his arrival the Germans requested asylum in Gaul, but Caesar refused. He suggested the two tribes share the land of the Ubii, another German tribe on the eastern bank of the Rhine who were hostile to the Suebi. The Usipetes and Tencteri delegations asked for three days to consider this. However, shortly after a skirmish broke out between the Roman Gallic allied cavalry and the German cavalry defending their nearby camp. Caesar viewed this as treachery and the following day ordered an all-out attack on the Germans, catching the entire Usipetes and Tencteri by surprise. A massacre followed, with archaeological finds recently found near the battle site at Kessel in the Netherlands showing as many 200,000 were slaughtered. No Roman casualties are known from the engagement, with even the Senate back in Rome recoiling at brutality on this scale. Not Caesar though, who revelled in it given he felt he had prevented another German incursion into Gaul similar to that of the Suebi in 57 BC.

Ignoring any criticism, he now decided on a show of strength to deter any further German action and for the first time crossed the Rhine into Germany proper, building a wooden military bridge downstream of modern Koblenz between Andernach and Neuwied. However his great feat of engineering came to nought as the local German tribes, including the Suebi, had already evacuated their lands. Given a free hand, Caesar ravaged them for eighteen days and then returned to Gaul. This was because he already had his eye on the next target in this intense campaigning year, fantastical Britain opposite the lands of the Menapii and Morani.

The conclusion of Caesar's Gallic campaigns are covered in detail in Chapter 8 in the context of my analysis of his specific campaigns and battles. There I detail his 55 BC and 54 BC incursions to Britain, and his final 'winner takes all' campaign against Vercingetorix, king of the Arverni tribe in Gallia Centrica, which culminated in the famous Siege of Alesia in 52 BC. However, to provide continuity, here I briefly touch on his last three years campaigning in Gaul.

Caesar was never to return to Britain after his 54 BC campaign. When he arrived back in Gaul it was on the verge of rebellion, and the final two years of his conquest there were spent in an increasingly brutal series of campaigns to stamp out the last embers of Gallic resistance. At first he suffered a number severe setbacks, including the wiping out of the entire *legio XIV* by the Eburones tribe in Gallia Belgica (which in true Caesarian fashion he immediately reformed in full). However, gradually the Romans asserted their authority in their usual sanguineous fashion and the final Great Revolt led by Vercingetorix was crushed at Alesia, bringing the conquests to a close. The scale of Caesar's eventual success in Gaul, but also the terrible price paid by the native Gauls, cannot be overestimated. To provide context, in Plutarch's analysis of his campaigns there he estimates one million natives were killed, and another million enslaved (*Lives*, Julius Caesar, 15.5 and Pompey, 67.10). By way of analogy, given the entire population of Late Iron Britain at this time was some two million (Elliott, 2020b, 90), the scale of devastation is clear.

As the decade progressed distractions back in Rome were also to divert Caesar's attention. Here, his triumvirate with Pompey and Crassus was coming to a crashing end. First, his ties with Pompey had begun to unravel as soon as Julia passed away in childbirth in 54 BC (Caesar had learned the dreadful news when campaigning in Britain), with the leading *optimates*' champion declining a subsequent offer of marriage to Caesar's great-niece. Further, when he returned from Britain to Gaul later in the year Caesar also learned that his mother Aurelia, with her strong family ties to the *optimates*, had also died. Finally, his relationship with Crassus and his supporters then dramatically ended when the fabulously rich patrician was killed leading his legions to their doom in the east against the Parthians. From now on, without the wealth of Crassus to provide a balance, Caesar and Pompey would increasingly be at odds, with matters coming to a head as the decade ended.

Crossing the Rubicon

Caesar's main issue now was the same one he had been facing when he left for Gaul in 58 BC, namely his vulnerability to private prosecution by his political enemies when out of office. While a proconsul in Gaul and Illyricum he was immune from this, and once he again became a consul back in Rome (as he expected on his return) he would also be immune. The time gap between was therefore where he was most susceptible to attack. If subject to legal action then he might be financially ruined. He knew there were plenty of *optimates* in Rome willing to try to make their names taking on the conqueror of Gaul. He therefore needed to keep one of his provinces until he next became consul.

This issue had already been the subject of much political manoeuvring in Rome. Caesar had had his proconsulships extended by a further five years at the Conference of Luca in 56 BC. Now that extension was coming to an end, just at the time when his Gallic conquests were also ending, making a further five year extension unlikely. He did think he had part solved the problem during Pompey's consulship in 52 BC when a law was passed allowing him to stand for the consulship *in absentia* while in Gaul. This was set for the consular elections in 49 BC, with the aim of him being consul in 48 BC. However, the timing of his leaving Gaul and Illyricum and then becoming consul still left him with a hiatus of ten months when he would be vulnerable to his enemies. Despite the increasing tensions with Pompey, an agreement seems to have been reached to mitigate this in the form of an understanding that no debates in the Senate to find a successor in Caesar's provinces would begin until 1 March 50 BC. With the cracks in his relationship with Pompey widening by the day though, these debates had actually begun as early as 51 BC. Each time they had had to be voted down by Caesar's supporters, led by Mark Antony who was one of Caesar's key supporters in the Republican capital. However, despite his best efforts, the issue finally came to a head in 50 BC when Gaius Claudius Marcellus, one of the consuls that year, had a resolution passed in the Senate saying that Caesar should lay down command of his provinces on the official final date, with no extensions. Mark Antony and Caesar's many *populares* supporters moved to block this again, and on 1 December Caesar's backer Gaius Scribonius Curio managed to obtain a resolution of 370 votes to 22 specifying both Caesar and Pompey lay down their proconsulships at the same time. The game was now afoot.

The following day, without any authorisation from the Senate, Marcellus made Pompey an offer to take command of all of the legions in Italy, with the ability to raise more legionaries if he wished. Pompey immediately accepted and Caesar, still in Cisalpine Gaul, now realised conflict was inevitable. He decided to act first to catch the *optimates* off guard and provoke the coming fight, writing to the Senate on 1 January 49 BC to say he would only resign his commands at a time of his choosing. He knew this tone would infuriate his opponents, and the Senate quickly declared he would be treated as a public enemy if he did not lay down his commands on a date to be fixed by them. He was also specifically told not to bring his troops across the Rubicon River just north of Ravenna which separated Cisalpine Gaul from Italy proper. This was all Caesar needed to make his move. On 11 January he led *legio XIII* across the shallow waterway, declaring *alea iacta est* (the die is cast) after a famous quote by the Athenian playwright Menander. Once over the waterway he then led the legion south for Rome at lightning speed. This was a clear act of war, with the *optimates* and *populares* once more set to come to blows after over a decade of relative peace (Plutarch, *Lives*, Julius Caesar, 45).

When Pompey received word of Caesar's lightning strike he fled Rome and headed south as fast as possible to the port of Brindisi (Roman *Brundisium*) on the Adriatic Sea. While his army heavily outnumbered Caesar's single legion, he believed some of his own troops would side with the *populares* when their champion arrived (Matyszak, 2003, 207). He knew that his most loyal veterans were in Greece so headed there. Caesar pursued and almost caught Pompey and his troops, but they just escaped. He now returned to Rome, facing down any *optimates*' opposition. Caesar was ever a pragmatic strategist and knew he would have to secure his rear before he chased Pompey across the Adriatic. The latter also had a strong power base in Spain where he remained proconsul, including seven legions. Caesar now targeted these in a rapid offensive that lasted until August 49 BC.

To ensure surprise he marched his legions day and night through Transalpine Gaul, taking only twenty-seven days to reach the Pyrenees. Speed was of the essence and he allowed nothing to stand in his way. When he reached the key city of Marseille (Roman *Massilia*) it rebelled under the leading Pompeian Lucius Domitius Ahenobarbus. Caesar marched straight past, leaving behind two of his *legates* with allied troops to besiege the port. He then sent three legions ahead of his main column under the *legate* Fabius to seize the Pyrenean mountain passes from Pompey's troops. This ensured a swift entry into Hispania Citerior where he re-formed the army and headed south.

Most of the Pompeian legions chose to make a stand on a hill near Lleida (Roman *Ilerda*) in north-eastern Catelonia, led by the *legates* Marcus Petreius and Lucianus Afrianus. When Caesar arrived he initially declined battle, halting short of the hill and deploying his first two lines in case of a surprise attack. He then deployed his third line out of sight of the Pompeians, they digging a deep 5m-wide ditch behind which he withdrew the first two lines after nightfall. He then kept his troops under arms overnight to guard against a surprise attack, the following day turning the ditch into a substantial fortified camp.

Caesar now scouted the wider area and found another hill between that occupied by Petreius and Afrianus and the town. He realised that if he occupied it he would block the Pompeian army from their lines of supply. He sent a swift detachment towards the new hill, with the Pompeian's countering with their own column. The latter, comprised of skirmishers, arrived first and used their missile weapons to drive off Caesar's initial force. However, the Pompeians then pursued too far and were caught be Caesar's *legio IX* which routed them and drove them to the walls of Lleida. Now Caesar's legionaries pursued too far and were in turn counter-attacked as they occupied yet another hill, this time beneath the town walls. Here a general meeting engagement developed with the Caesarians at a disadvantage due to terrain that allowed the Pompeians to feed in greater troop numbers. However, *legio IX* and the various detachments sent in to support them fought bravely, holding their ground for five hours. The Pompeian legionaries eventually tired. Sensing this, Caesar ordered his troops to charge with drawn swords, breaking the *optimates'* army. The survivors fled back to the town and their own camp.

A protracted stand-off followed through the spring, the Pompeians staying behind the town walls and in camp, with Caesar's troops remaining in their own camp. The latter, on lower terrain, particularly suffered from mountain-stream seasonal flooding. Once the weather improved, however, Caesar again formed up and offered battle. This time the Pompeians chose to withdraw, aiming to join up with another Republican force under Marcus Terentius Varro. Caesar again responded swiftly, overtaking their rearguard and forcing the retreating army to build another marching camp. Caesar then moved to their rear aiming to block their line of retreat. This forced the Pompeians to return to Lleida. Caesar now surrounded the town and began a full siege, his intelligence sources reporting that morale among the opposing legionaries was poor. Finally, on 2 August, the five Pompeian legions there surrendered. Caesar kept up the campaign momentum; now marching south into Hispania Ulterior where he had earlier raised his elite *legio X* while proconsul. His old province immediately submitted and Pompey's final two legions in Spain surrendered. The campaign was over. Leaving four legions in Spain to deter any future revolt, Caesar now turned his attention to Pompey in Greece (Goldsworthy, 2006, 401).

Greece and Egypt

There the *optimates'* champion had made Veria (ancient Greek *Beroea*) in Thessaly his headquarters, mustering nine legions and many allied troops. Back in Italy Caesar appointed Mark Antony to control the Senate and began to gather an invasion force.

Pompey got word of his plans and moved his legions to the western coast of Greece to counter any landing. When nothing happened by the end of the campaigning season he moved his troops into winter quarters. However, on 4 January 48 BC Caesar surprised all by mustering all the troops he had to make a surprise winter crossing of the Adriatic, even leaving his baggage train behind to save time. They avoided Pompey's Corfu-based fleet and landed without incident at Palasë (ancient Greek *Palaeste*) in Illyria. To draw Pompey's army out of their winter camps Caesar then began sacking the nearby cities that were nominally under Pompey's protection. The tactic worked and the Republican army moved to intercept Caesar, the two armies then facing off either side of the River Apsus. There they remained for four months, waiting for the campaigning season to begin.

In April Mark Antony arrived with reinforcements, boosting the number of Caesar's legions to eleven. These included his own and those which had come over to the *populares'* side in Italy. The two forces now broke camp, Pompey heading back to Thessaly and Caesar following. There they faced off again at Asparagium. Despite still outnumbering Caesar, many of whose legions were understrength and whose legionaries had been forced to make bread using local grasses (Matyszak, 2003, 207), Pompey still refused to engage in battle, confident that he could interdict Caesar's lines of supply. Pompey then moved on once more, this time back to the west coast at Dyrrachium. Caesar now began an audacious project to build an enclosing wall around Pompey's camp, aiming to box it in against the sea. Quickly realising the danger Pompey countered, sallying out with his troops, forcing Caesar to retreat. The Republican leader then established a new camp south of Caesar's siege lines, threatening his rear in a move which Sabin says was beginning to resemble an engineering contest (2006, 215). However, on 9 July when Pompey's forces were split between Dyrrachium and the new camp, Caesar attacked the former. Pompey was forced to send five of his legions to rescue the trapped troops. Both sides suffered heavy losses, particularly Caesar, though the action proved indecisive (2006, 414).

Caesar now abandoned his blockade and withdrew to the south, concerned at the increasing disparity in numbers as Pompey continued to receive reinforcements from his allies in Anatolia and the east. Pompey's cavalry pursued the withdrawal but Caesar escaped towards the east coast. On the way he set up camp on the north bank of the River Enipeus between Pharsalus and Palaepharsalus in central Greece. Pompey followed, setting up his own camp a kilometre to the west. For this the latter chose a range of low hills that provided a good strategic position and ensured a safe route for supplies to reach him from the coast. The two armies again faced off, with battle soon joined and Caesar winning a career-defining (at least to that date) victory of epic proportions. Today this decisive engagement is known as the Battle of Pharsalus and is fully detailed in Chapter 8.

Caesar was relentless in his pursuit of Pompey's army after his victory, wiping out his camp and then chasing what was left of his legions to a nearby hill called the Kaloyiros. This he besieged, and eventually Pompey's leaderless troops surrendered. Caesar claimed to have killed 15,000 of Pompey's soldiers, while losing only 1,200 himself. Pompey never recovered, fleeing to Egypt to seek sanctuary with the Ptolemaic boy co-regent Ptolemy XIII Theos Philopator who had been his supporter. To his great surprise, when he landed in the Egyptian capital of Alexandria he was summarily beheaded.

Back in Greece, unaware of his great rival's demise, Caesar promptly set sail for Egypt with a small squadron seeking to capture Pompey. There, the Ptolemaic dynasty continued its rule, with the young Ptolemy and Cleopatra VII joint rulers following the death of their father Ptolemy XII Auletes. Both had their own armies and strove to be sole ruler, with the former now in poll position given his links with Pompey. However, it was also Ptolemy who had ordered Pompey's execution as he had arrived fleeing Caesar. This had been at the suggestion of his guardian and key advisor, the eunuch Pothinus. The latter had received news of the outcome of Pharsalus before Pompey's arrival and thought the beheading would endear Ptolemy to Caesar.

The boy now sailed out to meet Caesar, presenting him with the severed head of his great rival aboard the Roman flagship. However, if he and Pothinus were expecting gratitude they were rudely awakened. Caesar was incandescent, demanding to know why a minor Hellenistic despot thought it fitting to murder one of the leading men of Rome. Caesar repaid the affront by announcing he would enact the will of Ptolemy XII. This would be to the detriment of Ptolemy XIII and Pothinus as it reinforced the co-regency with Cleopatra. Pothinus realised this and stirred up the mob in Alexandria against the Romans to deter Caesar from landing ashore. Caesar typically ignored them and arrived on the harbour front with a small force of legionaries which formed into a column and headed directly to the Palace. There he confronted both co-regents, insisting they disband their armies and reminding them they owed him money. This was the better part of 10 million *denarii* promised to Caesar by Ptolemy XII a decade earlier when Caesar was beginning his wars in Gaul. Pothinus kept his counsel here but afterwards quietly engaged with Achillas, commander of the main Ptolemaic army, to prepare for action against the Romans. Meanwhile, because of the fate of Pompey, Caesar now began to favour Cleopatra who moved ahead of her younger brother in the regency pecking order. Shortly afterwards the two became lovers.

Matters now quickly came to a head. When Ptolemy arrived for a meeting with Caesar he found Cleopatra with him. He promptly stormed out and ordered Pothinus to again raise the Alexandrian mob, this time against not only the Romans but also his sister. Caesar used his famous skills in rhetoric to calm the crowd, reading out the will of the dead king, announcing yet again that Ptolemy XIII and Cleopatra would be co-regents, and adding that Rhodes would be returned to Egyptian rule by the Romans. He knew the latter would make him even more unpopular with the *optimates* back in Rome, but correctly judged it would help win over the Alexandrians.

A banquet was now arranged to celebrate the newly founded, Roman sponsored peace between brother and sister. However, during the dinner Caesar received word that Pothinus and Achillas were plotting against himself and Cleopatra. The eunuch was executed there and then, though the latter escaped and rallied Ptolemy's army and the Alexandrian city guard who surrounded the palace. So began the Alexandrian War (Goldsworthy, 2006, 440).

Caesar, with only the force of legionaries he had landed with, decided to fortify the palace and a siege began. Inside he held not only Cleopatra but also Ptolemy XIII and their younger sister Arsinoe. He had more troops still aboard ship just outside the harbour with his fast squadron, but these would not be enough to mount a rescue if Achillas ordered the palace to be stormed. However, he also knew that a much larger force with much of his army was following his own rapid crossing, and would be there soon. He also knew that Achillas, an experienced commander, would attempt to stop this new force arriving. Caesar acted first, ordering the burning of the

Ptolemaic fleet in the harbour. This set fire to some nearby warehouses and in the confusion Arsinoe fled, joining Achillas who now declared her to be the new queen. They quickly fell out, however, and Achillas was beheaded, to be replaced by Ganymedes, another court eunuch and her former tutor.

Ganymedes now ordered that the water supply to the palace be poisoned in the hope of forcing Caesar and Cleopatra's surrender. The queen countered by having new wells cut. Caesar then released Ptolemy, hoping it would destabilize the relationship between Arsinoe and Ganymedes. It had the opposite effect, revitalising the anti-Cleopatra faction just at the point when their campaign was beginning to slow. At this point, when all seemed lost for Caesar and Cleopatra, she revealed to him that she was pregnant by him.

Then, at the last minute, all was saved when Caesar's main reinforcements arrived. They landed on the causeway linking the famous lighthouse in Alexandria to the harbour and a fierce battle took place there. Another Roman force then landed south of Alexandria and Ptolemy now turned his forces about and headed off to meet this. Caesar, having joined his legionaries on the harbour front in Alexandria, pursued them vigorously and the Ptolemaic army was caught in a pincer movement. In short order it was defeated with heavy losses, with Ptolemy himself drowning in the Nile. Caesar returned to Alexandria with the body to be met by Cleopatra, where another younger brother was proclaimed her new co-regent as Ptolemy XIV. To celebrate their victory Caesar and Cleopatra then carried out a triumphal voyage up the Nile with 400 vessels.

When they returned to Alexandria, no doubt Caesar took time to view the body of his hero Alexander the Great in its *Soma* mausoleum. He then began planning his return to Rome. There, despite being the last man standing in the most recent contest of late Republican warlords, he remained highly unpopular with the *optimates* who criticized his reticence to incorporate Egypt as a new Roman province, and the length of time he was staying there.

First though he had two more matters to deal with in the east. In the first instance he travelled to Judea where he thanked the Jewish allies who had supported him during the Alexandrian War. Then he received word that the new Bosporan king, Pharnaces II son of Mithridates, had used the distraction of the Alexandrian War to invade Anatolia. Caesar knew the last thing the Romans wanted was another Mithridatic War and rushed north where he crushed the Pontic forces. In his own words to the Senate after his victory he came, saw and conquered (*veni, vidi, vici*).

Now well into 47 BC, Caesar was at last free to turn his full attention to Rome (Matyszak, 2003, 206). He arrived back in Italy in September, leaving three veteran legions to protect Cleopatra and bringing back Arsinoe with him as a prisoner. As promised, he also gave Cyprus back to Egypt, which made him even more unpopular with the *optimates*. He was now dictator again, having already been appointed twice in his absence, and quickly appointed Mark Antony as his official deputy with the title Master of Horse. The latter had returned to Italy soon after Pharsalus and had been the effective ruler in Rome on Caesar's behalf since 47 BC. However, he lacked Caesar's leadership skills and was soon facing the twin threat of rebellious Caesarian legionaries awaiting their discharge gratuities after the civil war, and rioting in Rome by disgruntled *optimates*.

Rome and Africa

Caesar's arrival in the Republican capital at the beginning of October was well timed and the dictator soon restored order, though the mutinous soldiers were a different matter. They were still demanding their release from service so Caesar set out to address them directly. Here he listened to their grievances and then, calling them citizens rather than comrades as he had so many times before, dismissed them out of hand promising they would receive their promised rewards in good time. This shocked them and most begged to be returned to service which Caesar, with mock reluctance, agreed to.

He now moved against the last bastion of Pompeian supporters, led by Cato, who had fled to the province of Africa. As usual he moved quickly, ordering the six legions and 2,000 allied cavalrymen of his army to take only the most essential baggage. They set sail from Sicily on 25 December, though the fleet became scattered on the journey and when he landed near the enemy-held port of Hadrumentum south of Carthage he only had 3,500 legionaries and 150 cavalry with him. He demanded the town surrender but when ignored moved on, keen to seek out a meeting engagement to bring this new phase of civil war to a rapid end.

First he seized the ports of Ruspina and Little Leptis to allow the rest of his army to arrive. Within days he had three full legions ready for operations and marched them inland to gather supplies. While out foraging this column was ambushed by the Pompeian commander Labienus with a force of local light troops, including the famous Numidian skirmishing cavalry renowned for their skill with the javelin and for hamstringing fleeing opponents. Soon Caesar was surrounded and further Pompeian troops arrived under Marcus Petreius, Gnaeus Calpurnius Piso, Quintus Caecilius Metellus Scipio and the Numidian king Juba I. Eventually Caesar was able to extricate his force with great skill, but only after suffering heavily casualties. He knew he was lucky not to have been annihilated, and returned to Ruspina to begin training new recruits to replace those fallen in battle. He was still outnumbered by the *optimates*, however, and chose to remain in place until further reinforcements arrived in the form of his veteran *legios* XIII and XIV, 800 more allied cavalry and 1,000 skirmishing archers. The balance of power was further tipped towards parity when Juba had to return to Numidia to fend off a *populares*' inspired Mauretanian invasion.

In early Spring Caesar moved on to the offensive once more, advancing out of Ruspina. However, the Pompeian forces now led solely by Scipio declined battle. Caesar pressed on, now joined by two more legions including his elite *legio X*, and set up camp at Uzita. Again the Pompeians avoided battle so he pressed on south-east to Aggar. There he was joined by more reinforcements and decided now was the time to force the enemy to battle. He knew he needed level ground with defended flanks to negate the *optimates*' particular strength in Numidian elephants and cavalry. Scouting ahead he found that the nearby port city of Thapsus was an ideal location, and there battle was joined on 6 April. Once more Caesar was victorious after a hard fight (see Chapter 8 for full detail), with Thapsus falling soon afterwards and the Pompeian cause in Africa lost. Pompey's two sons Gnaeus Pompeius and Sextus Pompeius fled to Spain where opposition to Caesar was again emerging. However, Cato, Scipio and Juba took their own lives. Caesar then annexed Numidia and returned to Rome, victorious once more.

Triumphs and Spain

Caesar arrived back in Rome in July 46 BC to huge acclamation, being awarded no less than four triumphs in one go for his exploits in Gaul, Egypt, Asia, and over Juba in Africa (the leading role of the Pompeians in the last campaign was glossed over). The celebrations were enormous in scale and lasted from 21 September through to 2 October. During these celebrations various parades took place in which his famous captives, including Arsinoe, Juba's infant son and the once mighty Vercingetorix, were forced to participate. The latter was brutally strangled to death at the end of the Gallic parade in the traditional Roman way, though Arsinoe and the baby were spared during their parades. The canny Caesar also remembered to reward his legionaries for their loyalty, with Plutarch (*Lives*, Julius Caesar, 55) saying he gave them generous rewards. Caesar's celebrations made him wildly popular with the popular classes in Rome, the only jarring note being shock on the part of some at the sheer scale of bloodshed during the gladiator contests held in honour of his deceased daughter Julia. A particular complaint was that he continued to carry out his daily work as dictator while watching the shows.

In late 46 BC Caesar's popularity was seriously put to the test when Cleopatra and her co-regent Ptolemy XIV visited Rome. She had already given birth to their son in June 47 BC, who she named Ptolemy XV Caesarion and announced as her heir. The visit was treated as royal in every sense. Scandalously she was even installed in Caesar's fine new home on the Janiculum Hill, this despite the fact that Caesar was still married to Calpurnia, and welcomed as a friend and ally of the Roman people. Cleopatra was soon widely acknowledged as his mistress. In Caesar's villa she hosted a number of symposia for the great and the good of Rome.

Caesar raised more eyebrows by next building a temple to his 'ancestor' Venus Genetrix to celebrate his victory over Pompey. This included a statue of Alexander the Great's horse Bucephalus outside, a clear statement of ambition on Caesar's part. However, it was what he installed inside that proved even more controversial, namely a statue of Cleopatra in the form of Isis, immediately next to the statue of Venus. This was very un-Roman, troubling even his most ardent *populares* supporters. He also began placing statues of himself across Rome, one of them specifically linking himself to Alexander.

Caesar also started a building programme in Rome at this time, favouring a Graeco-Egyptian style. This included a new grand temple in the *Forum Romanum*. It was also now that he created the new Julian calendar in his role as *Pontifex Maximus*, almost certainly with the help of Cleopatra's astronomers. With its 365 days and leap years, it was to remain the standard calendar in the western world until superseded by the Gregorian calendar in 1582. After his death the Senate voted that the month of his birth should be named after him, today's July (Matyszak, 208, 2003).

Next Caesar started appointing a large number of new Senators given the legislative body had been severely depleted by the civil wars. From this point onwards it would have a big *populares* majority among a membership of over 900. He then had a piece of legislation passed which time limited a proconsul's period in office to ensure a provincial governor did not have time to create a powerbase with which to oppose him in future. He also gave himself the title of Prefect of the Morals, allowing him to wield censorial powers which meant that no magistrate could challenge him in court on matters relating to public morality and the public finances. Coins were also struck in his name and with his likeness, and he was given the power to speak first in the Senate. He also rewarded the supporters he had been unable to elevate to the Senate by increasing the number of magistrates. Finally in this burst of administrative reform, he set in train the reorganization of the whole of the territory of the Republic and its provinces into the single integrated unit that would eventually emerge in the reign of Augustus as the Roman Empire.

With matters well in hand in Rome, in late November 46 BC Caesar moved to address the final Pompeian bastion in Spain. There two legions in Hispania Ulterior had declared for Gnaeus Pompeius and Sextus Pompeius earlier in the year and had driven out Caesar's proconsul. The brothers then arrived there with the remains of the *optimates*' army from Africa, along with the *legate* Labienus who had caused Caesar so much trouble at the beginning of the war in Africa. They raised one more legion from the African troops and locals and now set about securing the province, with Caesar's generals Quintus Fabius Maximus and Quintus Pedius looking on and refusing to risk battle.

Caesar decided to intervene in person, knowing that if he dealt with Pompey's sons the *optimates*' cause should be lost for good. Taking two veteran legions with him, X *Equestris* and V *Alaudae* (the latter originally raised from Gallic natives during his later conquest of Gaul campaigns), together with the less experienced III *Gallica* and VI *Ferrata*, he marched 2,400km in less than a month, arriving in the campaigning theatre in late December.

Caesar was able to stop any further *optimates* expansion in the province, but the Pompeius brothers and Labienus avoided a meeting engagement, just as Scipio had in Africa. However, after a number of skirmishes their legionaries started to desert and they realised they had to engage now or all was lost. The ensuing engagement, the Battle of Munda, was Caesar's last and one of his most hard fought. Fully detailed in Chapter 8, once more he won through, again fighting in the front rank where combat was at its most dangerous. His victory here was total, with Labienus falling and the Pompeius brothers again fleeing. Gnaeus was later captured in a small engagement at the town of Lauro and executed, while Sextus survived, much later causing a rebellion in Sicily. There he was defeated by Marcus

Agrippa, and later executed by Mark Antony in Asia in 35 BC. Back in Spain, after the battle Caesar left Maximus to invest Munda and moved to restore the wider province, dealing severely with any surviving *optimates*.

Caesar then returned to Rome again, where he was once more greeted as the victor. However, now for the first time he seriously overplayed his hand, with Plutarch saying (*Lives*, Julius Caesar, 56):

> [T]he triumph he celebrated (after Munda)...displeased the Romans more than any other. For he had not defeated foreign generals or barbarian kings, but had destroyed the sons and family of one of the greatest men of Rome, who had met with misfortune, and it was not proper for him to lead a procession of celebration of the calamities of his country, rejoicing in things for which no other defence could be made to Gods or men than that they had been done out of necessity.

However, Caesar carried on with his pro-*populares* reforms regardless, continuing to take steps to ensure he remained in power as long as he wanted to, and on his own terms. He had already stepped down as the sole consul in October 45 BC to make ready for the Spanish campaign, making sure two supporters would be elected to replace him for the remainder of the year. Though in theory this restored the joint-consulship as the primary political executive in the Republic, he remained dictator. In effect, the consuls and Senate could therefore only act on his say so. Then in February 44 BC he was appointed dictator for life, which made him an absolute monarch in all but name. He then passed a law allowing him to appoint all magistrates in 43 BC, and consuls and tribunes in 42 BC. This was draconian indeed, though the context was to secure his political 'rear' for his next foreign campaign. Never one to rest on his considerable laurels, this was to be an invasion of the mighty Parthian empire in the east, the nemesis of his one-time triumvir colleague Crassus. For this Caesar planned to take an enormous force of 16 legions and 10,000 allied cavalry.

For many in Rome, despite the excesses of his triumphs and favouring of Cleopatra, Caesar's time as dictator was a prosperous one. Unlike the civil strife that marred the era of Marius and Sulla, most of the civil war campaigning in Caesar's time was abroad in Macedonia, Greece, Africa and Spain. There is also no doubt that the Roman popular classes loved a winner, particularly one who so overtly championed the *populares*' cause. However, Caesar's ascension to a position of absolute authority over the political classes in Rome was jarring to many of the Capital's leading Senators and equestrians. This was particularly the case with regard to the *optimates*, most of whose leaders had already perished or were in exile. Caesar's recent Pompeian triumph only exacerbated the issue. The Roman nobility were very proud of their forebears having thrown off the fetters of the monarchy of Tarquin the Proud in 509 BC. Many felt it was time to do so again.

Assassination

Plotting to assassinate Caesar began while he was away in Spain. His subsequent triumph, and being made dictator for life, then acted as the twin catalysts that finally drove his enemies, and even some former supporters, to act. The conspiracy featured more than sixty Senators and was led by Gaius Cassius Longinus (best known to posterity as Cassius), Decimus Junius Brutus Albinus and Marcus Junius Brutus (best known as Brutus). The group styled themselves Liberators and aimed to restore normal consular-led Senatorial governance to the Republic. After considering a number of plans of action, they decided to kill Caesar in the Senate itself where they could hide daggers under their heavy togas.

Opportunity soon presented itself. On the Ides of March (15th of March) 44 BC the dictator was set to preside over a session of the Senate. At the time this was being held in the *Curia* of Pompey within the larger Theatre of Pompey, given Caesar was having a new Senate house built to replace the previous *Curia Hostilia* which had burned down in 53 BC. Caesar is said to have been given a number of warnings about his impending demise, including by Calpurnia following a bad dream, his doctors who warned him of his ill health, and by religious sacrifices that had produced bad omens, including the famous one immortalized by Shakespeare regarding the Ides of March. However, he chose to ignore them and set off as normal.

While Caesar was travelling Mark Antony tried to intercept him, having heard in the night that an attack on Caesar was being planned. However, the plotters had planned for this and when he arrived at the steps of Pompey's Theatre one of the Liberators, either Brutus Albinus or Caesar's former *legate* Gaius Trebonius, detained him long enough for the deed to be carried out.

Plutarch (*Lives*, Julius Caesar, 60) says that when Caesar entered the Senate chamber the members rose out of respect for him. Then, as he sat, some of the conspirators fanned out behind his chair, while others approached to support the supposed petition of their fellow plotter Tillius Cimber to allow his exiled brother to be recalled to Rome. He rebuffed them, suspecting nothing, but then Cimber pulled Caesar's toga down by the neck. This was the signal to strike, with Publius Servilius Casca Longus, the Tribune of the People, stabbing him in the neck first. This was a non-mortal blow and, after a shocked pause, the other conspirators joined in. He was allegedly stabbed twenty-three times and even though he tried to get away there was no escape, he was eventually blinded by his own blood. Even if he had managed to fight his way out it would have been to no avail according to Suetonius who says the surgeon Antistius in his autopsy declared the second wound, to his chest, was ultimately the fatal one (*The Twelve Caesars*, Julius Caesar, 82). Caesar's last act was to pull his toga over his head when he saw Brutus among the assassins (Putarch, *Lives*, Julius Caesar, 66).

Immediately after the murder Brutus moved forward to say something, but his fellow conspirators panicked and fled. When some of them arrived in the *Forum Romanum* they proclaimed Rome to be free of a tyrannical monarch once more. However, they were met with a shocked silence by the crowd and knew immediately how badly they had judged the popular mood. Meanwhile, Mark Antony had fled the Theatre of Pompey as soon as he had heard the commotion inside. He stayed in hiding for a short while, before emerging to take centre stage in all that followed. Caesar's body was left where it fell for three hours until magistrates arrived to organise its removal. A few days later it was cremated in the *Forum Romanum* after Mark Antony's famous funeral oration from the *rostra*. The Liberators may have thought their deed had saved the Republic. Instead, it initiated its demise.

Chapter 7

The Republican Roman Army

Julius Caesar was a first class military leader who owed his success in both civilian and military life to the loyalty of the legions he led. Their actions under his command defined his career, for example when leading *legio XIII* across the Rubicon River on his way to Rome in 49 BC in defiance of the political classes of Rome. The exploits of his soldiers enthralled people across the Republic, with his *legio X equestris* being the most famous military unit of his day. Whether in his campaigns of conquest or in civil wars, Caesar was never shy in raising new legions, the troops often carrying his bull symbols on their shields. In times of crisis he even raised legions from non-Romanized natives, for example *legio V Alaudae* in Gaul in 52 BC. Yet the story of how these warriors became the elite soldiers of the ancient world is far from straightforward (Elliott, 2020b, 53). In this chapter I first trace the development of the legionary from before the time of the Republic, examining how their equipment evolved to that used by Caesar's legionaries. I then look at how Caesar led his legions on campaign, before finally considering the warrior's life experiences. This will give the reader insight into how Caesar was able to attract such intense loyalty from his troops, thus enabling his success as a political and military leader.

Evolution of the Caesarian Legionary

The first insight we have into Roman military tradition comes from a time when the city was under Etruscan rule before the days of the Republic. This Etrusco-Roman army adopted the Greek-style hoplite phalanx as its main line-of-battle formation. This was introduced to the region when the Etruscans met the Greek colonies of southern Italy and eastern Sicily. As detailed in Chapter 3, the term phalanx references a deep formation of armoured spearmen whose front ranks fought with their *doru* long spears (usually) in an overarm thrusting position, with each front rank warrior protected by interlocking large round *aspis* body shields.

The Etrusco-Roman phalanx was supported on its flanks by Roman/ Latin troops who still fought in a loose formation as did their Villanovan ancestors. Common weapons for these troops were spears, axes and javelins (Connolly, 1989, 136). This way of fighting, with a solid phalanx of hoplites in the centre and lighter troops either side, was formalized by Servius Tullius, the first of the great reforming Roman military leaders. He instituted the Servian Constitution in the mid-sixth century BC which divided Roman society into seven different classes. Each had a different military commitment to the Roman state based on wealth. The classes were:

- The *equites*, the wealthiest citizens who could afford a mount and thus formed the cavalry.
- The First Class, the next wealthiest forming eighty centuries of hoplite-equipped spearmen fighting as a phalanx. Most troops here would have been of Etruscan origin.
- The Second Class, twenty centuries of spearmen with helmet, greaves and the *scutum* rectangular shield.
- The Third Class, twenty centuries of spearmen with helmet and *scutum*.
- The Fourth Class, twenty centuries of spearmen with *scutum* only.
- The Fifth Class, twenty centuries of missile troops with slings and javelins.
- The *capite censi*, this translating as head count and referencing those in Etrusco-Roman society with little or no property. This class had no military commitment.

This system was put to the supreme test in conflict with the Senones Gauls when, at the Battle of Allia in 390 BC, it catastrophically failed. The Romans were not only defeated, but nearby Rome sacked soon after. In short order the Tullian system was dumped in favour of the much more flexible manipular system introduced by Marcus Furius Camillus. This initially featured two legions, each commanded by a consul, with six *tribuni militum* subordinates serving beneath him (Connolly, 1989, 136). These new legions numbered 3,000 men each, though this quickly increased to 6,000 over time. Within the Camillan legion there were three classes of line-of-battle troops, all called for the first time legionaries. Their classification was based on experience and age rather than wealth. The specific classes were the *triarii*, *principes* and *hastati*. The first were veterans wearing helmet and body armour and carrying the new *scutum* full body shield. They were armed with the *hasta* thrusting spear (the direct equivalent of the hoplite *doru*), featuring a socketed iron spearhead up to 30cm in length and a bronze butt-spike, the latter acting as a counterweight to the spearhead. Each also carried a sword. They replaced, in part, the old Tullian First Class. Meanwhile, the *principes* were older warriors, also wearing helmet and body armour and carrying the *scutum*. Initially armed with the *hasta*, they replaced these with *pila* heavy throwing javelins of Etruscan origin (though some think Spanish) as the Republic progressed. The latter were javelins with a barbed head and a long iron shank, a lead weight sitting behind the latter in the socket where it joined the wooden shaft of the weapon. This combination gave the *pilum* tremendous penetrating power, with the shank designed to bend on impact so that even a simple hit on a shield would make the latter's use impossible. Each legionary carried two, one lighter and one heavier, the first thrown at range and the latter immediately prior to impact before swords were drawn. The *principes* also replaced, in part, the old Tullian First Class. Finally came the *hastati*, 'the flower of young men'. Again equipped with helmet though with less body armour, they too carried the *scutum*, initially the *hasta* and later *pila*, together with sword. They replaced the old Tullian Second Class.

The Camillan legion was completed with three lesser classes of warrior. These were the *rorarii*, *accensi* and *leves* who replaced, sequentially, the old Tullian Third, Fourth and Fifth classes. They were support troops rather than line-of-battle troops and became less important as the Republic progressed.

The *triarii*, *principes* and *hastati* all formed up in a looser formation than the old Tullian phalanx. This allowed free use of the sword and *scutum* body shield, something impossible in the dense phalanxes of old. This change was directly related to the height of the Gallic warriors faced at Allia and later by the legions of Rome, and their fighting technique. The Gauls were taller than their Roman counterparts and fought with long iron swords, utilizing a downward slashing technique. This rendered the Tullian First Class hoplite's *aspis*, designed to defend the user and his neighbours from frontal attack, less practical (Elliott, 2018, 30). The new *scutum*, thought to be of Samnite origin, was used in a much more proactive way. It could be pushed forward offensively or raised to take the blow from an opponent's sword. The veteran *triarii* with their *hasta* did retain the ability to deploy in a dense formation if needed. They were traditionally held back in reserve (often kneeling on their right knee), and could form a hedge of spears against mounted opponents or to cover a retreat.

The original Camillan legionary *scutum* was a large curved rectangle, up to 120cm in length and 75cm in width. Made from planed wooden strips that were laminated together in three layers, the shield featured an *umbones* iron boss attached to the centre where the shield was slightly thicker. It was completed by fitting a calf-skin/felt facing. The legionary *scutum* was very heavy and could weigh up to 10kg, being held by a horizontal grip using a straightened arm.

For body armour Camillan legionaries of all three classes wore a square, round or triple disc bronze pectoral covering their heart and upper chest, often with a matching back plate. This was held in place with leather straps. As the Republic progressed, those who could afford it (usually *triarii* and *principes*) increasingly replaced these primitive pectorals with *lorica hamata* chainmail shirts. Of Gallic origin and weighing up to 15kg, these offered greatly improved protection, covering the torso from shoulder to hip. They were made from interlinked iron rings 1mm thick and up to 9 mm in external diameter, with up to 20,000 being needed for each shirt.

This Camillan legionary defensive panoply was completed with a helmet. Polybius (*The Rise of the Roman Empire*, 6.23.14) says these were made from bronze, fitting the cranium and providing good overall protection. Popular designs among the legionaries included those called Etrusco-Corinthian, Attic and Montefortino.

The principal weapon of the Camillan *principes* and *hastati*, and sidearm of the spear-armed *triarii*, was his sword, with all legionaries trained to fight with a particular fencing technique. This involved taking the blow of an opponent on the *scutum*, they then being dispatched with a swift upward or downward stabbing action to their exposed midriff or neck. Throughout much of the Camillan period such swords were comparatively simple leaf-shaped iron blades or the curved *kopis* detailed in Greek armies in Chapter 3.

The Camillan manipular legion deployed in the *acies triplex* formation of three lines, the first having fifteen maniples of *hastati* comprising sixty men and two officers. Each of these maniples had twenty *leves* attached to act as skirmishers. The second line comprised fifteen maniples of *principes*, again each of sixty men and two officers. The third line was formed by fifteen *ordines*, each *ordo* comprising a *vexilla* of *triarii*, a *vexilla* of *rorarii* and a *vexilla* of *accensi*. These *vexilla* numbered sixty warriors and two officers, with the *triarii* additionally having a standard-bearer.

A final innovation of Camillus would have been very popular with Caesar's later legionaries. This was because it was he who for the first time paid the legionaries for their service. This was in the context of the long siege of the Etruscan city of Veii, detailed in Chapter 4, which ended in 396 BC. This siege was of such length that the troopers (citizen soldiers at this time) were kept away from their normal work for lengthy periods of time. To compensate, Camillus introduced a legionary *stipendium* cash allowance.

The manipular legion further evolved into what historians call the Polybian system after Rome's conflict with Pyrrhus of Epirus and his Hellenistic army in the early third century BC. Polybius was the leading second-century BC Greek historian who narrated the story of Rome's conflicts in the third and second centuries BC. The Polybian legions were again deployed in the *acies triplex*, this time featuring 1,200 *hastati* in 10 maniples of 120. Next came 1,200 *principes* organised in the same way, and finally 600 *triarii* in 10 maniples of 60. Each of the maniples featured two centurions, two subordinates and two standard-bearers. The major change was the disappearance of the *leves*. These were later replaced by 1,200 *velites*, specialist skirmishers divided among the other maniples. Meanwhile, the *rorarii* and *accensi* also disappear at this time. The Polybian legion also featured a formal cavalry component, 300 strong and divided into 10 *turmae* of 30 troopers. These legions, used to such great effect in three Punic Wars, four Macedonian Wars and the Roman–Seleucid War, were highly efficient and adaptable, for example learning from their three defeats in Italy in the Second Punic War to ultimately beat Hannibal at the Battle of Zama in 202 BC and thus win the conflict.

The main weapon of the Polybian *principes* and *hastati*, and once more the sidearm of the *hasta*-armed *triarii*, was again the sword. However, by this time a true innovation had taken place with earlier designs replaced by the iconic *gladius Hispaniensis* whose use in the legions was ubiquitous by the mid-third century BC. It was to remain the standard legionary sword through to the time of Caesar and well into the Principate phase of Empire. As the name suggests, the *gladius* was of Spanish origin, and rather than being the short stabbing sword of popular legend, in the Polybian period it was instead a cut and thrust design up to 69cm long and 5cm in width. The *gladius* featured a tapering sharp stabbing point and was worn on the right-hand side unless by an officer who wore it on the left as a mark of differentiation. Many have questioned how a legionary could draw the weapon smoothly into an on-guard position from the right-hand side, especially as the pommel sat just below the armpit. However, in his detailed analysis of the weapon, Bishop (2016, 46) explains:

> In fact, the gladius can be easily drawn by inverting the right hand, thumb downwards, then grasping the handgrip and pulling straight upwards. It is a quite natural progression to continue this movement forwards to bring the sword down to the side, point forward, in the characteristic 'at the ready' position depicted on relief sculpture.

Those *gladii* used in the Polybian legions and later were also terror weapons in their own right, inflicting gaping injuries that shocked their opponents in the Second Macedonian War when its widespread use is first noted. This was because it lacked any blood runnels to let air into a wound. Therefore, the sword had to be viciously twisted to release it. Meanwhile, those Polybian legionaries who could afford it now also carried a *pugio* 30cm long dagger. The Polybian *principes* and *hastati* also carried two *pila* in the same manner as their Camillan forebears, one heavy and one light. Meanwhile, the *triarii* continued to use the *hasta* long thrusting spear.

For defensive equipment all three classes of Polybian legionary still carried the *scutum* shield, helmet, armour of some kind for the upper torso and often also the lower legs. The shield was the same as the earlier Camillan design, while more and more legionaries now wore the *lorica hamata* chainmail shirt. If the legionary could afford it, he also wore an iron or bronze greave on the leading left lower leg, both legs for the very well off. Meanwhile, a new innovation was with regard to the helmet. As the Republic progressed and the legionaries came into continued contact with the Gauls and later Galatians, two new types appeared. These were the Coolus design with a round cap of bronze and small neck guard, and the iron Port type with a deep neck guard. The latter developed into the classic 'Imperial' Gallic helmet often associated with the Principate Roman legionary of the first and second centuries AD. Etrusco-Corinthian, Attic and Montefortino designs continued to be used by the Polybian legionary, but most had disappeared by the beginning of the first century BC excepting the former as a design still often worn by officers (Elliott, 2020b, 60).

The final reform of the legions prior to Caesar's day were those carried out by Marius, he completely reorganizing the Roman military establishment in 107 BC following Rome's repeated humiliation in the early stages of the Cimbrian War. His aim was to turn each individual legion into a self-contained fighting force. To do this he standardised the legionary on the *gladius* and *pilum*-armed *principes* and *hastati* (these terms now being dropped), with the spear-armed *triarii* and javelin-armed *velites* disappearing entirely. From this point, all of the fighting men in the legion were simply called legionaries, numbering 4,800 out of a total 6,000 men in each legion. The remaining 1,200 troopers were support personnel who carried out a wide variety of roles that enabled the legion to function autonomously. Paternus (in extracts detailed in Justinian, *The Digest of Justinian*, 50.6.7) usefully details that these included ditch diggers, farriers, pilots, master builders, shipwrights, *ballista* makers, glaziers, arrow makers, bow makers, smiths, coppersmiths, helmet makers, wagon makers, roof-tile makers, water engineers, swordcutlers, trumpet makers, horn makers, plumbers, blacksmiths, masons, woodcutters, limeburners, charcoal burners, butchers, huntsmen, sacrificial animal keepers, grooms and tanners. Additionally, the specialist military personnel in the legions also included *agrimensor* land surveyors, *librator* land levellers and *mensor* quantity measurers (and in the case of the military building aqueducts *aqualegus* aqueduct inspectors). These legionaries were the supreme surveyors of the ancient world, putting the stamp of Rome in a very physical way everywhere they went. Highly skilled professionals, they used a number of tools, instruments, and techniques to plan the settlements, farmland, courses for roads and aqueducts and fortifications that were an everyday part of the experience of living within the Roman Empire. All such specialist legionaries were dubbed *immunes* – soldiers exempted from general duties because of their skills.

Marius also replaced the old Camillan and Polybian manipular system with centuries, each comprising eighty legionaries and twenty support staff, sub-divided into units of ten (eight legionaries and two non-combatants). Each century was commanded by a centurion, they having specific titles which reflected their seniority based on the old Camillan and Polybian manipular legions. The names, with seniority in ascending order, were:

- *hastatus posterior*
- *hastatus prior*
- *princeps posterior*
- *princeps prior*

- *pilus posterior*
- *pilus prior*.

The legionaries lived, fought and ate together, with each legion developing their own identity around the new *aquila* eagle standards introduced by Marius. Training was also regularized, with Marius insisting on frequent fitness drills to ensure the legionaries were always physically fit. This was to ensure the legionary could carry his own equipment on campaign, with the troops earning the nickname *muli mariani* (Marius' mules). One should perhaps envision the Marian legionary as having the same body shape as a 165cm tall modern Olympic weight lifter, square and all muscle. His training particularly focused on martial skills, based on the methods used to instruct gladiators. As an example, for sword drill a large stake the size of an opponent was set up in the training ground. The trooper then practised his *gladius*- and *scutum*-based fencing technique using a wooden replica sword and wicker shield, with the stake being 'the enemy'.

The main advantage of the new Marian legions was that they did not have to rely on long lines of supply given they were self-contained units with integral specialists. This allowed late Republican warlords like Caesar and Pompey to amalgamate a large number into huge armies owing their loyalty to a specific leader, especially when campaigning on the frontiers of the growing Republic well away from Rome. In such circumstances it became common for the various warlords to actually raise their own legions without the approval of the Senate, often using their own or supporter's money to finance them.

In terms of equipment, these Marian legionaries were all equipped in the same way, with *scutum*, *lorica hamata* chainmail hauberk, Coolus and Port type helmets, two *pila* javelins, the *gladius* sword and the *pugio* dagger. By doing away with differentially armed troop types within the legions, Marius therefore made them much easier to maintain in the field.

The standard deployment in battle for the Marian legions, including those of Caesar and Pompey, remained the *acies triplex* of the earlier manipular system. Under Caesar as with most seasoned Roman commanders, the first two were deployed to sequentially engage the enemy (second line units replacing the front line units as the latter tired), while the third acted as a reserve, just as the *triarii* had in the manipular legions. Caesar himself provides direct insight into this tactical approach, describing how when fighting the supporters of Pompey in Spain in 49 BC he deployed four cohorts of legionaries in his front line and three in the second and third.

A final short consideration here of the auxiliary troops who completed the military forces deployed by Caesar in his campaigns across the Republic and beyond. Their complement would have depended on whether the theatre of engagement was in the western or eastern Mediterranean, but could have included heavy Gallic, German, Spanish and Macedonian cavalry, light Numidian and Syrian cavalry, Gallic and Ligurian warriors, Hellenistic *thureophoroi* spearmen, Spanish, Illyrian and Thracian loose order foot, and skirmishing foot from Gaul, Germany, Spain, the Balearic isles, Numidia, Macedonia, Greece and Crete.

There is some debate about whether Caesar also used war elephants. These beasts of war had first been encountered by Rome when fighting Pyrrhus in the early third century BC, and later in the Punic Wars and when fighting the Hellenistic kingdoms and the Numidians (see Chapter 3 for full detail). African forest elephants were soon adopted by mid- and late-Republican Roman armies. The second-century AD Macedonian author Polyaenus (*Stratagems*, 8.23.5) records that 'Caesar' himself had one large elephant when campaigning in Britain, which he used to force a crossing over a large river, often identified as the River Thames. Caesar himself does not mention this, which I believe he would have given his obsession with prestige, and most historians do not give the reference any credit. Polyaenus was most likely either confusing his source material with Claudius' successful AD 43 invasion when elephants are certainly recorded arriving with the emperor prior to the submission of the regional British tribes engaged (these likely from the Imperial menagerie rather than war elephants), using 'Caesar' to directly refer to Claudius.

During his Thapsus campaign in North Africa in 46 BC Caesar did actually obtain elephants from Italy, using them to train his troops in how to engage the beasts. However, these are not thought to have been trained war elephants and may have been animals originally destined for the arena. Caesar subsequently captured Pompey's elephants after defeating him at Pharsalus in 48 BC, which had been supplied by the latter's Numidian ally Juba. These are last mentioned at the Battle of Mutina in 43 BC after Caesar's death. It is of course possible Caesar intended to take these elephants to Parthia with him where he next intended to campaign. However, as detailed in Chapter 3 war elephants were always a two-edged sword in the ancient world, difficult to control and expensive to maintain. Often a bigger threat to their own troops than the enemy, it seems likely that the pragmatic Caesar distrusted them and preferred to rely on his legionaries and supporting auxiliaries.

How Caesar Led his Legions

Caesar was a very shrewd political and military operator who knew that he could only achieve his personal ambitions if backed by loyal legions. His campaigns in Gaul from 58 to 50 BC, and later in the civil war against Pompey and his supporters from 49 to 45 BC, are excellent examples of this. Many of these legions were founded under his leadership, and went on to have long and successful histories of service well into the Principate Empire.

Caesar was particularly adept at accruing legions to ensure weight of numbers told in his favour. For example, when given the governorship in Gaul in 59 BC he inherited four legions. These were legions VII, VIII, IX and X, the latter effectively his own personal legion. This was because it was the first he had personally founded, in 61 BC when governor of Hispania Ulterior, as detailed in Chapter 6. At the time of Caesar's accession to the governorship of Gaul these four legions were deployed defensively in northern Italy in Cisapline Gaul. However, with destiny calling, Caesar immediately set his sights on conquering the remainder of Gaul in the name of Rome. He was keenly aware of the difficulty of the task and immediately began recruiting new legions before launching his first offensive north of the Alps in 58 BC. These new legionaries were most often Roman citizens recruited in Cisalpine Gaul. His first new foundings here were legions XI and XII in 58 BC, then *legio XIII* and *legio XIV* in 57 BC, *legio XIV* again in 53/52 BC after it had been destroyed, *legio XV* in 53/52 BC and finally the native Gallic *legio V Alaudae* and also *legio VI* in 52 BC (the whole process detailed in full in Chapter 6).

Caesar first shows an ability to concentrate his legions into a single striking force in these Gallic campaigns. For example, all eight of his then extant legions were involved when fighting the Belgic Nervii near the River Sambre in 57 BC. Caesar also made use of the tactical flexibility of the Marian legions during his Gallic campaigns. For example he only took legions VII and X to Britain during his first incursion in 55 BC, with the other six left in Gaul as a garrison. When he returned to Britain in 54 BC with a point to prove, he still only took five of his eight legions (see Chapter 8 for detail). In these Gallic campaigns the legions would have stayed in marching camps built at the end of every day's march when in enemy territory, later being dispersed among friendly (at least ostensibly) Gallic *oppida* during the winter months.

Caesar again showed his propensity for recruiting new legions, often against the wishes of the Senate, during his civil war with Pompey and his supporters. This began in 49 BC when he crossed the Rubicon River just south of Ravenna with *legio XIII Gemina*. The bold move disconcerted the political classes of Rome, and their champion Pompey fled to Greece. Caesar then set about building up his power base in Italy. He was already able to field legions V to XV, which he used to defeat Pompey's supporters in Spain in later 49 BC. He then made full use of his unchallenged access to the recruiting grounds of Italy. As consul in 48 BC he recruited legions I, II, III and IV. He then began extending the sequence past XV, possible up to *legio XXX*. This gave him an enormous number of troops to command, ultimately leading them to victory over Pompey in later 48 BC, and his supporters by 45 BC.

Talk of leadership brings us onto Caesar's personal relationship with his legionaries. In that regard he was a first-class leader of men, both at a strategic level when planning and effecting his campaigns, and tactically when fighting his battles. This reflected his skill as a communicator, naturally knowing how to engage subordinates of all levels to ensure victory. The most extreme form of this would be leading his men from the front at crucial times in the heat of battle, *scutum* raised and *gladius* in hand. As Suetonius explains (*The Twelve Caesars*, Julius Caesar, 62): 'If Caesar's troops gave ground he would often rally them in person, catching individual fugitives by the throat and forcing them round to face the enemy again.' He later adds (*The Twelve Caesars*, Julius Caesar, 67): 'He always addressed his soldiers not with "My men", but with "Comrades" ... which put them into a better humour.'

Caesar was certainly a man of the people, at least when it came to his soldiers, and this committed engagement paid dividends throughout his many years of campaigning when he was always able to rely on their dedication and devotion. As Plutarch (*Lives*, Julius Caesar, 16) explains:

> He could so count on the goodwill and zeal of his soldiers, that those who in other campaigns had been in no way superior to the rest were invincible and irresistible when facing any danger on behalf of Caesar's glory.

The Life of Caesar's Legionaries

Until the reforms of Marius, the Camillan and Polybian manipular legions were formed by a compulsory levy of Roman citizens who met a minimum wealth/property qualification. These formations were raised whenever necessary rather than being forces in being. Recruitment into their ranks was usually authorized by the Senate, with the legion later being disbanded once the need for its existence had passed.

A key aspect of Marius' reforms in 107 BC at the height of the Cimbrian War was to realise that, given Rome's by then widespread military responsibilities, this early Republican system was no longer sustainable. He determined standing units were required that could remain in existence for years or even decades, and thus were born the Marian legions. To man these he principally relied on volunteer recruits usually aged between 17 and 23, though some were as young as 13 or as old as 36. Additionally, in times of crisis, the number of legionaries was bolstered by conscription under a levy called the *dilectus*.

Each Marian legionary, whether recruit or conscript, signed up for a minimum term of six years. This length of service lasted until at least the Battle of Actium in 31 BC. Land was also offered to them upon their retirement, the veterans often settled in colonies. Caesar provides a good example, his retirees after the campaign in Greece against Pompey being settled at the Hellenistic city of Butrint (Roman *Buthrōtum*) in modern Albania.

Marius also abolished the property requirement to join the legions, and from that point the majority of recruits came from the landless lower classes. This was a shrewd move that increased the sense of identity within each individual legion, with the legionaries now increasingly 'other' when compared to the rest of society. At a stroke the warlords of the later Republic were therefore able to wield armies that owed more loyalty to them than to the Senate and people of Rome. Caesar also cannily ensured he promoted the senior officers in his existing legions to become the *legates* in new ones, and similarly experienced centurions to also become the new senior officers in his new foundings, both further ensuring the enduring loyalty of the new units.

Caesar was ever sensitive to the needs of his legionaries and set their pay at 225 denarii a year, a sure means of ensuring their loyalty given that this was a very good middle-class salary in the late Republic. It is unclear if his opponents immediately copied the move, but this amount became standard legionary pay through to the time of the Emperor Domitian in the late first century AD. Plutarch (*Lives*, Julius Caesar, 17) adds that Caesar was also adept at spreading the plunder from his campaigns among his troops.

He always went out of his way to ensure he did not appear to be amassing wealth for his own ends, even when trying to stay ahead of his many creditors.

Like all armies, Caesar's legions marched on their stomachs. Later the fourth century AD writer Vegetius (1996, 3.3) said in his military manual that troops should never be without corn, salt, wine and vinegar and that would certainly have been the case for Caesar's legions, with beans, bread, porridge, vegetables and eggs forming the core diet. Meat would be added on feast days, with the wider diet supplemented by local produce and hunting. On campaign, as Caesar's legions so often were, the daily staples were whole-wheat biscuits and hard tack, together with bread baked in the marching camp at the end of the day's march.

Religion was a key feature in the daily lives of Caesar's legionaries, playing a major role in their appreciation of belonging and belief. Roman society, within the military and without, was very conservative and in that regard each legionary was obliged to honour the Gods of the Roman pantheon, in particular the Capitoline triad of Jupiter, Juno and Minerva given their association with Rome. We can add to these Mars given he was the God of war. The worship of Gods associated with a given legion's place of origin, often a local deity assimilated into the Roman pantheon in some way, was also common.

For non-military kit all of Caesar's legionaries carried their equipment on a T-shaped pole resting on their shoulders when on the march, with the shield held in place across the back. Helmets were usually strung from the neck across the chest. The marching kit also included a *paenula* hooded, woollen bad-weather cloak made from thick wool that fastened with a button or toggles on the centre of the chest. The officers wore a shorter rectangular cloak called a *sagum* which fastened on the right shoulder with a brooch.

A very important piece of kit for the legionary, including Caesar himself when minded to march with his troops, were the hobnailed *caligae* sandals. Typically these featured a leather upper made from a single leather piece which was sewn at the heel. This was then stitched to a multiple-layer hide sole shod with many iron studs, each sandal weighing up to 1kg. Caesar's legionaries also carried a sturdy cross-braced satchel for their personal effects, a water skin in a net bag, a *patera* bronze mess tin, a cooking pot, canvas bags for grain rations, spare clothing, and bespoke engineering equipment.

This brings us onto the engineering prowess of Caesar's legionaries. In the first instance every Marian legion included 1,200 specialists within the overall complement of 6,000 as detailed above. It is these specialists who were able to facilitate Caesar's great engineering feats in the field, for example the bridges over the River Rhine and siege lines at Alesia, the latter fully detailed in Chapter 8.

Meanwhile, Caesar's legionaries themselves were skilled engineers in their own right, able to support the specialists in the legion with any task ordered. Each of the front line legionaries, as part of their personal engineering equipment, carried a saw, stake, chain, pickaxe, sickle, basket, and leather strap. Such construction and engineering work often involved backbreaking physical hard labour, and is a further example of the fitness of the soldiers of the Marian legions.

Chapter 8

On Campaign and In Battle: Caesar

Gaius Julius Caesar was the greatest warlord of the later Roman Republic. A renowned risk-taker, he often acted unpredictably, catching opponents off-guard time and again in war and politics. These traits are evident in all of his campaigns and battles, and in this final Chapter I choose five examples to show his martial prowess as a counterpoint to those earlier detailed for Alexander the Great. Given the latter's *anabasis* was in effect one long campaign ranging through the Achaemenid Persian Empire through to India, in Chapter 4 I considered five of Alexander's specific engagements. However, Caesar's military career was very different in that instead of one long major campaign, his life featured at least seven over a period of around twenty years. These included his early campaigns in Spain, his conquest of Gaul, the civil war campaign against Pompey in Macedonia and Greece, the Alexandrian War, his brief Pontic campaign, and finally the separate civil war campaigns in North Africa and Spain. Therefore there is no easily accessible narrative thread to allow us to follow the evolution of his military prowess given the very different nature of many of these conflicts. I have therefore decided to choose five examples that shed light on different aspects of his military leadership. These are his 55 BC and 54 BC invasions of Britain at the height of his Gallic conquests (detailed at length given the many leadership traits he displayed here), the winner-takes-all siege of Alesia in 52 BC, and then the civil war battles of Pharsalus in 48 BC, Thapsus in 46 BC and Munda in 45 BC.

Caesar's Invasions of Britain in 55 BC and 54 BC

Caesar's outlandish decision to invade mysterious Britain across terrifying *Oceanus* in 55 BC was, to that point, the most perilous decision in his military career. It was a move fraught with danger and great personal risk both to his life and reputation. He had already displayed the key traits as a leader that were to later define him. These included speed of thought and action, personal bravery, being a first class leader of men in battle, military skill at a strategic and tactical level, and grit and determination. Yet his decision to lead his troops to Britain was to test all of these to the absolute limit, in a move that Mattingly describes as 'treading a thin line between qualified success and outright disaster' (2006, 64). It is difficult to explain to a modern audience what an outlandish adventure he planned here. In the first instance his force would have to cross *Oceanus*, a sea frightful to contemporary audiences used to the comparatively benign Mediterranean. Then, once there he would be campaigning in a land of which the Romans knew little. This was truly a leap in the dark.

So why did he choose to invade Britain in the first place? There was still plenty of time in the campaigning season of 55 BC for Caesar to seek out new opponents on the continent, or even travel to his other province of Illyricum in the north-eastern Balkans. In the first instance, basic geography may have played a part. At this point, after three years of brutal campaigning and with hundreds of thousands of Gallic and German warriors dead, he (mistakenly as it turned out) believed Gaul and Germany pacified. Meanwhile, Illyricum was too far away for the next quick victory he craved. He therefore turned his attention to the nearest suitable target in his ongoing quest for wealth and glory, namely nearby Britain. Next, Caesar himself acknowledged that Britain remained a source of instability in Gaul, saying that (Julius Caesar, *The Conquest of Gaul*, 5.1) 'in almost all the Gallic campaigns the Gauls had received reinforcements from the Britons.'

The Cantiaci in Kent were only 33km across *Oceanus* from the nearest point of Gallia Belgica. Meanwhile, a number of other British tribes had direct links with their counterparts in Gaul, with some even sharing a name. Examples included the Parisii above the Humber, the Atrebates in the Thames valley and the Belgae on the south coast. Caesar himself confirms the latter, saying (*The Conquest of Gaul*, 5.2) 'The Suessiones (a Belgae tribe)…possessed huge tracts of very fertile territory… ruling not only much of Belgic territory but of Britain as well.'

The tribes in Britain were also increasingly taking in large numbers of refugees from Gaul, particularly tribal elites fleeing the predations of the Romans. These and their descendants continued to be a thorn in the side of Roman Gaul until the Claudian invasion of Britain in AD 43.

Additionally, thanks to the few pieces of intelligence provided by the Mediterranean merchants and geographers of prior centuries, and also news gathered from those Gallic tribes with maritime contacts there, Caesar knew Britain was rich in raw materials. He himself noted that 'Tin is found inland, and small quantities of iron near the coast' (*The Conquest of Gaul*, 2.4). The Greek geographer Strabo, writing slightly later, confirmed iron as a key export from Britain (*Geography*, 4.5), while Mattingly adds silver as a desirous commodity from the islands (2006, 64). Aside from *metalla* goods, Britain was also known in the classical world for its wool, arable, hunting dog and slave exports. The latter indicates tribal relations in Britain were far from stable, this adding to Rome's sense of instability there.

Finally, and most importantly, Britain presented Caesar with his ultimate challenge. A chance of unmatchable, divine glory. As seen, he was a man driven by destiny and a need for prestige amongst both peers and the popular classes back in Rome, as well as with his legionaries. Just landing in Britain, let alone its conquest, would set him above all of his Republican warlord rivals and predecessors, including Crassus, Pompey, the great Marius and unbeaten Sulla. This is important as it sets Caesar's exploits in Britain firmly in the context of the winner-takes-all battle between the *optimates* and *populares* back in Rome that would eventually see the Republic implode within thirty years (Mattingly, 2006, 65).

Caesar states his first visit to Britain was more an armed reconnaissance than an attempt at conquest. This was because of the lateness of the campaigning season in 55 BC. Specifically, he says that he (*The Conquest of Gaul*, 5.1) 'thought it would be of great advantage to him to merely visit the island, to see what its inhabitants were like, and to make himself acquainted with the lie of the land, the harbours, and the landing places'.

So what exactly would Caesar have known of Britain prior to deciding to cross *Oceanus*? Aside from the tribal links, *metalla* resources and exports detailed above, very little it appears. He says he knew the Cantiaci occupied the area now called Kent and had closest ties with the continent, and that Britain more broadly was densely populated (Julius Caesar, *The Conquest of Gaul*, 5.1). Further, he was also aware that bronze coins and iron ingots were used as currency in the south-east. These coins were called 'staters' and were copies of Greek coins of the same name, imported to Britain from Gaul and then minted in increasingly poorer copies as time progressed. He also knew from the commentaries of the Mediterranean merchants and geographers that many of the natives used woad blue natural dye to paint their bodies, and about the differential in the length of the days at this higher latitude when compared to much of the continent. However, he was incorrectly informed that many Britons lived on meat and milk and did not grow corn, wore only skins, and rather outlandishly that British wives were shared between groups of up to twelve men.

By now a seasoned commander, Caesar realised his lack of intelligence about the mysterious island across *Oceanus* presented a serious problem. He quickly set out to remedy this. In the first instance, he says he (*The Conquest of Gaul*, 5.1)

> summoned to his presence traders from a wide area, but he was unable to gain any intelligence whatsoever from them: nothing about the size of the island; nor the nature or numbers of the tribes who inhabited it; nor their customs nor about such harbours as might be suitable for a sizeable fleet of large ships.

Moorhead and Stuttard (2012, 13) argue this actually amounted to a deliberate policy of disinformation by the Gauls and Britons he interviewed to deter him from invading. This is understandable given the severity with which Caesar had dealt with the Veneti leadership the previous year, the tribe with the strongest maritime links to Britain.

This lack of intelligence is just one manifestation of what many modern commentators say was Caesar's uncharacteristic lack of detailed planning for his 55 BC expedition, which is what makes it such a useful campaign to study when considering his military prowess. This sparse attention to detail is surprising given the level of jeopardy involved. Mattingly says this lack of preparation was the principal shortcoming of what proved a flawed campaign (2006, 65), while Moorhead and Studdard say the lack of planning was an unusual mistake for the otherwise canny Caesar (2012, 13).

More mistakes followed. First, he sent the wrong man to reconnoitre potential landing beaches on the eastern coast of Kent. This was Gaius Volusenus Quadratus, the *Tribunus Militum* of the XIIth legion who had served with distinction in the 57 BC campaign against the Belgae. Caesar thought he was courageous and had good strategic sense, dispatching him with a single galley. However, even though he spent four days scouting the region, in which time he 'sailed as far as he could without actually disembarking and risking contact with the barbarians' (Julius Caesar, *The Conquest of Gaul*, 5.1), the most suitable place he could find was the strip of beach beneath the White Cliffs of Dover. This was a bizarre choice for such an experienced warrior, given the impossibility of getting off the invasion beaches if the cliff tops were defended. Just to the north were much more appropriate landing places, including the 14km broad expanses of beach ranging from modern Walmer through Deal up to Richborough, and the natural sheltered harbourage of the then navigable Wantsum Channel. Caesar clearly made a bad error selecting Volusenus.

A further miscalculation was the odd decision to send Commius, king of the Gallic branch of the Atrebates, to Britain to win over hearts and minds among the tribal ruling families ahead of his arrival. Commius owed his position to Caesar, having been appointed king after the Romans had defeated the Atrebates' tribal confederation during his 57 BC campaign in northern Gaul. Caesar says he was (*The Conquest of Gaul*, 5.1) 'a man whose bravery, good sense and loyalty he had a high opinion (of) and whose authority was well respected in Britain.'

This mission was a spectacular failure, with Commius arrested and tied up as soon as he arrived in Britain. This had major repercussions when Caesar actually landed as he appears to have been relying on the natives to supply his troops with food, not carrying enough provisions himself to keep his army in the field.

The campaign began in earnest when Caesar ordered his '...whole army...' (Julius Caesar, *The Conquest of Gaul*, 5.1), by now numbering eight legions with up to 48,000 legionaries plus allied troops, to march into the territory of the Morini tribe in north-eastern Gaul, closest to Britain. These were one of the few tribes to refuse to submit to Rome in the 56 BC Atlantic coast campaign. However, seeing the scale of Caesar's military might, they now did so, handing the Romans a large number of hostages.

Caesar decided he only needed two of his legions for the first expedition to Britain and chose his own elite *legio X equestris* and *legio VII*. He then selected an embarkation point, unspecified in this campaign, where he gathered a fleet of eighty transports and some war galleys to carry the legionaries. An additional eighteen transports were modified to carry horses, though these were prevented from joining the fleet due to a change in wind direction. The vessels therefore waited 13km further along the coast to await the arrival of the allied cavalry. To protect his rear Caesar then appointed the *legates* Sabinus and Cotta to lead the six remaining legions north into the land of the Menapii who were still refusing to submit to Roman rule. There they spent the rest of the campaigning year seeking out the elusive Gauls who concealed themselves in dense forest, the Romans eventually resorting to a slash-and-burn strategy to destroy their crops and villages. Meanwhile, Caesar appointed another *legate* called Publius Sulpicius Rufus with orders to build defences around, and then to protect, his main port of embarkation.

Caesar now waited for favourable weather conditions before setting off across *Oceanus* to Britain, departing just before midnight on the chosen day. His cavalry transports had orders to follow, but were too late in departing and missed the tide, being carried back to the Gallic coast. An attempt to transport the cavalry four days later also failed, leaving Caesar to fight the forthcoming campaign in unknown territory without his cavalry. These would have provided his main scouting function, as well as the means to pursue a broken enemy to prevent them regrouping. Both were to prove serious shortcomings in the coming campaign.

His main fleet began to arrive off the White Cliffs of Dover around 9am the following morning, with Caesar in one of the lead ships. The flawed choice of landing place by Volusenus was immediately clear, as was the failure of the hearts and minds gamble with Commius, given the cliff and hilltops were swarming with native British warriors. These were armed and organised in a very similar manner to their Gallic counterparts, with a light-chariot and horse-riding aristocracy leading spear- and sword-armed bands of followers. The major point of difference was that the Britons had far more chariots and far fewer cavalry, being much later in the process of transitioning from the former to the latter.

Viewing the arrayed enemy, Caesar immediately decided this first choice of landing place was highly impractical and ordered the arriving fleet to drop anchor just off the coast out of missile range. By 3pm all of the main force transports and warships had arrived. Caesar now gathered his officers to consider their options. After taking counsel he decided to act quickly, setting off northwards to find an uncontested landing place before nightfall. The fleet eventually anchored off Deal where the fine, evenly-sloped expanse of beach was undefended (Julius Caesar, *The Conquest of Gaul*, 5.1). However, when the Romans tried to run the transports aground to allow the legionaries to disembark they found the size of the vessels made this impractical in the shallow foreshore. To compound his difficulties, by the time Caesar became aware of this the Britons had begun to arrive, first the chariots and cavalry and then the foot troops. Soon the native army was once more arrayed to oppose his landing.

Caesar was now forced to carry out a full amphibious assault. For this he drove his war galleys hard ashore to the north of the landing beaches where he aimed to turn the Britons' right flank. From here the galleys enfiladed the landing area with *ballista*, bows and slings to try to drive the natives from the shore. He then ordered the transports to get as close to the beach as possible. However, even with the covering fire from his war galleys the legionaries were reluctant to land. An iconic incident now occurred when the *aquilifer* standard-bearer of *legio X*, carrying the legion's gold *aquila* eagle standard, leapt into the shallows, shouting (Julius Caesar, *The Conquest of Gaul*, 5.1): 'Leap, fellow soldiers, unless you wish to betray your eagle to the enemy. I, for my part, will perform my duty to the Republic and to my general.'

The shamed legionaries now jumped into the shallows and swarmed ashore to protect their eagle, this taking longer than expected given the larger transports continued to struggle to get close to the beach. Once ashore the legionaries rallied to the nearest unit standard rather than their usual *vexilla* given the confusion, with the Britons trying to isolate small groups as they landed and kill them. Caesar countered by ordering the *myoparo* and *scapha* cutters and skiffs supporting the fleet to be loaded with troops and used as a maritime mobile reserve, deploying here and there where the fighting was fiercest (Elliott, 2016, 43). The picture painted by Caesar is of a very confusing battle, often the case with contested beach landings, and the engagement was clearly a close-run thing. Caesar himself admits that both sides fought hard (*The Conquest of Gaul*, 5.1). However, eventually the legionaries' better training and equipment came to the fore and they pushed the Britons back off the beach. Soon the native troops began to flee and the Romans secured the landing zone. As night fell they could claim victory given they had control of the battlefield, though the lack of cavalry prevented the Romans from pursuing the beaten enemy who soon re-formed close by.

Having been on the receiving end of the Roman military machine for the first time the British leaders quickly decided that peace, at least in the short term, was the most desirable outcome and sent envoys to Caesar. These stated that they had only attacked the Romans through ignorance, and to show their good intentions handed over Commius, Caesar's failed envoy. The Romans demanded more hostages to secure the agreement, and when these started to arrive an uneasy peace settled in eastern Kent.

The beachhead secure, Caesar now ordered the building of a large marching camp for his two legions. However, the British weather now intervened. While Caesar's legionaries were well protected in their new camp, the vessels used by the Romans to travel from the continent were not. On the fourth day ashore a violent storm arose, which together with a high tide damaged many of the Roman ships riding at anchor, some being destroyed. It was this event that prevented the cavalry transports arriving on their second attempt to cross to Britain. It also presented Caesar with a conundrum as he had travelled without any significant food stores, hoping to rely on the natives or on his fleet ferrying provisions from the continent. He was now forced to divide his army into two, the Xth legion to repair his ships and the VIIth to forage locally for what he describes as corn. The former were successful at their task, with all but twelve ships successfully repaired. However, the latter presented the native Britons with too tempting an opportunity. Their leadership, having learned of Caesar's misfortune, now resumed their hostility.

Caesar narrates that as the VIIth legion went about their business gathering food they were ambushed by the Britons and found themselves in danger of being overwhelmed. The Roman marching-camp guards noticed the native advance in the distance as a large dust cloud and Caesar ordered two cohorts of the Xth legion, led by him in person, to march to the relief of the VIIth. This they did, the Romans then withdrawing in good order back to the safety of their camp. For some reason the Britons did not press their attack and withdrew. The Roman lack of cavalry is again evident here as this would have provided both an early warning of the initial attack and then been in place to pursue the Britons as they departed.

More bad weather followed, allowing the British leadership to send messengers far and wide to gather an army large enough to challenge Caesar's two legions. They impressed on the neighbouring tribes the small size of the Roman force and the chance for booty, encouraged no doubt by the Gallic refugees within their midst. Caesar decided to draw them to him rather than risk another ambush and deployed his two legions in front of his marching camp, bolstered by the arrival of thirty horsemen from Gaul (not his actual cavalry contingent, these instead from his legionary port of embarkation). The Britons took the bait and attacked, though once again the Romans were victorious. The Britons again fled, pursued by Caesar as far as possible before he once more withdrew his troops back to camp.

The defeated natives now sued for peace again. As before Caesar agreed, but this time asked for twice as many hostages. Soon after this he decided to withdraw back to Gaul, knowing he lacked the provisions to overwinter in Britain and not wanting to subject his repaired ships to a crossing of *Oceanus* any later in the year. A favourable wind made the return crossing a success, excepting two transports that were blown too far to the north. These landed among Morini still hostile to Rome and soon 300 legionaries were surrounded by an increasingly large force of natives keen on booty.

They held out for four hours until Caesar's rescue force of cavalry arrived, at which point the Morini fled. Caesar then sent the *legate* Labienus with the VIIth and Xth legions, newly back from Britain, to attack the rebellious Morini who were all killed or captured. Caesar then gathered his scribes once more and sent further dispatches back to Rome. As usual these portrayed his campaigns in a positive light and were well received given the Senate decreed twenty days of public thanksgiving. However, looking back across *Oceanus* towards Britain, Caesar knew he still had unfinished business there.

The ambitious warlord made his decision to carry out a second expedition to Britain before the end of 55 BC, giving orders to his *legates* to start building a bespoke fleet of ships more appropriate for a large invasion than those used in his first incursion. He then headed back to Cisapline Gaul to winter in his usual quarters there.

Early in the New Year, after a brief visit to his other province of Illyricum, he returned to the territory of the Morini where he gathered his entire army of 8 legions, together with 4,000 Gallic allied cavalry. This time we learn the name of the chosen port of embarkation for Britain, *Portus Itius*. Grainge (2005, 90) usefully sets out the various candidate sites in the region, all to the south of modern Calais with its short journey across *Oceanus* to Britain. The most northerly is Wissant near Cap Gris Nez, while the most southerly is the later major port site at Boulogne (Roman *Gessoriacum*, the future headquarters of the *Classis Britannica* regional fleet). The latter seems the most likely given the fine harbourage there in the estuary of the River Liane.

When Caesar arrived he was pleased with the work of his *legates* and their shipbuilders, with 600 specially-built vessels ready for service. These, based on designs of the Veneti, featured lower freeboards than his earlier Mediterranean designs to enable easier disembarkation, banks of oars as well as a large sail to give good manoeuvrability in shallow waters, and wider beams to carry bulkier loads (Julius Caesar, *The Conquest of Gaul*, 5.2). To these he added 200 locally chartered transports, over 80 Roman transport ships that had survived the previous year's incursion, and his 28 remaining war galleys.

Before starting his second British campaign Caesar quickly moved to secure his rear once more, mounting a brief campaign against the Treveri tribe to the north bordering the Rhine. These were famous for their cavalry, and here he helped resolve a leadership dispute. All was now set for his second invasion.

Caesar's force this time was far bigger, consisting of five entire legions with 30,000 legionaries and 2,000 cavalry. He left the remainder, 3 legions and 2,000 more cavalry, under the command of the *legate* Labienus with orders to protect the regional ports on the Gallic coast, ensure a regular supply of provisions to Caesar in Britain and generally keep an eye on Gaul.

The fleet set sail northwards on 6 July at sunset using a light south-westerly breeze. At first progress across *Oceanus* was good, but around midnight the wind dropped and Caesar's fleet began to drift with the tide northwards. At daybreak on 7 July it became evident that the fleet had drifted 'far out of his course by the tidal current… (with) Britain left behind on the port side' (Julius Caesar, *The Conquest of Gaul*, 5.2). Modern interpretations, based on knowledge of the then tidal streams and weather have interpreted Caesar's location at this point anywhere from Dover to north of the treacherous Goodwin Sands off eastern Kent and Isle of Thanet (Grange, 2005, 102). Wherever they were as the sun rose, this expedition was far better prepared than that of the previous year and Caesar calmly gave orders for the transports and warships to deploy their oars and row for the British coast. He aimed for the invasion beaches of 54 BC, greatly aided by a far better knowledge of the tidal streams in the Dover Straits than the previous year. The rowers worked in shifts and soon the large fleet made landfall near Deal again.

This time Caesar's far bigger force intimidated the Britons and the landing was unopposed. Later intelligence indicated a native army had gathered on the high ground above the invasion beaches, but when the leaders saw the size of the Roman fleet they withdrew inland. Once ashore the Romans looked to build a large marching camp, and here new archaeological evidence has enabled us to piece together the strategy followed by Caesar.

Roman marching camps are of great use to the archaeologist and historian when attempting to understand a specific military campaign. This is because even though deliberately slighted after use to prevent exploitation by the enemy, they frequently leave very noticeable crop marks outlining their playing-card shape, not surprising given their substantial nature when in use. Matching these to the known size of the campaigning force allows us to track the routes taken by various campaigning armies, for example in a British context those in Scotland of Agricola in the late first century AD or Severus in the early third century AD. In that regard, there should therefore be three such routes visible in Kent, namely those of Caesar in his 55 BC and 54 BC campaigns, and that of the AD 43 Claudian invasion. Surprisingly, until recently none have been found.

However, we are today fortunate in that one has now been found, and identified in the context of Caesar's first 54 BC incursion.

The camp in question is 20 ha in size, large enough to accommodate two legions. It was first located in 2010 when archaeologists found a large defensive ditch 5 metres wide and 2 metres deep during a rescue archaeology project in advance of the building of a road at Ebbsfleet near Pegwell Bay. The ditch is the standard size for one protecting a Roman marching camp. Later investigations at the site by University of Leicester archaeologists funded by the Leverhulme Project using geophysical surveys in 2015–16 and trial excavations in 2016–17 confirmed it as such. The geophysical survey revealed the plan of the western part of the camp including two standard entrances. The overall design is very similar to those later used by Caesar in his Alesia campaign in 52 BC. Meanwhile, the excavations found coins and pottery that have been used to date it to the 54 BC campaign. A discarded *pilum* head, and human bones showing signs of combat trauma, were also found there. The latter are likely the remains of British dead hastily buried in the ditch when the camp was abandoned. However, its location is the most interesting factor as it is actually on what was then the island of Thanet, separated from the British mainland by the Wantsum Channel, then a substantial waterway. This is some way from the invasion beaches at Deal, and therefore presents a conundrum as at no time does Caesar indicate that he built his landing marching camp away from the native Britons across a substantial waterway.

There are two explanations for this perceived discrepancy. First, Caesar was being deliberately disingenuous in his narrative of *The Conquest of Gaul* and actually started his 54 BC campaign on a defensive footing, mindful of difficulties the previous year. Or secondly, the camp on Thanet is of a different nature, namely a supply base to ensure Caesar had sufficient provisions in a defendable location to support his second campaign. Analogously this is a common feature of many Roman campaigns where a significant commitment was made in terms of manpower. Good examples include the fortified supply bases at Cramond on the River Forth and Carpow on the River Tay. The former, just over 2 ha in size, was first built in the Antonine period as part of the Antonine Wall construction programme for which it played a major supporting role. It was later used as a key node in the east-coast supply chain during the attempts by Septimius Severus to conquer Scotland in AD 209 and AD 210. Meanwhile, Carpow was built to support the Agricolan attempts to conquer Scotland in the Flavian period, later again being used during the campaigns of Severus. The implication of this latter interpretation is that Caesar may have actually been planning to stay in Britain in 54 BC, his invasion a full attempt at conquest.

If the camp on Thanet was a supply depot, then the marching camp he references would have been opposite on the mainland, to the south nearer the invasion beaches. Here Caesar left a force of 10 cohorts of legionaries and 300 of his allied cavalry under the *legate* Quintus Atrius to protect his invasion fleet. These vessels had all been anchored in a sheltered location. This was almost certainly in the Wantsum Channel itself, to the north of the invasion beaches. The aim here was to avoid the damage suffered the previous year during bad weather.

Caesar set off at midnight the day after landing, his cavalry quickly locating the gathered Britons 20km inland. The British leaders tried to halt Caesar's advance on a river line, probably one of the branches of the River Stour. Here they deployed their chariots and cavalry forward. These were quickly driven back by Caesar's cavalry and soon the Romans were across the river line and heading for the major Cantiaci settlement where Canterbury is located today. There he learned that the British force had withdrawn to the nearby hill fort at Bigbury 3.2km to the west. Here they had blocked up the two main entrances with felled logs. This 10.7 ha fortification, atop high ground overlooking modern Canterbury, presented Caesar with a significant obstacle. He decided to storm it at once and ordered the VIIth legion into the attack. The veteran legionaries used their *testudo* tortoise formation with interlocked shields around and above them to force the gates under cover of a missile bombardment of *ballista* bolts and slingshot. The Britons quickly capitulated, those able to do so escaping to nearby woods. Caesar ordered his cavalry to pursue for a short distance. He then reformed his force to build a marching camp for the night.

Next morning Caesar resolved to force a meeting engagement with the Britons, dividing his force into three columns of march. However, as he progressed and with the enemy now in sight, he got word from Atrius that the fleet had yet again been devastated by a violent overnight Channel storm. This had been so severe that the anchors and cables holding them in place, even in the sheltered waters where they were located, had broken or snapped. Many had been driven hard ashore or against each other with every ship damaged in some way. Some forty vessels were totally wrecked and unsalvageable. Caesar therefore left a holding force facing the Britons near Bigbury and then sent all of his remaining legionaries back to the ships to begin urgent repairs. He also sent word by swift galley to Labienus in Gaul to send more specialist carpenters and to build more vessels to replace those damaged. When this vessel returned it was with very sad news for Caesar as it was now he learned that his daughter Julia had died during childbirth, with her baby dying shortly afterwards. Caesar set aside his grief for the moment and focused on the campaign at hand. The ship repairs took ten days and once complete Caesar had all the vessels hauled on to the nearby beaches. He then extended his coastal marching camp around them to provide protection. This huge undertaking complete, he left the same 10 cohorts and 300 cavalry to guard the site and set off once more inland (Julius Caesar, *The Conquest of Gaul*, 5.2).

This time Caesar kept his legions together as one large legionary spearhead which started to make serious headway into Kent. Here it faced a combined British tribal army commanded by a king called Cassivellanus. In his *Conquest of Gaul* Caesar does not reference his tribe, but does say the River Thames divided the lands he ruled. He adds that in recent inter-tribal conflict Cassivellanus had beaten the Trinovantes who were located in eastern Essex. This seems to indicate he was the king of the Catuvellauni to their west. The description of the Thames dividing the lands he ruled would indicate the Cantiaci in Kent were his vassals at the time.

The Britons avoided a set piece battle at this stage, relying on hit-and-run tactics by their chariots and cavalry to engage the Romans on the march. Their infantry also ambushed out of woodland when the Romans were building their marching camps. Caesar says that on every occasion his troops bested the Britons, though it did test the discipline of the Romans who were eager to pursue their defeated opponents. He realised the enemy were trying to lure small parties into ambushes and ensured that the order of march was maintained. Only on one occasion did he feel his forces endangered, this being when a large British force attacked a part-built marching camp. Caesar responded quickly, sending two cohorts (the first of their respective legions, so larger than usual) to their rescue. They themselves then came under pressure, with a military tribune called Quintus Laberius Durus killed during the fighting. Caesar was forced to send in more cohorts to stabilize the situation, and eventually the Britons were driven off again.

Caesar describes the Britons using complex tactics in these engagements, always trying to lure the Romans away in small numbers and using concealed troops to screen any advances or retreats. He notes particularly that when the enemy were operating in this fluid way the legionaries in their heavy *lorica hamata* mail hauberks were at a disadvantage as they simply could not keep up with their elusive foe. He adds that even his allied cavalry were at a disadvantage against the British chariots as his Gauls often pursued them into terrain unsuitable for mounted troops. At that point the charioteers would dismount and fight on foot where they had the advantage.

The following day Caesar got his meeting engagement, though not on his own terms. The combined British force under Cassivellanus had re-gathered and deployed on high ground some distance from Caesar's overnight marching camp. The Romans felt secure enough to send three legions out to forage, together with all of the cavalry. This force was put under the command of the experienced *legate* Gaius Trebonius. However, as soon as the foraging column had travelled some distance from the camp the Britons attacked in a fluid movement that enveloped the head and both flanks of the column. Caesar describes the fighting as so fierce that the Britons came close to capturing the legionary *aquila* eagle standards (Julius Caesar, *The Conquest of Gaul*, 5.2). This battle was clearly a close-run thing, far too close for comfort for Caesar. However, Roman discipline again won out and eventually a ferocious charge by Caesar's cavalry routed the Britons who fled in panic, thousands being cut down in the ensuing pursuit by his headhunting allied Gallic cavalry. Any surviving Britons returned to their respective tribes as quickly as possible, with Cassivellanus unable to gather a combined army from that point. He fled back north over the Thames, with Caesar in hot pursuit.

At this point Caesar gives the first insight into the likely route taken by his legionary spearhead as there is no mention of any other river than the Thames. This is in direct contrast to the AD 43 Claudian invasion. Here, Cassius Dio in his *Roman History* describes the famous river-crossing battle where the Roman advance through central Kent was almost halted at a defended river line bisecting the modern county (Cassius Dio, *Roman History*, 60.19). This was almost certainly the River Medway, with Aylesford located as the battle site (Elliott, 2016, 115). The lack of any mention of this natural defensive feature by Caesar indicates he was operating north of the North Downs along the northern coast of Kent where the Romans later built Watling Street. Here he would have been able to rely on his fleet to protect his littoral flank and keep him supplied if necessary.

Caesar now decided to force a crossing of the Thames in pursuit of Cassivellanus. He chose a place he describes as the only one fordable by his army. Again, analogy with the later Claudian invasion is useful here to enable this location to be identified. It has recently been determined that the AD 43 invasion force under the *legate* Aulus Plautius crossed the Thames at a location between Higham on the south bank and Tilbury on the north, the line of the later medieval ferry there and the lowest fordable point during the Roman period when it was marshy and featured many islands, particularly at low tide (Elliott, 2016, 116). This site was almost certainly where Caesar chose to cross, taking him into the lands of the Trinovantes. These were now allies of Cassivellanus given his recent victory over them when he had killed their king and replaced him with a supporter.

Cassivellanus had not been idle and had gathered a new army from among his own Catuvellauni and his Trinovantian allies. This he arrayed on the north bank of the Thames to oppose any crossing by Caesar. The latter knew momentum was the key to success here, though he checked his advance for a short time to scout the crossing, wary of further British ambushes. This proved a shrewd move as his reconnaissance, together with intelligence from captive Britons, revealed the north side of the crossing was protected by sharpened stakes. These had been placed both along the bank and below the waterline. Caesar therefore deployed his legionary pioneers and engineering specialists in the vanguard of the assault. He then ordered a general advance, his cavalry following the pioneers as the latter opened routes through the British defences. To cover this operation he deployed his war galleys where the *ballistae*, archers and slingers of the marines kept the heads of the Britons defenders down. Caesar then ordered his legionaries forward. These were so eager to get to grips with the enemy that, even though up to their necks in the river as they crossed, they soon caught up with the cavalry. Both the mounted troops and foot thus hit the Britons on the north bank at the same time. The defenders were soon overpowered and again fled.

Caesar pursued a short distance, then recalled his troops to build a marching camp again, his first north of the Thames. Cassivellanus, defeated again and again when the Romans could get to grips with his warriors, now disbanded his foot troops and headed westward to his own Catuvellaunian territory. Here he changed his strategy back to the use of hit-and-run ambushes using only his chariots. Caesar says he retained 4,000 charioteers to man them (*The Conquest of Gaul*, 5.2). These repeatedly attacked Roman scouting cavalry and foraging parties, using pathways they knew well through local woodland to mask their approach and make their escape.

Given his enemy was now avoiding open battle, as Caesar passed through the territory of the Catuvellauni he instigated a scorched earth policy burning settlements and crops and totally destroying the local economy. At this point, a delegation arrived in his camp from the

Trinovantes to the east. This was led by Mandubracius, a young prince who had fled to seek protection from Caesar on the continent earlier in the decade. It was his father who had been killed by Cassivellanus. He asked that Caesar allow him to return home to rule his lands as an ally of Rome. Caesar agreed, in return for forty hostages and grain. When these arrived Mandubracius was duly installed as the new Trinovantian king, with Cassivellanus' candidate deposed. When word of this spread elsewhere other tribes now came forward to surrender to Caesar. From these he learned that Cassivellanus had retreated to his capital. This was a heavily fortified *oppidum* featuring substantial surrounding ditches, earthen banks, palisades and defended gateways. Its location has long been contested, with candidate sites including Gatesbury, Redbourn, Baldock, Ravensburgh Castle and Wallbury Camp (Moorhead and Stuttard, 2012, 33). The most likely location, however, is Wheathampstead in the upper Lea valley in modern Hertfordshire. Here, the Late Iron Age defences were so impressive that some remain visible today, particularly the 30m wide and 12m deep Devil's Dyke.

Keen to bring the campaign to a conclusion, Caesar headed straight for the *oppidum*. Given it was now late in the campaigning season he resolved to immediately assault the fortification rather than risk a lengthy siege. His legionaries attacked on two sides in *testudo* formation, forcing the gateways under covering fire from *ballistae* and slingers. Soon, despite the impressive defences, Caesar was again victorious. Those Britons that could fled through the gateways on a side the Romans had yet to attack.

Cassivellanus once more sought sanctuary in nearby woodland. He now changed tactics yet again, this time sending word to his Cantiaci vassals back in Kent to attack Caesar's 'naval camp'. This was either the mainland camp that had been extended to protect the beached ships or the supply base on Thanet detailed earlier. Caesar here names four Cantiaci kings as the recipients of the new orders, these being Cingetorix, Carvilius, Taximagulus and Segovax. They were singularly unsuccessful, the 10 cohorts and 300 cavalry defending the landing area intercepting the British force and quickly defeating it. Again many were killed as they fled, including a leading noble called Lugotorix.

This was the last attempt by Cassivellanus to resist the Romans. Having suffered so many reverses on the battlefield, seen his allies desert him, his capital captured and his lands ravaged, he now sued for peace. Terms were quickly agreed, including Cassivellanus supplying more hostages and agreeing to pay an annual tribute to Rome. The Catuvellauni king also pledged to leave the Trinovantes unmolested. Honour satisfied, Caesar now returned to the landing zone in Kent. Here he determined to return to Gaul for the winter, having received word that some of the Gallic tribes were again considering rebellion. Given the large number of hostages, the captives due to be sold into slavery and his earlier ship losses, he decided to embark in two waves. The first travelled to the continent safely, but these vessels were prevented from returning by more bad weather. Caesar then decided to risk packing his remaining troops onto the few serviceable vessels left in Britain, the war galleys that had supported his Thames operation. These arrived back safely at the end of September, and thus ended Caesar's adventures in Britain.

Caesar was never to return to the mysterious island across *Oceanus*. When he arrived back in Gaul it was indeed on the verge of rebellion, and the final two years of his conquest of Gaul was spent in an increasingly brutal series of campaigns to stamp out the last embers of Gallic resistance. This culminated in the famous siege of Alesia in 52 BC, this considered next.

The Siege of Alesia

By 52 BC Caesar's conquest of Gaul was almost complete. However, many of the Gallic tribes remained rebellious. They found a new leader in Vercingetorix of the Averni tribe, around whom resistance coalesced. A mass revolt followed prompting Caesar to target the Averni capital Gergovia with typical speed. Though repulsed, Roman grit showed through again, the legions fighting a prolonged campaign that forced Vercingetorix and 60,000 of his men to take shelter in the fortified hilltop town of Alesia. Here Caesar determined to starve Vercingetorix into surrender, and we see Roman siege warfare at its best (Elliott, 2020b, 191). He ordered his men to construct ditches and an earthen bank topped by a palisade, just as with the marching camps but far grander in scale, an astonishing 18km long. This wall was interspersed with timber towers, enabling legionaries and archers to enfilade any attackers to the front or rear. The whole enclosed the town in a circumvallation.

We have great insight here into the sophistication of this fortification thanks to Caesar's detailed description (*The Conquest of Gaul*, 7.9). The bank and palisade was 3.6m high, with sharpened forked branches projecting outwards towards Alesia. Beyond this, two ditches were dug, each 4.4m wide and 2.4m deep. The one nearest the bank and palisade featured an 'ankle breaker' in the bottom, a step cut into its base designed to trap the feet of those scrambling to get up the other side which would snap ankle bones if due care was not taken. The ditch further out was filled with water wherever possible, requiring the Roman engineers to line it with clay. Further out from the bank and palisade, another shallower trench 1.5m deep was dug into which were placed five rows of sharpened stakes. Beyond these were formations of pits up to 1m wide in repeating *quincunx* formation (four in the corners of a square and one in the centre) featuring more stakes, this time concealed. These were nicknamed 'lilies'. Finally, even further out, there was a band of *stimuli*, wooden blocks embedded in the ground into which iron barbs had been placed.

The Gauls responded with constant raids against the building works, but failed to slow progress. Then, as construction neared completion, a large force of Gallic cavalry burst through and made off. Caesar, guessing they had been sent to fetch assistance, began a second ditch, bank and palisade fortification to the rear of the first, matching the one facing Alesia. At 22km long this wall was even grander, facing outward to cover his rear and forming a contravallation. There was only one area of weakness in this outer wall, a section where large boulders and a deep ravine made it impossible to build a continuous fortification. Caesar decided to mask the spot with a kink in the wall.

An incident next occurred which showed the Romans at their most brutal and determined. Vercingetorix, to save whatever food remained for his warriors, forced all of the women and children out of the gates of Alesia. He hoped the Romans would let them pass through Roman lines. However, Caesar refused and they had no choice but to camp between the town and the fortifications. Here they slowly starved, this episode showing Caesar at his most brutally pragmatic.

In late September a Gallic relief army arrived. It quickly launched an attack on the contravallation outer wall. Vercingetorix then also attacked from Alesia against the circumvallation inner wall. The legionaries fought off both attacks, but the assaults were renewed the following night and continued over the next few days. The Roman besiegers thus found themselves the besieged, between their two siege lines. Then, on 2 October, the Gauls attacked the weak spot in the Roman outer wall, with Vercingetorix again coordinating his assault against the inner wall. Caesar quickly realised the attack would be difficult to defend and poured in reinforcements, while distracting Vercingetorix against the inner wall by sallying legionaries out into the open. Despite valiant efforts in both areas Caesar now saw both of his lines were in danger of breaking. To save the day he personally led

6,000 cavalry from the outer walls. These rode to the rear of the Gauls there, attacking them as they assaulted the palisade. The Gauls were butchered, the survivors breaking and routing. The Roman cavalry pursued them closely, causing more slaughter, eventually overrunning the Gallic camp.

With little food remaining and no prospect of escape Vercingetorix now knew he was defeated and began negotiating with Caesar who agreed to spare the lives of his men, though the Gallic leader was sent to Rome in chains (Goldsworthy, 2006, 342). It was to be a dramatic fall from grace, the one-time king held captive for five years before forming the centrepiece of Caesar's triumphal parade where he was executed by strangulation as detailed in Chapter 6. Such was the lot of those who opposed Rome and lost.

The Battle of Pharsalus

Pharsalus, in Thessaly in north-eastern Greece, was the location of the decisive battle on 9 August 48 BC between Caesar and Pompey at the height of the civil wars of the first century BC. Previous encounters between the two had been indecisive, despite the bloody encounter at Dyrrhachium, and matters now came to a head in the largest encounter between Roman armies to that date.

The campaigning theatre in the Balkans was chosen by Pompey who fled Italy in 49 BC rather than confront Caesar, as detailed in Chapter 6. He believed some of the local legions there would side with his younger rival. This reflected the autonomous nature of the Marian legions as outlined in Chapter 7, each of which had a very distinct sense of identity and loyalty.

After the engagement at Dyrrhachium Caesar withdrew south, worried about the increasing disparity in numbers as Pompey continued to receive reinforcements. The latter's cavalry pursued Caesar but he escaped to Thessaly where he set up camp on the north bank of the River Enipeus between Pharsalus and Palaepharsalus. Pompey now followed with his whole force, setting up his own camp a kilometre to the west on a range of low hills that provided a good strategic position which ensured a safe route for his supplies from the coast. With both armies now in camp, they faced off.

Both armies featured a core of legions together with allies, though Pompey had the greater force and slightly more allies. By this time Caesar had with him elements of nine of his legions numbering some 23,000 legionaries in 80 cohorts (many of which were understrength). He also had between 5,000 and 10,000 allied foot and around 1,000 Gallic and German cavalry. Pompey had elements of 12 legions together with seven cohorts of legionaries from Spain in his force, in total numbering 50,000. He also had 4,200 allied foot and 7,000 allied horse including Galatians, Macedonians, Cappadocians, Gauls and Germans (Sabin, 2007, 237).

Caesar, clearly outnumbered, was keen to settle the issue immediately given he felt that his men were better rested than those of Pompey, and that their morale was higher (Goldsworthy, 2006, 425). However, Pompey, on the range of hills, was unwilling to abandon his advantage of high ground despite the weight of numbers in his favour. Several days passed before Caesar decided to fall back in the hope of drawing Pompey from his camp. On the morning of 9 August Pompey took the bait and moved his troops out onto the plain. Caesar pounced immediately, abandoning his baggage and even destroying his own field defences to get more of his legionaries onto the battlefield.

Pompey was the first to begin deploying, with 110 cohorts of legionaries plus line-of-battle allies lined up along a 4km front in the standard *acies triplex* formation. He deployed most of his cavalry, archers and slingers on his left flank hard up against the low hills where his camp was, with a smaller cavalry and light infantry force on the right against the River Enipeus. His veteran legionaries were dispersed throughout his force to support newly recruited troops. Pompey's plan was for his cavalry to circle around Caesar's flanks and attack his rear while his infantry pinned Caesar's centre. Pompey positioned himself at the rear of the left wing.

Meanwhile, Caesar, beginning his deployment later, lined up his troops parallel to Pompey's but with his three lines somewhat thinner given his numerical disadvantage. He was keen to avoid a hanging flank that Pompey's legionaries could exploit. Next he positioned himself opposite Pompey, behind the veteran and highly motivated *legio X*, the best legion on the field. He then deployed his cavalry on his right, and to harass the opposing legionaries positioned his light missile troops across his centre. As a precaution against Pompey's superior cavalry numbers he also moved six cohorts of legionaries from his rear line, positioning them as a reserve on his extreme right flank at an oblique angle.

The armies now closed to within 140m and faced off, Pompey then ordering the first attack with his cavalry where he held the numerical advantage. Caesar's cavalry counter-charged and a melee ensued. Meanwhile, Caesar's first two lines of infantry approached Pompey's foot who stood their ground rather than advancing to meet the oncoming enemy. Seeing Pompey's lines were not advancing, Caesar halted his legions just out of range of the legionaries' lighter *pila*. He then redressed his ranks, before ordering a charge by his first two lines (the third being held in reserve). The legionaries surged forward, each unleashing both *pila* before drawing their *gladii* and closing. Pompey's legionaries countered, both sides finally meeting in a savage crescendo.

On the left flank Pompey's cavalry were beginning to make their weight of numbers tell and Caesar ordered his mounted troops to withdraw, leaving Pompey in control of the flank. However, Caesar now ordered his right flank reserve of six cohorts forward to engage Pompey's cavalry who were re-forming. They charged to close quarters, hurling their *pila* into the faces of their opponents who broke in short order. The Republican cavalry fled the field in confusion, leaving Caesar in control of the whole flank.

In the centre Caesar now committed his third line to prevent Pompey from redeploying his own legionaries. He then wheeled the six cohorts on his right into the exposed left flank of Pompey's legionaries. Butchery ensued and Pompey's army broke, the allied troops fleeing first before the legionaries routed. The latter retreated headlong for the hills, with Pompey retreating to his camp before leaving the field completely. The one-time champion of the Republic now rode for Larissa with a small escort, disguising himself as an ordinary soldier. As detailed in Chapter 6 Caesar was ruthless in his pursuit, wiping out Pompey's camp, and with his opponent later fleeing to Egypt to his doom.

What is clear from the primary sources regarding this battle is that the élan of Caesar's legions, particularly *legio X*, more than made up for his numerical disadvantage. Pompey, dubbed the Great by contemporaries, was far from it in this campaign and once Caesar had destroyed his rival's left flank, the command and control he exercised over his legions ensured Pompey's army was quickly rolled up. Caesar also made much better use of reserves, knowing that with the legionaries of both sides evenly matched (at least in terms of equipment) the ability to exploit success would be vital. So it proved.

The Battle of Thapsus

Caesar's engagement at Thapsus on 6 April 46 BC was the culmination of his hard fought North African campaign against the leading *optimates* seeking refuge there after his defeat of Pompey two years earlier.

After his near entrapment at Ruspina earlier in the year he now moved onto the offensive, seeking a decisive meeting engagement given the recent arrival of significant reinforcements including his elite *legio X equestris*. Caesar was aware that his opponent Quintus Caecilius Metellus Scipio had a significant advantage in mounted troops given the elephants and skirmishing light cavalry provided by the *optimates*' Numidian ally Juba I (still with the army despite the king having to return to Numidia, see Chapter 6). He therefore sought an ideal location to negate this and, scouting ahead, found it at the nearby port city of Thapsus given it could only be approached by two isthmuses either side of a very wide, deep lagoon. Caesar's strategy was to advance on the town's Pompeian garrison along one of the isthmuses, drawing Scipio after him. Aware this would leave his rear exposed he built a strong marching camp at the head of this strip of land as he passed through it, manning it with three cohorts of highly reliable and well-led legionaries. He then invested Thapsus and waited for the *optimates*' relief force to arrive, with Scipio promptly falling for the trap. Arriving at the head of Caesar's chosen isthmus the *optimates* found it blocked by his marching camp and withdrew to the shores of the lake, here building their own camp. Caesar now had him trapped and pounced immediately. Scipio had no choice but to accept battle as his line of retreat was blocked by the lake.

The exact numbers engaged at Thapsus are unclear, though Caesar could have fielded anything up to 50,000 foot (we know for a fact he left two legions of recent recruits in the siege lines around Thapsus) and 5,000 cavalry, while Scipio's force could draw on 72,000 foot, 14,500 cavalry and 60 elephants.

Forced into an engagement he did not want, Scipio formed his legionaries in front of the palisade of his camp, with the elephants and cavalry he had been left by Juba on his wings. Caesar countered with his usual *acies triplex*, deploying his skirmishers and an extra fourth line of legionaries on the flanks to counter the elephants. Unusually he then deployed some of his war galleys onto one of the nearby waterways to enfilade the rear of the Pompeian forces once the battle began (Goldsworthy, 2006, 464).

When the battle opened Caesar's archers immediately targeted the elephants, many of which panicked and started to trample their own men. Meanwhile, a separate elephant charge into Caesar's centre from one of the wings hit the now veteran *legio V Alaudae* who fought so bravely that from that point their legionary symbol was an elephant (one interpretation actually has a legion split into two to form the fourth-line of flank-cover legionaries). Across the wider battlefield Caesar's better troops were soon triumphant, and the battle was quickly over. When the Pompeian legionaries tried to surrender many were cut down where they stood, with the primary sources talking of a fierce pursuit in which even some of Caesar's own officers were killed when trying to control the troops. This was true civil war red in tooth and claw, with the Pompeians losing over 10,000 men to Caesar's alleged 50 in a massacre that Holland describes as a terrible slaughter (2003, 334). Thapsus fell soon after and the Pompeian cause in Africa was lost, with Pompey's two sons Gnaeus Pompeius and Sextus Pompeius fleeing to Spain along with the *legate* Labienus who had caused Caesar so many problems at the beginning of his North African campaign. Meanwhile, Cato (in command of the city of Utica), the defeated Scipio and Juba (who may have returned in time to see the defeat, but did not participate) committed suicide by various means.

The Battle of Munda

Caesar's final battle was once more against remnant Pompeains, this time in Spain at the conclusion of his 45 BC campaign. It was also yet another brutal encounter, and one he came close to losing.

Caesar had made his move to deal with the Pompeians' final stronghold in Spain in November 46 BC, where Gnaeus Pompeius, Sextus Pompeius and Labienus had fled after the disaster in North Africa. There they had joined two Pompeian legions in Hispania Ulterior, then raised another from local recruits and survivors from the war in North Africa, with Caesar's generals Quintus Fabius Maximus and Quintus Pedius looking on and refusing to risk battle.

Caesar travelled from Italy to Spain by a series of forced marches, taking two veteran legions, *X equestris* and *V Alaudae*, and also the less experienced *III Gallica* and *VI Ferrata*. Arriving in December, he immediately blocked any further *optimates* expansion in Spain, though struggled to force a meeting engagement as the Pompeius brothers and Labienus chose to avoid battle. However, after a number of indecisive skirmishes some of the Pompeian legionaries began to switch sides, knowing their fate if Caesar was ultimately victorious. This forced the hands of the *optimates* who now offered battle, with Gnaeus leading his troops out of their marching camp near the town of Munda on the morning of 17 March 45 BC, they deploying in the usual *acies triplex* on a nearby hill (Goldsworthy, 2006, 483). Caesar saw his chance to bring matters to an end with the Pompeains once and for all and deployed his force, again in the *acies triplex*, immediately opposite.

Here Caesar fielded a total of 8 legions, with 4 more from Spain joining the 4 that had travelled with him, together with 8,000 allied cavalry. The Republicans fielded 13 legions, though a number had suffered badly from the earlier desertion, along with 6,000 horse and 6,000 light foot. In the coming battle many of the Pompeians would fight with desperation, knowing they could expect no mercy.

After a failed attempt to lure the Republicans into a trap Caesar ordered his troops into a general attack with the watchword 'Venus'. Both armies fought toe-to-toe for eight hours, with all the commanders joining in the fighting. Caesar based himself on his right flank where he joined *legio X* again.

Although initially the Pompeians made good progress, with Caesar at one point having to advance to within ten paces of the Pompeian battle line to rally his weary legionaries, the elite Xth eventually began to push back the Pompeian legion opposite. This caused Gnaeus Pompeius to withdraw a legion from his own right flank to bolster his left. The weakened right flank was now exploited by Caesar's allied cavalry there, commanded by King Bogud of Mauritania, who wheeled round its furthest extremity and charged the Pompeian camp to the rear of their battle line. Labienus now ordered his own cavalry to the rear to counter Bogud's men, but the Pompeian legionaries – already heavily engaged and falling back on their left – thought Labienus was retreating and gradually broke, then fled in disorder. As usual Caesar pursued vigorously. A few of the Pompeians were able to make the safety of Munda, though not many.

An estimated 30,000 were left dead on the battlefield amid another unforgiving slaughter, with all 13 of their legionary standards being captured. Caesar claimed that he lost only 1,000 men. The outcome was total victory for the *populares*, with Labienus falling in the battle and the Pompeius brothers once more fleeing. It also seems that Caesar really wanted to send a message to any potential future rebels in the aftermath of battle, refusing to recognise the fallen Pompeian legionaries as Roman citizens with their bodies used as building material and their severed heads stuck on poles (Holland, 2003, 341). Faced with such savage brutality, the Pompeians were to all intents and purposes finished, though the civil war was to dramatically flare up again after Caesar's assassination a year later.

Conclusion

In this work I have considered the lives and martial careers of the two men I believe were the greatest military commanders in the ancient world. Such were the astonishing achievements of Alexander the Great and Julius Caesar when on campaign and in battle that their feats and triumphs stand up against those of any military leader from any period in history. Therefore, determining which of the two was pre-eminent in their martial careers is difficult. Fortunately, both were very different men in terms of their backgrounds and the lives they lived, and it is that which allows us to address the question set out in the title of this work.

To do that, I firstly consider the legacies of Alexander and Caesar, both in their own time and in the modern world. I then set out a number of traits that I believe provide a framework allowing us to determine their success or otherwise as military leaders in the ancient world. Finally, I use this template to reach my conclusion, explaining to the reader why.

The Legacies of Alexander and Caesar

Alexander the Great was the ultimate young man in a hurry. A leader who, in his own lifetime, came to believe he was a demi-God, the conqueror of his known world. A warrior who always led from the front, the very idea he should hold back an affront to his visceral martial nature. As Plutarch says (*Lives*, Alexander, 41): 'Alexander made a point of risking his life…both to exercise himself and to inspire others to acts of courage…'

Yet his immediate legacy in the aftermath of his death was one of failure, given he neglected to set in place a succession plan fit to maintain the integrity of his vast conquests. Indeed, as the key players at the very birth of the Hellenistic world stared uneasily at each other over the dying king in the smoky dimness of his bedchamber in Babylon, Alexander's alleged last words only fuelled uncertainty over the future. This was because, according to Diodorus Siculus, when asked to whom he left his kingdom he said (*Library of History*, 18.1): '...to the strongest, for I foresee that a great combat of my friends will be my funeral games.'

In the ancient world such games were the athletic events held in honour of a recently deceased dignitary, the more senior the grander. Given his then stature as the world's greatest conqueror, those of Alexander were indeed fitting given they now set alight his empire for over thirty years.

When the king passed away many of the key players from the years of conquest were already gathered in Babylon, including his seven bodyguards who were also the leading nobles and holders of high command in the Macedonian army. At this time these were Aristinous, Lysimachus, Peithon, Leonnatus, Ptolemy, Peucestas and Perdiccas. We also know of several other leading figures from the military leadership there at the time, including Attalos, Demephon, Cleomenes, Menidas and Seleucus, given they all joined Peithon and Peucestas in spending the night before Alexander died praying for his recovery, unsuccessfully as it turned out, in the temple of Serapis. Other key figures were absent at this crucial moment though, most notably Antipater (the regent in Macedon), Antigonus *Monophthalmus* in his satrapy of Greater Phrygia in central Anatolia where he had the key task of keeping open the lines of communication with Babylon, and Craterus who was on his way back to Macedon with returning veterans.

Most of these characters, whether in Babylon or elsewhere, were to play a leading role in the subsequent Wars of the Successors that ran through various phases from 323 BC to 281 BC. When this succession of conflicts ended, Alexander's empire was no more, split asunder into various Hellenistic kingdoms striving to maintain his legacy, at least in name, until the Romans in the west and Parthians in the east in turn defeated them.

Fortunately for Alexander, this failed Hellenistic attempt at imperial longevity proved a distraction in terms of his legacy, given subsequent generations saw it very differently. This was because his astonishing conquests were later viewed with awe, truly capturing the imagination of millions and creating a legend that set the bar impossibly high for all future conquerors, kings and military leaders. All such aspirants failed in comparison, at least in the eyes of their contemporaries, and often themselves. The many we could list in the ancient world include Antiochus the Great, Pompey, Julius Caesar (who wept at the statue of Alexander in Cadiz), Augustus, Nero, Septimius Severus, Caracalla, Alexander Severus, and later Justinian the Great and Charlemagne. There have been far more subsequently, all striving to emulate the success of the boyish world conqueror, but failing.

Thus Alexander's conquests, for good or ill, have become a metaphor for imperial over-achievement.

However, if we move forward in time to today, at this chronological distance it is difficult to determine the legacy of Alexander in our own world. Individual views tend to be bi-polar, based on one's personal politics and geographical origin, as I set out with regard to my own experiences in the Introduction. The king is either eulogised or demonised, with the popular trend today towards the latter. For example, as Bosworth explains (1993, 180): 'The abiding importance of Alexander (today) lies more in the field of moral and philosophical debate than in practical politics.'

This modern view totally ignores a vast swathe of contemporary nuancing. Foremost was the unending threat perceived by the Greek-speaking world from the Achaemenid Persian Empire. Challenging this provided both Philip II and Alexander with their primary motivation as they sought glory in the east. Alexander's success here cannot be underestimated. It lifted forever the eastern threat to the Greek-speaking world. It also removed the main barrier preventing the spread of Greek culture and settlement eastwards. For the first time the Mesopotamian frontier became part of the Greek world, while in Bactria and India Hellenistic settlement was profligate. Thus the combined results of his conquests in halting the spread of Persian influence westwards, and spreading Greek culture eastwards (for good or ill) as far as India for the next 500 years, is Alexander's most tangible historical achievement. Certainly the failure of his *anabasis* would have seen the western world far different today.

Moving on to Caesar, we are again faced with an equally complex legacy both then and now. However, here we are fortunate in having more detail about what happened in the immediate aftermath of his death, and its impact on the Roman world. Caesar's funeral ceremony sounded the death knell of the Republic. The Senate, seeking to encourage almost immediate reconciliation between the *optimates* and *populares*, voted that it should be public. The event duly took place on 18 March, with Mark Antony giving the eulogy from the *rostra* in the forum. There he reminded the huge crowd, which included thousands of Caesar's veterans, of the dictator's many achievements. He then read Caesar's will, which included the gift of a huge new garden complex along the Tiber for the citizens of Rome, and 75 *denarii* for each Roman citizen (Caesar also naming his grand-nephew Octavian as his sole heir). Mark Anthony then showed off Caesar's bloody toga, before the body was finally lifted up by magistrates to be carried to a site next to the tomb of his daughter Julia on the Campus Martia where it was due to be cremated and interred. However, having been whipped into a frenzy by Mark Antony, the crowd would have none of it. They seized the body and cremated it there and then on a pyre built in front of the *rostra*. Veterans and citizens alike threw their precious goods into the huge blaze as a sign of their grief, with the flames quickly flaring out of control. In short order many of the buildings in the forum were badly damaged.

Violence then erupted against the *optimates*, with the huge funeral crowd turning into a rampaging mob that attacked the houses of Cassius, Brutus and the other Liberators. In the frenzy Caesar's loyal supporter Helvius Cinna was killed by rioters who mistook him for the plotter Cornelius Cinna. It took days for order to be restored in the capital, by which time Caesar's immediate legacy as the leading man of Rome murdered by bitter *optimates* was firmly established. On the site of his cremation the Temple of Caesar was later erected on the eastern side of the main square of the *Forum Romanum*, featuring a life-size wax statue of the dictator. He was also later deified in 42 BC as the Divine Julius. However, this initial legacy soon span out of control, with full civil war once more breaking out between the *optimates* and *populares*.

The first act here was the flight of the leading *optimates*, including Cassius and Brutus, to Greece to avoid the anger of the Roman mob. The *populares* had already dealt with key plot-leader Decimus Junius Brutus Albinus who initially fled north to Cisapline Gaul where he survived a number of attempts to defeat him, only to be executed by a Gallic chief loyal to Caesar when he tried to reach Greece. There Cassius and Brutus were raising an enormous army which Mark Antony in Italy countered by gathering an equally large force using the immense wealth of Caesar's own war chest. He legitimised his actions by saying he was acting in the name of Caesar. Then, on 27 November 43 BC, the *lex Titia* law was passed which established the Second Triumvirate of Mark Antony, Octavian and Caesar's loyal commander Lepidus. This ensured the continued rule of the *populares*, with their first action being to reinstate the policy of proscription last used under Sulla. Soon those *optimates* still in Rome were being rounded up and executed. Their estates and wealth were then confiscated to fund the raising of even more legions. Eventually the triumvirate took the war to the *optimates* in Greece where Cassius and Brutus were heavily defeated at the Battle of Phillipi by Mark Antony and Octavian in October 42 BC. Both Cassius and Brutus committed suicide in the aftermath.

However, as with the First Triumvirate, the second was not to last. In the mid-30s BC Octavian accused Lepidus of trying to usurp power, stripping him of all titles and exiling him after most of his troops defected to Octavian. Meanwhile, Mark Antony campaigned in the east, suffering a big defeat in his invasion of Parthia after over-extending his lines of supply. He now increasingly came under the influence of Cleopatra in Egypt with whom he formed an alliance, though he still styled himself a triumvir even after the time period agreed in the *lex Titia* expired in 33 BC. A new and final civil war soon broke out between himself with Cleopatra against Octavian. The latter was the ultimate victor at the climactic Battle of Actium in 31 BC, his fleet under Marcus Agrippa destroying that of Mark Antony and Cleopatra who fled to Egypt where they later famously committed suicide in 30 BC. This left Octavian as the last man standing after the turbulent civil wars that had plagued Rome throughout the first century BC. He was already able to call himself *Divi Filius* ('son of a God') given Caesar's deification, and by 27 BC the Senate was calling him *Caesar Augustus*. The Republic was no more, and the Roman Empire now came into being.

This elevation of Octavian to Augustus saw him styled as the *princeps*, a title designed to project him officially as the first among equals within the now defunct Republic. This was clearly a conceit given in reality he was far more of a dictator that Caesar had ever been. Augustus was also the first to style himself *imperator*. Overall this process had a huge impact on the Roman psyche as, from that point, in the Roman world the first emperor Augustus was viewed the greatest Roman, not Caesar. Indeed his enormous success at home and abroad, despite the occasional setback, set the standard by which all future emperor's measured themselves. This was writ large when, later, senior and junior imperial titles were introduced. From that point the senior emperor was called the Augustus, and his junior partner the Caesar. Thus Caesar's legacy was reduced to a supporting role.

However, in the post-Roman world this diminishing of the legacy of Caesar set against the rise of Augustus was dramatically reversed. Now, Caesar and his epic story was that by which rulers began to measure themselves. This was particularly the case from the time of the later Middle Ages and Renaissance, perhaps peaking with William Shakespeare's contemporary blockbuster *Julius Caesar*. It was Caesar who gave his name to the rulers of the Russian and Slavic world with their Tsars, and to the Germanic Kaiser. And it was Caesar on whom future would-be conquerors styled themselves, for example the Ottoman Sultan Mehmed II who was the ultimate nemesis of the Roman Empire when he finally captured the Byzantine capital of Constantinople in 1453, Charles VIII of France who ordered a translation of *The Conquest of Gaul*, and the Holy Roman Emperor

Charles V who ordered a map to be made of France to better understand Caesar's Gallic wars. Meanwhile, the latter's contemporary Suleiman the Magnificent translated Caesar's commentaries into Turkish and catalogued the surviving editions. Later, the French kings Henry IV, Louis XIII and Louis XIV all had Caesar's commentaries translated into French. Into the nineteenth century Napoleon Bonaparte studied not only Caesar's military prowess but also his skill as a strategic communicator, while later in the century Caesar's style of leadership inspired a political ideology called Caesarism based on unrestricted rule by a charismatic strongman. One adherent, unsurprisingly, was the Italian fascist leader Benito Mussolini.

More broadly in terms of Caesar's legacy, the Julian calendar was that used throughout the western world until the advent of the Gregorian calendar in 1582, while his campaigning in Spain and conquests in Gaul facilitated the spread of the Latin language and Roman law which still influence linguistics and legal systems there to this day. Through later Roman *imperium* one can add the Catholic Church. Thus, for all of these reasons, we still live in the shadow of this great figure of Roman history today.

Finally, as a concluding aside when comparing Caesar with Alexander, it seems that in recent years the Roman dictator has suffered far less from revisionist reinterpretations of his life story than the Macedonian king. This might seem odd, though in mitigation Roman leaders of both the Republic and Empire have always had the negative aspects of their rule factored into wider popular appreciations, certainly to a greater extent than with Alexander.

Key Traits of Great Military Leaders in the Ancient World

Having considered the contemporary and modern legacies of Alexander and Caesar, we can now focus more tightly on their abilities as military leaders in the ancient world. To provide a structure for this, here I set out seven traits that I believe allow their skills in that regard to be considered. These traits are their sense of self-belief and destiny, strategic and tactical prowess, personal bravery, attention to detail, the ability to be brutal when necessary, ability to communicate with audiences high and low, and grit and personal charisma.

Sense of Self-Belief and Destiny

At first sight this seems a close-run thing between the two leaders, with both displaying an innate sense of self-belief and destiny. Certainly Alexander, as the son of Philip II (the greatest Argead king to that point), was raised to believe a Homeric destiny awaited him. This was writ through all that followed in his incredible career of conquest. However, there is also no doubt that as his *anabasis* progressed, this innate sense of divine purpose was twisted, despite the many attempts by his Macedonian contemporaries to keep his feet on the ground. Soon, especially after his visit to the desert oracle of Zeus Ammon at Siwa in Egypt, he began to overtly claim descent from the line of Hercules, and increasingly Zeus. As his life came to a close many feel he clearly believed he was a living demi-God, though one should consider here the state of his mental health. His adult life, short as it was, was one of constant fighting and physical effort. Alexander was wounded numerous times, including severely at least twice. He also suffered numerous bouts of fever and ill health, with exhaustion from these tribulations a key factor contributing to his early demise. Overall, it seems likely that his life experiences led to some kind of psychosis in his later years where, rather than his sense of self-belief and destiny being a positive driving force, they became something far darker.

Meanwhile, Caesar also claimed that from an early age he believed he would live a life of greatness. However, at least initially he was far more grounded than Alexander given his family origins in an unremarkable branch of the Julii *gentes*. Not for Caesar the benefits of being born the heir to the throne. Instead, he spent a lifetime militarily and politically hacking his way to the top, facing down opponent after opponent, whether they be foreign kings and tribal leaders, or rival politicians and warlords. At each stage of Caesar's career, as one adversary was defeated, others emerged, until he finally met his match in the Liberators when his total dominance in Rome threatened the very survival of the Republic.

Strategic and Tactical Prowess

Both Alexander and Caesar were inspirational commanders on campaign and in battle. Yet once more a clear difference is evident. In Alexander's case, once he initiated his *anabasis*, his strategy was at first glance simple. Head ever eastwards until he had finally defeated Darius III in a set piece battle of such significance that it would bring down the mighty Achaemenid Persian Empire once and for all. Then, with his primary objective achieved, keep going east until he reached the ends of the known world. Yet the simplicity of its description defies the true enormity of this campaign, which Alexander pursued almost to perfection until his ever-loyal troops finally lost patience with his limitless vision. By way of example, consider his strategic decision to follow the Tigris rather than Euphrates routes to bring Darius to battle at Gaugamela in 331 BC. Even when presented with unexpected challenges, for example having to react to Darius' strategic initiatives in the Granicus River and Issus campaigns, Alexander coped admirably. Thus, at a strategic level he is often called a military genius whose skills would grace any age.

Moving on, at a tactical level Alexander's skill-set was again perfect for the age. He devised thoughtful battle plans (note the complexity of his deployment at Gaugamela, designed to mitigate his inferiority in numbers), taking into account intelligence, logistics and the strengths and weaknesses of his foes. He then ensured his subordinates were very clear regarding their orders. In this way he always found a way to win. A key final point here is that, at a tactical level, Alexander always chose to lead from the front on the battlefield, as a true Argead king should. For him to do otherwise would have been unthinkable, both for himself and his men, no matter what the risk. However, even when at the fulcrum of battle, he always maintained control of the forces he was commanding. Thus in all of his set piece battles, instead of pursuing defeated opponents, he ensured his initial success in breaking the enemy's battle line became total victory by striking the exposed flanks and rears of intact enemy formations.

Meanwhile, Caesar also illustrated the highest level of skill as a military commander at a strategic and tactical level. Again though, we see a clear differential when compared to Alexander. First, although the latter put his own stamp on his astonishing *anabasis*, he inherited the basic strategy from his father Philip II. However, in Caesar's case he devised his own strategies when campaigning across the breadth of the Mediterranean and north-western Europe. Caesar's success speaks for itself, especially given the greater number of serious opponents he fought. Notable examples include Ariovistus, Cassivellanus, Vercingetorix, Pompey, Pharnaces II, and any number of the surviving Pompeain leaders in his final North African and Spanish civil war campaigns.

Caesar also proved a supreme tactical leader on the battlefield, where he faced opponents who presented a symmetrical threat more often than Alexander. Certainly the Gallic and German tribes proved difficult to overcome time and again, as did the Pompeain legionaries in his brutal civil war campaigns. At this tactical level, a further point of difference also emerges between Alexander and Caesar. This was in how they positioned themselves on the battlefield. As detailed, Alexander always led from the front. Not so with Caesar, who only chose to join the fighting when necessary. This was in no way shirking his martial responsibilities, but simply reflected the changed nature of tactical leadership by the time of the later Roman Republic. Thus at Pharsalus in 48 BC he positioned himself behind his elite Xth legion, where he was best placed to direct matters as required, rather than in the front rank. This was very much in line with late Republic/Imperial Roman doctrine, as set out by the first century AD historian Onasander (*Strategicos*, 10.2.7):

> The general should fight cautiously rather than boldly, or should keep away altogether from a hand to hand fight with the enemy. For even if in battle he shows that he is not to be outdone in valour, he can aid his army far less by fighting than he can harm it if he should be killed, since the knowledge of a general is far more important than his physical strength. Even a soldier can perform a great deed by bravery, but no one except the general can by his wisdom plan a greater one.

Roman generals continued to follow this pragmatic approach to battlefield leadership well into the next millennium, with Elliott citing Septimius Severus in the Principate and Julian in the Dominate as prime examples (2018, 14).

Personal Bravery

Here there is much commonality between Alexander and Caesar. Both displayed great personal bravery on multiple occasions, the former suffering many wounds as a result and the latter never afraid to mount a charger or carry a *scutum* and *gladius* in the front rank of legionaries. They instinctively knew the value of inspiring their men by martial example, and never avoided this responsibility.

Attention to Detail

Here I focus on logistics given the geographic enormity of the conquests of Alexander and Caesar. The former's skill in maintaining his snaking lines of supply from central Asia and the Punjab back to the Balkans cannot be overestimated. Even today, this achievement is truly astonishing. As Goldsworthy says (2020, 298): 'Alexander's boldness and personal heroism can all too easily mask the methodical way in which he waged war, and much that seems reckless was based on careful judgement...'

Even when able to live off the land in enemy territory, itself always fraught with uncertainty (especially over such vast distances), this cultural umbilical back home was key to maintaining the morale of Alexander's Macedonian and Greek soldiers, fighting for their king so far from home.

However, if anything Caesar was even more the master of logistics when on campaign, often criss-crossing enemy territory time and again to hunt down his opponents and force a meeting engagement, or to crush a rebellion. Extreme examples include his outlandish amphibious landings in Britain in 55 BC and 54 BC, and his North African campaign in early 46 BC when chasing down the Pompeains in the most hostile of territories. Caesar's minute attention to detail is well-illustrated in this Thapsus campaign when he used elephants obtained from Italy to train his troops in how to engage the beasts fielded by the *optimates*' Numidian allies.

Brutality

This may seem an odd trait to reference, but is actually a key facet of conquest in the ancient world. Here both protagonists never stepped back when an example was needed *pour encourager les autres*. Think of Alexander's treatment of Darius' Greek mercenaries after Granicus River and Issus, and the unfortunate defenders of Tyre who suffered so terribly after daring to resist him. Meanwhile, for Caesar consider his sanguineous slaughter in Gaul, and treatment of the Pompeian legionaries after Thapsus and Munda when he needed to stamp out Pompeain resistance once and for all.

Communications Skills

Alexander and Caesar were superb communicators, with both able to inspire audiences high and low. They understood the importance of ensuring their audiences heard news and information from their own perspective first. Thus we have Alexander sending news of his shattering defeat of Darius III at Issus back to Macedonia and Greece at the first opportunity, knowing this would mitigate scepticism amongst the *poleis* about the feasibility of his *anabasis*. Similarly, we have Caesar communicating the 'success' of each year's campaigning in his conquest of Gaul back to the Senate and people of Rome, this in such detail that collectively we can still read his own missives today in *The Conquest of Gaul*. Indeed, so successful was Caesar in that regard that even today many still believe it was he who successfully invaded Britain to create the Roman province here, rather than Claudius ninety-seven years later.

Grit and Personal Charisma

Again here, we have two leaders who were closely matched. In the first instance, both had the personal resilience to always come back from adversity, learning from their mistakes to ensure final victory on campaign and in battle. Similarly, both were extraordinarily gifted in terms of natural charisma, able to inspire audiences of all kinds. When reading contemporary narratives of Alexander and Caesar, both display a crackling charm which they used to great effect, convincing their men to follow them time and again to overcome even the greatest of challenges.

Who Was the Greatest Commander in the Ancient World?

Having considered the legacies of Alexander and Caesar and then compared their careers set against a template of seven traits, we can now determine who, of the two, the greatest commander in the ancient world was.

Starting with Alexander, he was truly great by the standards of any age if military conquest, ambition and force of personality were the key determinants. Further, he personally overcame the pro–philhellene bias of his own day, with his worldview evolving as his *anabasis* progressed eastwards to encompass the creation of one homogenous Empire. While certainly Macedonian and Greek culture was at the centre of his vision, this was not to the detriment of every other ethnicity encountered and conquered. Indeed, his leaning away from his own Greek-speaking Balkans origins caused huge friction time and again with the Macedonians and Greeks in his army, and also at home.

However, we have one inescapable fact to consider when discussing Alexander as a military leader. This was that he won his astonishing victories with a military machine created by his father. Indeed, Philip II is in many ways the third protagonist in this debate about great military leaders in the ancient world. It was on his watch that the Kingdom of Macedon went from being a bit-part player among the Greek *poleis* to becoming the dominant regional military power. In particular, the creation of the Macedonian pike phalanx proved one of the greatest innovations in military history, especially when paired with the 'hammer' to its 'anvil', Philip's lance-armed companion shock cavalry.

Caesar's rise to the top was very different. Though he was born into the patrician level of Roman society, his family branch within the Julii *gentes* was relatively unknown until his father's generation. Further, the cultural norms within elite levels of Roman society worked against the rise to power of one dominant individual, except in times of extreme crisis. In that regard, the overthrow of Tarquin the Proud in 509 BC still resonated forcefully among Rome's political classes almost 500 years later, hence Caesar's success jarring as it did.

Finally, there was also a key specific point of difference between Caesar and Alexander when on campaign and in battle. The latter, while incredibly successful in his martial achievements, most often fought opponents who were (often significantly) weaker in every aspect except numerical superiority. That was not the case with Caesar, who fought a broader range of opponents usually far more symmetrical in their capabilities.

Taking all of the above into account, I can now answer the question I set out in the title of this book. There is no doubt in my mind that Alexander's achievements were truly prodigious set against any criteria of any age. Yet Caesar's journey from being just another ambitious son of a Senator to mastering his known world was far longer, and harder, and his military career much wider in scope. Therefore, I believe that while Alexander was great, Caesar was greater, and it is therefore he who was the greatest commander in the ancient world.

Bibliography

Ancient Sources

Appian, *Roman History*, trans. B. McGing (Harvard: Loeb Classical Library, 2020)

Apuleius, *The Golden Ass*, trans. P.G. Walsh (Oxford: Oxford World Classics, 2008)

Aristotle, *The Politics*, trans. T.A. Sinclair (Oxford: Oxford University Press, 2009)

Arrian, *Anabasis Alexandri*, trans. R. Arrian (London: Forgotten Books, 2018)

Caesar, Julius, *The Conquest of Gaul*, trans. S.A. Handford (London: Penguin Classics, 1951)

Cato, Marcus, *De Agri Cultura*, trans. H.B. Ash and W.D. Hooper (Harvard: Loeb Classical Library, 1934)

Chrysostom, Dio, *Orations*, D.A. Russell (ed.) (Cambridge: Cambridge University Press, 2010)

Cicero, Marcus Tullius, *The Orations of Marcus Tullius Cicero*, trans. C.D. Yonge (London: George Bell & Sons, 1891)

Dio, Cassius, *Roman History*, trans. E. Cary (Harvard: Loeb Classical Library, 1925)

Greek Elagiac Poetry: From the 7ᵗʰ to the 5ᵗʰ Century BC, trans. D.E. Gerber (Harvard: Loeb Classical Library, 1999)

Herodian, *History of the Roman Empire* trans. C.R. Whittaker (Harvard: Loeb Classical Library, 1989)

The Holy Bible, King James Version

Homer, *The Iliad*, trans. E.V. Rieu (London: Penguin Classics, 1950)

Justin, *Epitome of the Philippic History of Pompeius Trogus*, trans. J. Yardley (Oxford: Oxford University Press, 1994)

Justinian, *The Digest of Justinian*, trans. A. Watson (Philadelphia: University of Pennsylvania, 1997)

242 Alexander the Great versus Julius Caesar

Livy, *The History of Rome*, trans. B.O. Foster (Cambridge, MA: Harvard University Press/Loeb Classical Library, 1989)

Onasander, *Strategicos*, trans. T. Page (Cambridge, MA: Harvard University Press/Loeb Classical Library, 1923)

Pausanias, *Guide to Greece: Central Greece*, trans. P. Levi (London: Penguin Classics, 1979)

Pliny the Elder, *Natural History*, trans. H. Rackham (Harvard: Harvard University Press, 1940)

Pliny the Younger, *Epistularum Libri Decem*, R.A.B. Mynors (ed.) (Oxford: Oxford Classical Texts/Clarendon Press, 1963)

Plutarch, *Lives of the Noble Grecians and Romans*, A.H. Clough (ed.) (Oxford: Benediction Classics, 2013)

Plutarch, *The Education of Children*, trans. S. Ford (Boston: Little, Brown and Co., 1878)

Polyaenus, *Stratagems* Dr. F.R.S. Shepherd (Michigan: Gale ECCO, 2010)

Polybius, *The Rise of the Roman Empire*, trans. I. Scott-Kilvert (London: Penguin Classics, 1979)

Sallust, *The War with Jugurtha*, trans. J.C. Rolfe (Harvard: Loeb Classical Library, 2013)

Strabo, *The Geography of Strabo*, trans. D.W. Roller (Cambridge: Cambridge University Press, 2014)

Thucydides, *The Peloponnesian War*, trans. M. Hammond (Oxford: Oxford University Press, 2009)

Vegetius, *Epitome of Military Science*, N.P. Milner (Liverpool: Liverpool University Press, 1996)

Victor, Aurelius, *De Caesaribus*, trans. H.W. Bird (Liverpool: Liverpool University Press, 1994)

Xenophon, *The Persian Expedition*, trans. R. Warner (London: Penguin Classics, 1949)

Modern Sources

Bardunias, P.M. and Ray, F.E., *Hoplites at War: A Comprehensive Analysis of Heavy Infantry Combat in the Greek World* (Jefferson, North Carolina: McFarland, 2016)

Barker, P., *The Armies and Enemies of Imperial Rome* (Cambridge: Wargames Research Group, 1981)

Bar-Kochva, B., *The Seleucid Army* (Cambridge: Cambridge University Press, 1976)

Bishop, M.C., *The Gladius* (Oxford: Osprey Publishing Ltd, 2016)

Bonner, S., *Education in Ancient Rome* (London: Routledge, 2014)

Bosworth, A.B., *Conquest and Empire: The Reign of Alexander the Great* (Cambridge: Cambridge University Press, 1993)

Bradley, K., *Slavery and Society at Rome* (Cambridge: Cambridge University Press, 1998)

Buckler, J., *Philip II and the Sacred War* (Leiden: Brill, 1989)

Cartledge, P., *Alexander the Great: The Hunt for a New Past* (London: Macmillan, 2004)

Caven, B., *The Punic Wars* (London: Weidenfeld & Nicolson, 1980)

Connolly, P., *Greece and Rome at War* (London: Macdonald & Co. (Publishers) Ltd., 1988)

Connolly, P., 'The Early Roman Army' in Hackett, J. (ed.) *Warfare in the Ancient World* (London: Sidgwick & Jackson, pp.136-148, 1989)

Cornell, T.J. and Matthews, J., *Atlas of the Roman World* (Oxford: Phaidon Press Ltd, 1982)

Cowan, R., *Roman Legionary, 58 BC–AD 69* (Oxford: Osprey Publishing, 2003)

Cowan, R., *Roman Battle Tactics 109 BC–AD 313* (Oxford: Osprey Publishing, 2007)

Dahm, M., 'The 300 Thebans?' *Ancient Warfare* magazine, V.14, Issue 2, pp. 50-55, 2020

Devine, A., 'Alexander the Great' in Hackett, J. (ed.) *Warfare in the Ancient World* (London: Sidgwick & Jackson, pp. 104-129, 1989)

Elliott, A., 'The Art of Command: Why Military Commanders of the Classical and Medieval World Fought the Way They Did in Battle and What Effect Did This Have on the Wars They Fought?' – BA Dissertation. (Unpublished, University of Wales Trinity Saint David, 2018)

Elliott, S., *Sea Eagles of Empire: The Classis Britannica and the Battles for Britain* (Stroud: The History Press, 2016)

Elliott, S., *Empire State: How the Roman Military Built an Empire* (Oxford: Oxbow Books, 2017)

Elliott, S., *Roman Legionaries: Soldiers of Empire* (Oxford: Casemate Publishers, 2018)

Elliott, S., *Julius Caesar: Rome's Greatest Warlord* (Oxford: Casemate Publishers, 2019)

Elliott, S., *Old Testament Warriors* (Oxford: Casemate Publishers, 2020a)

Elliott, S., *Romans at War* (Oxford: Casemate Publishers, 2020b)

Erdkamp, P., (ed.), *The Cambridge Companion to Ancient Rome* (Cambridge: Cambridge University Press, 2013)

Fields, N., *Tarentine Horseman of Magna Graecia* (Oxford: Osprey Publishing, 2008)

Fields, N., *Roman Republican Legionary 298 BC–105 BC* (Oxford: Osprey Publishing, 2012)

Frere, S., *Britannia: A History of Roman Britain* (3rd edn) (London: Routledge, 1974)

Goldsworthy, A., *Roman Warfare* (London: Cassell, 2000)

Goldsworthy, A., *The Complete Roman Army* (London: Thames and Hudson, 2003)

Goldsworthy, A., *Caesar* (London: Weidenfeld & Nicolson, 2007)

Goldsworthy, A., *Philip and Alexander* (London: Head of Zeus, 2020)

Golvin, J. C., *Ancient Cities Brought to Life* (Ludlow: Thalamus Publishing, 2003)

Grainge, G., *The Roman Invasions of Britain* (Stroud, Tempus, 2005)

Green, P., *Alexander to Actium* (London: Thames and Hudson, 1990)

Green, P., *Alexander of Macedon, 356–323 BC: A Historical Biography* (Berkeley: University of California Press, 1992)

Green, P., *The Greco-Persian Wars* (Berkely: University of California Press, 1998)

Green, P., *Alexander the Great and the Hellenistic Age* (London: Weidenfeld & Nicolson, 2007)

Hall, J.R., 'The Siege of Veii, 406–396 BC', *Ancient Warfare* magazine, V.14, Issue 24-33, 2020

Haywood, J., *Atlas of the Classical World* (London: Cassell, 1998)

Haywood, J., *The Historical Atlas of the Celtic World* (London: Thames and Hudson, 2009)

Head, D., *Armies of the Macedonian and Punic Wars* (Cambridge: Wargames Research Group, 2016)

Heckel, W., *The Wars of Alexander the Great 336–323 BC* (Oxford: Osprey Publishing, 2002)

Herrmann-Otto, Elizabeth, 'Slaves and Freedmen', in Erdkamp, P. (eds) *The Cambridge Companion to Ancient Rome* (Cambridge: Cambridge University Press, pp. 60-76, 2013)

Holland, T., *Rubicon: The Triumph and Tragedy of the Roman Republic* (London: Abacus, 2003)

Hornblower, S. and Spawforth, A., *The Oxford Classical Dictionary* (Oxford: Oxford University Press, 1996)

James, S., *Rome and the Sword* (London: Thames and Hudson, 2011)

Jones, B. and Mattingly, D., *An Atlas of Roman Britain* (Oxford: Oxbow Books, 1990)

Kiley, K.F., *The Uniforms of the Roman World* (Wigston: Lorenz Books, 2012)

Lane Fox, R., *Alexander the Great* (London: Penguin, 1986)

Lane Fox, R., *The Classical World* (London: Penguin, 2006)

Lazenby, J., 'Hoplite Warfare', in Hackett, J. (ed.) *Warfare in the Ancient World* (London: Sidgwick & Jackson, pp.54-81, 1989)

Manning, S., 'So You Want to Be a Hoplite: Reviving an Ancient Fighting Style', *Ancient Warfare* magazine, V.11, Issue 2, pp.44-48, 2017

Matthew, C., *An Invincible Beast: Understanding the Hellenistic Pike-Phalanx at War* (Barnsley: Pen & Sword, 2015)

Mattingly, D., *An Imperial Possession, Britain in the Roman Empire* (London: Penguin, 2006)

Matyszak, P., *Chronicle of the Roman Republic* (London: Thames and Hudson, 2003)

Matyszak, P., *Roman Conquests: Macedonia and Greece* (Barnsley: Pen & Sword, 2009)

Millett, M., *The Romanization of Britain* (Cambridge: Cambridge University Press, 1990)

Millett, M., *Roman Britain* (London: Batsford, 1995)

Moorhead, S. and Stuttard, D., *The Romans Who Shaped Britain* (London: Thames and Hudson, 2012)

Morkot, R., *The Penguin Historical Atlas of Ancient Greece* (London: Penguin, 1996)

Mouritsen, H., *The Freedman in the Roman World* (Cambridge: Cambridge University Press, 2015)

Murphy, K., 'The Role of Elephants in the Seleucid Army'. *Ancient Warfare* magazine, V.14, Issue 1, pp.26-33, 2020

Nagle, D.B., 'The Cultural Context of Alexander's Speech at Opis'. *Transactions of the American Philological Association*, V.126, pp.151-172, 1996

Nikonorov, V.P., *The Armies of Bactria 700 BC–450 BC: Volume 1* (Stockport: Montvert Publications, 1997)

Oleson, J.P., *The Oxford Handbook of Engineering and Technology in the Classical World* (Oxford: Oxford University Press, 2009)

Pietrykowski, J., *Great Battles of the Hellenistic World* (Barnsley: Pen & Sword, 2009)

Pitassi, M., *The Roman Navy* (Barnsley: Seaforth, 2012)

Pollard, N. and Berry, J., *The Complete Roman Legions* (London: Thames and Hudson, 2012)

Potter, D., *Rome in the Ancient World: From Romulus to Justinian* (London: Thames and Hudson, 2009)

Robinson, A., *The Story of Writing* (London: Thames and Hudson, 1995)

Rodgers, N. and Dodge, H., *The History and Conquests of Ancient Rome* (London: Hermes House, 2009)

Rubin, Z., *Civil-War Propaganda and Historiography* (Leuven: Peeters, 1980)

Rufus, Quintus Curtius, *The History of Alexander*, trans. J. Yardley (London: Penguin Classics, 1984)

Sabin, P., *Lost Battles* (London: Hambledon Continuum, 2007)

Salway, P., *Roman Britain* (Oxford: Oxford University Press, 1981)

Scarre, C., *The Penguin Historical Atlas of Ancient Rome* (London: Penguin, 1995)

Schmitz, M. and Sumner, G., *Roman Conquests: The Danube Frontier* (Barnsley: Pen & Sword)

Sekunda, N., *The Seleucid Army* (Stockport: Montvert Publications, 1994)

Sekunda, N., *The Ptolemaic Army* (Stockport: Montvert Publications, 1995)

Sekunda, N., *Macedonian Armies after Alexander 323–168 BC* (Oxford: Osprey Publishing, 2012)

Sekunda, N., *The Army of Pyrrhus of Epirus* (Oxford: Osprey Publishing, 2019)

Sheppard, R., *Alexander the Great at War: His Army – His Battles – His Enemies* (Oxford: Osprey Publishing, 2011)

Siculus, Diodorus, *Library of History*, trans. C.H. Oldfather (Harvard: Loeb Classical Library, 1939)

Simpson, S.J., 'The Scythians: Discovering the Nomad Warriors of Siberia', *Current World Archeology*, Issue 84, V.7, pp.14-19, 2017

Southern, P., *Roman Britain* (Stroud: Amberley Publishing, 2013)

Starr, C.G., *The Roman Imperial Navy 31 BC–AD 324* (New York: Cornell University Press, 1941)

Wallace-Hadrill, A., (ed.), *Patronage in Ancient Society* (Routledge: London, 1989)

Warry, J., *Warfare in the Classical World* (London: Salamander, 1980)

Wilcox, P., *Rome's Enemies (3): Parthians and Sassanid Persians* (Oxford: Osprey Publishing, 1986)

Wilkes, J.J., 'Provinces and Frontiers', in Bowman. A.K., Garnsey, P. and Cameron, A. (eds.) *The Cambridge Ancient History Vol. XII, The Crisis of Empire, AD 193-337* (Cambridge: Cambridge University Press, pp.212-268, 2005)

Windrow, M. and McBride, A., *Imperial Rome at War* (Hong Kong: Concord Publications, 1996)

Index

18/4
↓
04/05